LR/LEND/001

UNIVERSITY OF
WOLVERHAMPTON

COMPUTERS,
ETHICS,
AND SOCIETY

THIRD EDITION

Edited by

M. David Ermann

Michele S. Shauf

New York   Oxford

OXFORD
UNIVERSITY PRESS

2003

Oxford University Press

Oxford   New York
Auckland   Bangkok   Buenos Aires   Cape Town   Chennai
Dar es Salaam   Delhi   Hong Kong   Istanbul   Karachi   Kolkata
Kuala Lumpur   Madrid   Melbourne   Mexico City   Mumbai
Nairobi   São Paulo   Shanghai   Taipei   Tokyo   Toronto

Copyright © 1990, 1997, 2003 by Oxford University Press, Inc.

Published by Oxford University Press, Inc.
198 Madison Avenue, New York, New York, 10016
http://www.oup-usa.org

Oxford is a registered trademark of Oxford University Press

Library of Congress Cataloging-in-Publication Data

Computers, ethics, and society / edited by M. David Ermann, Michele S. Shauf.—3rd ed.
    p. cm.
    Includes bibliographical references and index.
    ISBN 0-19-514302-7
        1. Computers and civilization. 2. Computer security. 3. Human-computer interaction.
    I. Ermann, M. David. II. Shauf, Michele S.

QA76.9.C66 C572 2003
303. 48′34—dc21   2002072283

9 8 7 6 5 4 3 2 1

Printed in the United States of America
on acid-free paper

For Natalie, Mike, and Marlene

Contents

Preface   vi

I. Ethical Contexts

Philosophical Ethics

1. The Best Action Is the One with the Best Consequences   3
   John Hospers

2. The Best Action Is the One in Accord with Universal Rules   12
   James Rachels

3. The Best Action Is the One That Exercises the Mind's
   Faculties   16
   Aristotle

Professional Ethics

4. ACM Code of Ethics and Professional Conduct   23
   Association for Computing Machinery

5. Using the ACM Code   31
   *Ronald E. Anderson, Deborah G. Johnson, Donald Gotterbarm,
   Judith Perolle*

6. Can We Find a Single Ethical Code?   42
   Robert N. Barger

7. The Morality of Whistle-Blowing   47
   Sissela Bok

8. The Ethics of Systems Design   55
   Batya Friedman and Peter H. Kahn, Jr.

9. Are Hacker Break-ins Ethical?   64
   Eugene H. Spafford

10. Using Computers as Means, Not Ends   74
    Herbert L. Dreyfus and Stuart E. Dreyfus with Tom Athanasiou

II. Historical and Cultural Contexts

11. Technology Is a Tool of the Powerful   85
    Phillip Bereano

12. A History of the Personal Computer   91
    Robert Pool

13. Informing Ourselves to Death   101
    Neil Postman

14. Why the Future Doesn't Need Us   110
    Bill Joy

15. Boolean Logic   123
    Michael Heim

III. Social Contexts

16. Privacy in a Database Nation   137
    Simson Garfinkel

17. The GNU Manifesto   153
    Richard M. Stallman

18. Crossing the Digital Divide   162
    Jessica Brown

19. Gender Bias in Instructional Technology   171
    Katy Campbell

20. Computers and the Work Experience   184
    Anthony M. Townsend

21. Information Technologies and Our Changing Economy   190
    Martin Carnoy

22. Music: Intellectual Property's Canary in the Digital
    Coal Mine   202
    National Research Council

23. The Case for Collective Violence   214
    Craig Summers and Eric Markusen

24. Activism, Hacktivism, and Cyberterrorism   231
    Dorothy E. Denning

Preface

Too often, good people do things with computers that disturb other good people. Our ethical standards and social institutions have not yet adapted, it seems, to the moral dilemmas that result from computer technology. By the time our students reach decision-making positions, some of these problems will have been resolved, while different moral dilemmas will have been generated by further technological change. Hence, the responsibility of the computer professional to maximize the good consequences of computerization and minimize the bad will require not only technical skill, but also skill in recognizing and handling moral dilemmas.

We have chosen readings that will help students understand and resolve ethical issues in at least one of the following ways:

1. Acquaint students with contemporary and possible future moral problems that arise due to computerization
2. Give students a deeper understanding of the nature of moral choices
3. Help students understand the social, economic, legal, and cognitive effects of technology

Computers have already had an enormous impact on personal and professional life, as well as society at large, and their influence will only increase exponentially in the coming decades. This collection of readings is designed to help students evaluate this impact and, as computing professionals, steer information technologies toward positive effects.

The readings, annotated throughout with Internet references for further study, are designed for computing students and for students with computer-related interests. They include both scholarly works and lay articles to provide an engaging variety of material, as well as to demonstrate that the ethical consequences of computing is hardly an esoteric subject studied by academics alone. The broader implications of advancing technological development are of concern to everyone and have been thoughtfully considered by many writers over the years. It is for this reason that we include selections on very new conflicts (copyright infringement in the music industry, for example), as well as selections on lingering debates (for instance, the open source movement).

Unlike computer technology itself, which quickly becomes dated or obsolete, essays on the ethical questions surrounding technological advancement can remain relevant for decades. These questions are always complex, requiring careful examination from historical, philosophical, and sociological vantage points. Our goal has been to provide a framework for such a thoroughgoing examination.

M. David Ermann
Newark, Delaware

Michele S. Shauf
Atlanta, Georgia

I

Ethical Contexts

Philosophical Ethics

What constitutes an ethical choice? Does an ethical choice maximize happiness? Goodness? Does it follow some other universal principle? Is a universally applicable principle even possible? Ethical philosophers have long wrestled with these questions.

This section examines three ethical models: utilitarian, Kantian, and Nicomachean. In studying the following selections, consider how they might be applied to computer technologies. Following Aristotle's thinking, for example, can one conclude that hacking is ethical when it stems from a rational challenge conquered by a clever programmer? (See also Spafford, "Are Hacker Break-ins Ethical?")

1

The Best Action is the One with the Best Consequences

Of those actions available to you, you are morally obliged to choose that action which maximizes total happiness (summed over all affected persons) according to utilitarian ethical theory. The utilitarian model is particularly useful in illuminating instances when many people are affected in different ways by an action; for example, a utilitarian analysis may be useful in deciding what the laws ought to be on copyright (see National Research Council, "Music: Intellectual Property's Canary in the Digital Coal Mine") and privacy (see Garfinkel, "Privacy in a Database Nation").

John Hospers

Once one admits that one's own personal good is not the only consideration, how can one stop short of the good of everyone—"the general good"? This conclusion, at any rate, is the thesis of the ethical theory known as *utilitarianism*. The thesis is simply stated, though its application to actual situations is often extremely complex: whatever is intrinsically good should be promoted, and, accordingly, our obligation (or duty) is always to act so as to promote the greatest possible intrinsic good. It is never our duty to promote a lesser good when we could, by our action, promote a greater one; and the act which we should perform in any given situation is, therefore, the one which produces more intrinsic good than any other act we could have performed in its stead. In brief, the main tenet of utilitarianism is the maximization of intrinsic good.

Excerpt from *Human Conduct: Problems of Ethics,* Shorter Edition by John Hospers, Copyright © 1972 by Harcourt Brace & Company, reprinted by permission of the publisher.

The description just given is so brief that it will almost inevitably be misleading when one attempts to apply it in actual situations unless it is spelled out in greater detail. Let us proceed at once, then, to the necessary explanations and qualifications.

1. When utilitarians talk about right or wrong acts, they mean—and this point is shared by the proponents of all ethical theories—*voluntary* acts. Involuntary acts like the knee jerk are not included since we have no control over them: once the stimulus has occurred the act results quite irrespective of our own will. The most usual way in which the term "voluntary act" is defined is as follows:[1] an act is voluntary if the person *could* have acted differently *if* he had so chosen. For example, I went shopping yesterday, but if I had chosen (for one reason or another) to remain at home, I would have done so. My choosing made the difference. Making this condition is not the same as saying that an act, to be voluntary, must be *premeditated* or that it must be the outcome of *deliberation,* though voluntary acts often are planned. If you see a victim of a car accident lying in the street, you may rush to help him at once, without going through a process of deliberation; nevertheless your act is voluntary in that if you had chosen to ignore him you would have acted differently. Though not premeditated, the action *was* within your control. "Ought implies can," and there is no ought when there is no can. To be right or wrong, an act must be within your power to perform: it must be performable as the result of your choice, and a different choice must have led to a different act or to no act at all.

2. There is no preference for immediate, as opposed to remote, happiness. If Act A will produce a certain amount of happiness today and Act B will produce twice as much one year hence, I should do B, even though its effects are more remote. Remoteness does not affect the principle at all: happiness is as intrinsically good tomorrow or next year as it is today, and one should forego a smaller total intrinsic good now in favor of a larger one in the future. (Of course, a remote happiness is often less certain to occur. But in that case we should choose A not because it is more immediate but because it is more nearly certain to occur.) . . .

3. Unhappiness must be considered as well as happiness. Suppose that Act A will produce five units of happiness and none of unhappiness and Act B will produce ten units of happiness and ten of unhappiness. Then A is to be preferred because the *net* happiness—the resulting total after the unhappiness has been subtracted from it—is greater in A than in B: it is five in A and zero in B. Thus the formula "You should do what will produce the greatest total happiness" is not quite accurate; you should do what will produce the most *net* happiness. This modification is what we shall henceforth mean in talking about "producing the greatest happiness"—we shall assume that the unhappiness has already been figured into the total.

4. It is not even accurate to say that you should always do what leads to

the greatest *balance* of happiness over unhappiness, for there may be no such balance in any alternative open to the agent: he may have to choose between "the lesser of two evils." If Act A leads to five units of happiness and ten of unhappiness and Act B leads to five units of happiness and fifteen of unhappiness, you should choose A, not because it produces the most happiness (they both produce an equal amount) and not because there is a greater balance of happiness over unhappiness in A (there is a balance of unhappiness over happiness in both), but because, although both A and B produce a balance of unhappiness over happiness, A leads to a *smaller* balance of unhappiness over happiness than B does. Thus we should say, "Do that act which produces the greatest balance of happiness over unhappiness, or, if no act possible under the circumstance does this, do the one which produces the smallest balance of unhappiness over happiness." This qualification also we shall assume to be included in the utilitarian formula from now on in speaking of "producing the greatest happiness" or "maximizing happiness."

5. One should not assume that an act is right according to utilitarianism simply because it produces more happiness than unhappiness in its total consequences. If one did make this assumption, it would be right for ten men collectively to torture a victim, provided that the total pleasure enjoyed by the sadists exceeded the pain endured by the victim (assuming that pain is here equated with unhappiness and that all the persons died immediately thereafter and there were no further consequences). The requirement is not that the happiness exceed the unhappiness but that it do so *more* than any other act that could have been performed instead. This requirement is hardly fulfilled here: it is very probable indeed that the torturers could think of something better to do with their time.

6. When there is a choice between a greater happiness for yourself at the expense of others, and a greater happiness for others at the expense of your own, which should you choose? You choose, according to the utilitarian formula, whatever alternative results in the greater total amount of *net* happiness, precisely as we have described. If the net happiness is greater in the alternative favorable to yourself, you adopt this alternative; otherwise not. Mill says, "The happiness which forms the utilitarian standard of what is right in conduct, is not the agent's own happiness, but that of all concerned. As between his own happiness and that of others, utilitarianism requires him to be as strictly impartial as a disinterested and benevolent spectator."[2] To state this in different language, you are not to ignore your own happiness in your calculations, but neither are you to consider it more important than anyone else's; you count as one, and only as one, along with everyone else. Thus if Act A produces a total net happiness of one hundred, and Act B produces seventy-five, A is the right act even if you personally would be happier in consequence of B. Your choice should not be an "interested"

one; you are not to be prejudiced in favor of your own happiness nor, for that matter, against it; your choice should be strictly *dis*interested as in the case of an impartial judge. Your choice should be dictated by the greatest-total-happiness principle, not by a *your*-greatest-happiness principle. If you imagine yourself as a judge having to make a decision designed to produce the most happiness for all concerned *without* knowing which of the people affected would be *you,* you have the best idea of the impartiality of judgment required by the utilitarian morality.

In egoistic ethics . . . your sole duty is to promote your own interests as much as possible, making quite sure, of course, that what you do will make you really happy (or whatever else you include in "your own interest") and that you do not choose merely what you *think* at the moment will do so; we have called this policy the policy of "*enlightened* self-interest." In an *altruistic* ethics, on the other hand, you sacrifice your own interests completely to those of others: you ignore your own welfare and become a doormat for the fulfillment of the interests of others. . . . But the utilitarian ethics is neither egoistic nor altruistic: it is a *universalistic* ethics, since it considers your interests equally with everyone else's. You are not the slave of others, nor are they your slaves. Indeed, there are countless instances in which the act required of you by ethical egoism and the act required by utilitarianism will be the same: for very often indeed the act that makes you happy will also make those around you happy, and by promoting your own welfare you will also be promoting theirs. (As support for this position, consider capitalistic society: the producer of wealth, by being free to amass profits, will have more incentive to produce and, by increasing production, will be able to create more work and more wealth. By increasing production, he will be increasing the welfare of his employees and the wealth of the nation.) Moreover, it is much more likely that you can effectively produce good by concentrating on your immediate environment than by "spreading yourself thin" and trying to help everyone in the world: "do-gooders" often succeed in achieving no good at all. (But, of course, sometimes they do.) You are in a much better position to produce good among those people whose needs and interests you already know than among strangers; and, of course, the person whose needs and interests you probably know best of all (though not always) is yourself. Utilitarianism is very far, then, from recommending that you ignore your own interests.

It is only when your interests cannot be achieved except at the cost of sacrificing the *greater* interests of others that utilitarianism recommends self-sacrifice. When interests conflict, you have to weigh your own interest against the general interest. If, on the one hand, you are spending all your valuable study time (and thus sacrificing your grades and perhaps your college degree) visiting your sick aunt because she wants you to, you would probably produce more good by spending your time studying. But on the other hand, if an undeniably greater good will result from your sacrifice, if, for instance, your mother is seriously ill and no one else is available to care for her, you might have to drop out of school for a semester to care for her. It might even, on occasion, be your utilitarian duty to sacrifice your very life for a cause, when the cause is extremely worthy and requires your sacrifice for its fulfillment. But your must first make quire sure that your sacrifice will indeed produce the great good intended; otherwise you would be throwing your life away uselessly. You must act with your eyes open, not under the spell of a martyr complex.

. . . . .

7. The general temper of the utilitarian ethics can perhaps best be seen in its attitude toward moral rules, the traditional dos and don'ts. What is the utilitarian's attitude toward rules such as "Don't kill," "Don't tell lies," "Don't steal"?

According to utilitarianism, such rules are *on the whole* good, useful, and worthwhile, but they *may* have exceptions. None of them is sacrosanct. If killing is wrong, it is not because there is something intrinsically bad about killing itself, but because killing leads to a diminution of human happiness. This undesirable consequence almost always occurs: when a man takes another human life, he not only extinguishes in his victim all chances of future happiness, but he causes grief, bereavement, and perhaps years of misery for the victim's family and loved ones; moreover, for weeks or months countless people who know of this act may walk the streets in fear, wondering who will be the next victim—the amount of insecurity caused by even one act of murder is almost incalculable; and in addition to all this unhappiness, every violation of a law has a tendency to weaken the whole fabric of the law itself and tends to make other violations easier and more likely to occur. If the guilty man is caught, he himself hardly gains much happiness from lifelong imprisonment, nor are other people usually much happier for long because of his incarceration; and if he is not caught, many people will live in fear and dread, and he himself will probably repeat his act sooner or later, having escaped capture this time. The good consequences, if any, are few and far between and are overwhelmingly outweighed by the bad ones. Because of these prevailingly bad consequences, killing is condemned by the utilitarian, and thus he agrees with the traditional moral rule prohibiting it.

He would nevertheless admit the possibility of exceptions: if you had had the opportunity to assassinate Hitler in 1943 and did not, the utilitarian would probably say that you were doing wrong in *not* killing him. By not killing him, you would be stealing the death of thousands, if not millions, of other people: political prisoners and Jews whom he tortured and killed in concentration camps and thousands of soldiers (both Axis and Allied) whose lives would have been saved by an earlier cessation of the war. If you had refrained from killing him when you had the chance, saying "It is my duty never to take a life, therefore I shall not take his," the man whose life you saved would then turn around and have a thousand others killed, and for his act the victims would have you to thank. Your conscience, guided by the traditional moral rules, would have helped to bring about the torture and death of countless other people.

Does the utilitarian's willingness to adopt violence upon occasion mean that a utilitarian could never be a pacifist? Not necessarily. He *might* say that *all* taking of human life is wrong, but if he took this stand, he would do so because he believed that killing *always* leads to worse consequences (or greater unhappiness) than not killing and *not* because there is anything intrinsically bad about killing. He might even be able to make out a plausible argument for saying that killing Hitler would have been wrong: perhaps even worse men would have taken over and the slaughter wouldn't have been prevented (but then wouldn't it have been right to kill *all* of them if one had the chance?); perhaps Hitler's "intuitions" led to an earlier defeat for Germany than if stabler men had made more rationally self-seeking decisions on behalf of Nazi Germany; perhaps the assassination of a bad leader would help lead to the assassination of a good one later on. With regard to some Latin American nations, at any rate, one might argue that killing one dictator would only lead to a revolution and another dictator just as bad as the first, with the consequent assassination of the second one, thus leading to revolution and social chaos and a third dictator. There are countless empirical facts that must be taken into consideration and carefully weighed before any such decision can safely be made. The utilitarian is not committed to saying that any one policy or line of action is the best in any particular situation, for what is best depends on empirical facts which may be extremely difficult to ascertain. All he is committed to is the statement that when the action is one that does not promote human happiness as much as another action that he could have performed instead, then the action is wrong; and that when it does promote more happiness, it is right. Which particular action will maximize happiness more than any other, in a particular situation, can be determined only by empirical investigation. Thus, it is possible that killing is always wrong—at least the utilitarian could consistently say so and thus be a pacifist; but *if* killing is always wrong, it is wrong not because killing is wrong per se but because it always and without exception leads to worse consequences than any other actions that could have been performed instead. Then the pacifist, if he is a consistent utilitarian, would have to go on to show in each instance that each and every act of killing is worse (leads to worse consequences) than any act of refraining from doing so—even when the man is a trigger-happy gunman who will kill dozens of people in a crowded street if he is not killed first.

That killing is worse in every instance would be extremely difficult—most people would say impossible—to prove.

Consider the syllogism:

The action which promotes the maximum happiness is right.

This action is the one which promotes the maximum happiness.

Therefore, *This action is right.*

The utilitarian gives undeviating assent only to the *first* of these three statements (the major premise); this statement is the chief article of his utilitarian creed, and he cannot abandon it without being inconsistent with his own doctrine. But this first premise is not enough to yield the third statement, which is the conclusion of the argument. To know that the conclusion is true, even granting that the major premise is, one must also know whether the second statement (the minor premise) is true; and the second statement is an empirical one, which cannot be verified by the philosopher sitting in his study but only by a thorough investigation of the empirical facts of the situation. Many people would accept the major premise (and thus be utilitarians) and yet disagree among themselves on the conclusion because they would disagree on the minor premise. They would agree that an act is right if it leads to maximum happiness, but they would not agree on whether this action or that one is the one which *will* in fact lead to the most happiness. They disagree about the empirical facts of the case, not in their utilitarian ethics. The disagreement could be resolved if both parties had a complete grasp of all the relevant empirical facts, for then they would know *which* action *would* lead to the most happiness. In many situations, of course, such agreement will never be reached because the consequences of people's actions (especially when they affect thousands of other people over a long period of time, as happens when war is declared) are so numerous and so complex that nobody will ever know them all. Such a disagreement will not be the fault of ethics, or of philosophy in general, but of the empirical world for being so complicated and subtle in its workings that the full consequences of our actions often can not be determined. Frequently it would take an omniscient deity to know which action in a particular situation was right. Finite human beings have to be content with basing their actions on estimates of probability.

According to utilitarianism, then, the traditional moral rules are justified for the most part because following them will lead to the best consequences far more often than violating them will; and that is why they are useful rules of thumb in human action. But, for the utilitarian, this is *all* they are—rules of thumb. They should never be used blindly, as a pat formula or inviolable rule subject to no exceptions, without an eye to the detailed consequences in each particular situation. The judge who condemned a man to death in the electric chair for stealing $1.95 (as in the case in Alabama in 1959) was probably not contributing to human happiness by inflicting this extreme penalty, even though he acted in accordance with the law of that state. The utilitarian would say that if a starving man steals a loaf of bread, as in Victor Hugo's *Les Miserables,* he should not be condemned for violating the rule "Do not steal"; in fact he probably did nothing morally wrong by stealing in this instance because the effects of not stealing would . . . have meant starvation and preserving a life (the utilitarian would say) is more important to human happiness than refraining from stealing a loaf of bread—especially since the man stole from one who was far from starving himself (the "victim" would never have missed it). He is probably blameless furthermore because the whole episode was made possible in the first place by a system of laws and a social structure which, by any utilitarian standard, were vicious in the extreme. (But see the effects of lawbreaking, below.)

Moral rules are especially useful when we have to act at once without being able adequately to weigh the consequences; for *usually* (as experience shows) better—i.e., more-happiness-producing—consequences are obtained by following moral rules than by not following them. If there is a drowning person whom you could rescue, you should do so without further investigation; for if you stopped to investigate his record, he would already have drowned. True, he might turn out to be a Hitler, but unless we have such evidence, we have to go by the probability that the world is better off for his being alive than his being dead. Again, there may be situations in which telling a lie will have better affects than telling the truth. But since, on the whole, lying has bad effects, we have to have special evidence that this situation is different before we are justified in violating the rule. If we have no time to gather such evidence, we should act on what is most probable, namely that telling a lie in this situation will produce consequences less good than telling the truth.

The utilitarian attitude toward moral rules is more favorable than might first appear because of the hidden, or subtle, or not frequently thought of, consequences of actions which at first sight would seem to justify a violation of the rules. One might consider *all* the consequences of the action and not just the immediate ones or the ones that happen to be the most conspicuous. For example: the utilitarian would not hold that it is *always* wrong to break a law, unless, he had good grounds for saying that breaking the law *always* leads to worse consequences than observing it. But if the law is a bad law to begin with or even if it is a good law on the whole but observing the law in this particular case would be deleterious to human happiness, then the law should be broken in this case. You would be morally justified, for example, in breaking the speed law in order to rush a badly wounded person to a hospital. But in many situations (probably in most) in which the utilitarian criterion at first *seems* to justify the violation of a law, it does not really do so after careful consideration because of the far-flung consequences. For example, in a more typical instance of breaking the speed law, you might argue as follows: "It would make me happier if I were not arrested for the violation, and it wouldn't make the arresting officer any the less happy, in fact it would save him the trouble of writing out the ticket, so—why not? By letting me go, wouldn't the arresting officer be increasing the total happiness of the world by just a little bit, both his and mine, whereas by giving me a ticket he might actually decrease the world's happiness slightly?"

But happiness would be slightly increased only if one considers only the immediate situation. For one thing, by breaking the speed limit you are endangering the lives of others—you are less able to stop or to swerve out of the way in an emergency. Also those who see you speeding and escaping the penalty may decide to do the same thing themselves; even though you don't cause any accidents by your violation, *they* may do so after taking their cue from you. Moreover, lawbreaking may reduce respect for law itself; although there may well be unjust laws and many laws could be improved, it is usually better (has better consequences) to work for their repeal than to break them while they are still in effect. Every violation decreases the effectiveness of law, and we are surely better off having law than not having it at all—even the man who violently objects to a law and complains bitterly when he's arrested will invoke the law to protect *himself* against the violations of others. In spite of these cautions, utilitarianism does not say that one should *never* break a law but only that the consequences of doing so are far more often bad than good; a closer look at the consequences will show how true their reasoning is.

Notes

1. This term is most precisely defined by G. E. Moore in chapter 1, "Utilitarianism," of his book *Ethics*. [New York: Henry Holt and Company, 1912]. For the clearest and most rigorous statement of utilitarianism in its hedonistic form, see chapters 1 and 2 of [Moore's] book.
2. J. S. Mill, *Utilitarianism*. [ed. Oskar Piest (New York: Bobbs-Merrill, 1957; originally published 1863.], chap. 2.

2

The Best Action Is the One in Accord with Universal Rules

An important competitor to the utilitarian moral theory is the theory developed by Immanuel Kant. The fundamental ethical principle of Kantian theory is this: People should always be treated as ends, never as simply a means. In other words, it is wrong to ignore another person's legitimate desires and to use him or her just to get what you want. In the following essay James Rachels explains the Kantian view.

An example of Kantian thinking can be found in Stallman's argument that programmers should treat other computer users as persons whose desires should be respected, rather than as economic units (see "The GNU Manifesto").

James Rachels

The great German philosopher Immanuel Kant thought that human beings occupy a special place in creation. Of course he was not alone in thinking this. It is an old idea: from ancient times, humans have considered themselves to be essentially different from all other creatures—and not just different but *better*. In fact, humans have traditionally thought themselves to be quite fabulous. Kant certainly did. [I]n his view, human beings have "an intrinsic worth, i.e., *dignity,*" which makes them valuable "above all price." Other animals, by contrast, have value only insofar as they serve human purposes. In his *Lecture on Ethics* (1779), Kant said:

> But so far as animals are concerned, we have no direct duties. Animals . . . are there merely as means to an end. That end is man.

We can, therefore, use animals in any way we please. We do not even have a "direct duty" to refrain from torturing them. Kant admits that it is probably wrong to torture them, but the reason is not that *they* would be hurt; the reason is only that we might suffer indirectly as a result of it, because "he

From James Rachels, *The Elements of Moral Philosophy* © 1986. Reprinted by permission of The McGraw-Hill Companies.

who is cruel to animals becomes hard also in his dealings with men." Thus [i]n Kant's view, mere animals have no importance at all. Human beings are, however, another story entirely. According to Kant, humans may never be "used" as means to an end. He even went so far to suggest that this is the ultimate law of morality.

Like many other philosophers, Kant believed that morality can be summed up in one ultimate principle, from which all our duties and obligations are derived. He called this principle *The Categorical Imperative*. In the *Groundwork of the Metaphysics of Morals* (1785) he expressed it like this:

> Act only according to that maxim by which you can at the same time will that it should become a universal law.

However, Kant also gave *another* formulation of The Categorical Imperative. Later in the same book, he said that the ultimate moral principle may be understood as saying:

> Act so that you treat humanity, whether in your own person or in that of another, always as an end and never as a means only.

Scholars have wondered ever since why Kant thought these two rules were equivalent. They *seem* to express very different moral conceptions. Are they, as he apparently believed, two versions of the same basic idea, or are they really different ideas? We will not pause over this question. Instead we will concentrate here on Kant's belief that morality requires us to treat persons "always as an end and never as a means only." What exactly does this mean, and why did he think it true?

When Kant said that the value of human beings "is above all price," he did not intend this as mere rhetoric but as an objective judgment about the place of human beings in the scheme of things. There are two important facts about people that, in his view, support his judgment.

First, because people have desires and goals, other things have value *for them*, in relation to *their* projects. Mere "things" (and this includes nonhuman animals, whom Kant considered unable to have self-conscious desires and goals) have value only as means to ends, and it is human ends that *give* them value. Thus if you want to become a better chess player, a book of chess instruction will have value for you; but apart from such ends the book has no value. Or if you want to travel about, a car will have value for you; but apart from this desire the car will have no value.

Second, and even more important, humans have "an intrinsic worth, i.e., *dignity*," because they are *rational agents*—that is, free agents capable of making their own decisions, setting their own goals, and guiding their conduct by reason. Because the moral law is the law of reason, rational beings are the embodiment of the moral law itself. The only way that moral goodness can exist at all in the world is for rational creatures to apprehend what they should do and, acting from a sense of duty, do it. This, Kant thought, is the *only* thing that has "moral worth." Thus if there were no rational beings, the moral dimension of the world would simply disappear.

It makes no sense, therefore, to regard rational beings merely as one kind of valuable thing among others. They are the beings *from whom* mere "things" have value, and they are the beings whose conscientious actions have moral worth. So Kant concludes that their value must be absolute, and not comparable to the value of anything else.

If their value is "beyond all price," it follows that rational beings must be treated "always as an end, and never as a means only." This means, on the most superficial level, that we have a strict duty of beneficence toward other persons: we must strive to promote their welfare; we must respect their rights, avoid harming them, and generally "endeavor, so far as we can, to further the ends of others."

But Kant's idea also has a somewhat deeper implication. The beings we are talking about are *rational* beings, and "treating them as ends-in-themselves" means *respecting their rationality*. Thus we may never *manipulate* people, or *use* people, to achieve our purposes, no matter how good those purposes may be. Kant gives this example, which is similar to an example he uses to illustrate the first version of his categorical imperative. Suppose you need money, and so you want a "loan," but you know you will not be able to repay it. In desperation, you consider making a false promise (to repay) in order to trick a friend into giving you the money. May you do this? Perhaps you need the money for a good purpose—so good, in fact, that you might convince yourself the lie would be justified. Nevertheless, if you lied to your friend, you would merely be manipulating him and using him "as means."

On the other hand, what would it be like to treat your friend "as an end"? Suppose you told the truth, that you need the money for a certain purpose but will not be able to repay it. Then your friend could make up his own mind about whether to let you have it. He could exercise his own powers of reason, consulting his own value and wishes, and make a free, autonomous choice. If he did decide to give the money for this purpose, he would be choosing to make that purpose *his own*. Thus you would not merely be using him as a means to achieving *your* goal. This is what Kant meant when he said, "Rational beings . . . must always be esteemed at the same time as ends, i.e., only as beings who must be able to contain in themselves the end of the very same action."

Now Kant's conception of human dignity is not easy to grasp; it is, in fact, probably the most difficult notion discussed [here]. We need to find a way to make the idea clearer. In order to do that, we will consider in some detail one of its most important applications—this may be better than a dry, theoretical discussion. Kant believed that if we take the idea of human dignity seriously, we will be able to understand the practice of criminal punishment in a new and revealing way.

. . . . .

On the face of it, it seems unlikely that we could describe punishing someone as "respecting him as a person" or as "treating him as an end-in-himself." How could taking away someone's freedom, by sending him to prison, be a way of "respecting" him? Yet that is exactly what Kant suggests. Even more paradoxically, he implies that *executing* someone may also be a way of treating him "as an end." How can this be?

Remember that, for Kant, treating someone as an "end-in-himself" means treating him *as a rational being.* Thus we have to ask, What does it mean to treat someone as a rational being? Now a rational being is someone who is capable of reasoning about his conduct and who freely decides what he will do, on the basis of his own rational conception of what is best. Because he has these capacities, a rational being is *responsible* for his actions. We need to bear in mind the difference between:

1. Treating someone as a responsible being

and

2. Treating someone as a being who is not responsible for his conduct.

Mere animals, who lack reason, are not responsible for their actions; nor are people who are mentally "sick" and not in control of themselves. In such cases it would be absurd to try to "hold them accountable." We could not properly feel gratitude or resentment toward them, for they are not responsible for any good or ill they cause. Moreover, we cannot expect them to understand why we treat them as we do, any more than they understand why they behave as they do. So we have no choice but to deal with them by manipulating them, rather than by addressing them as autonomous individuals. When we spank a dog who has urinated on the rug, for example, we may do so in an attempt to prevent him from doing it again—but we are merely trying to "train" him. We could not reason with him even if we wanted to. The same goes for mentally "sick" humans.

On the other hand, rational beings are responsible for their behavior and so may properly be "held accountable" for what they do. We may feel gratitude when they behave well, and resentment when they behave badly. Reward and punishment—not "training" or other manipulation—are the natural expression of this gratitude and resentment. Thus in punishing people, we are *holding them responsible* for their actions, in a way in which we cannot hold mere animals responsible. We are responding to them not as people who are "sick" or who have no control over themselves, but as people who have freely chosen their evil deeds.

Furthermore, in dealing with responsible agents, we may properly allow *their conduct* to determine, at least in part, how we respond to them. If someone has been kind to you, you may respond by being generous in return; and if someone is nasty to you, you may also take that into account in deciding how to deal with him or her. And why shouldn't you? Why should you treat everyone alike, regardless of how *they* have chosen to behave?

Kant gives this last point a distinctive twist. There is [i]n his view, a deep logical reason for responding to other people "in kind." The first formulation of The Categorical Imperative comes into play here. When we decide what to do, we in effect proclaim our wish that our conduct be made into a "universal law." Therefore, when a rational being decides to treat people in a certain way, he decrees that in his judgment *this is the way people are to be treated.* Thus if we treat him the same way in return, we are doing nothing more than treating him as *he has decided* people are to be treated. If he treats others badly, and we treat him badly, we are complying with his own decision. (Of course, if he treats others well, and we treat him well in return, we are also complying with the choice he has made.) We are allowing *him* to decide how he is to be treated—and so we are, in a perfectly clear sense, respecting his judgment, by allowing it to control our treatment of him. Thus Kant says of the criminal, "His own evil deed draws the punishment upon himself."

3

The Best Action Is the One That Exercises the Mind's Faculties

The question of what constitutes ethical action has been a subject of discussion for millennia, as this selection from Aristotle (4th c. BCE) shows. Aristotle's answer is that ethical action consists in the active exercise of the mind's faculties. Those who are most involved with computerization, for whom reasoning and intellectual challenge are

From Aristotle, *Ethics for English Readers,* trans. H. Rackham. Oxford: Basil Blackwell, Publisher, 1952. Reprinted by permission.

highly valued, may well agree with Aristotle. (See also Dreyfus and Dreyfus, "Using Computers as Means, Not Ends.")

Aristotle

. . . Inasmuch as all study and all deliberate action is aimed at some good object, let us state what is the good which is in our view the aim of political science, and what is the highest of the goods obtainable by action.

Now as far as the name goes there is virtual agreement about this among the vast majority of mankind. Both ordinary people and persons of trained mind define the good as happiness. But as to what constitutes happiness opinions differ: the answer given by ordinary people is not the same as the verdict of the philosopher. Ordinary men identify happiness with something obvious and visible, such as pleasure or wealth or honor—everybody gives a different definition, and sometimes the same person's own definition alters: when a man has fallen ill he thinks that happiness is health, if he is poor he thinks it is wealth. And when people realize their own ignorance they regard with admiration those who propound some grand theory that is above their heads. The view has been held by some thinkers[1] that besides the many good things alluded to above there also exists something that is good in itself, which is the fundamental cause of the goodness of all the others.

Now to review the whole of these opinions would perhaps be a rather thankless task. It may be enough to examine those that are most widely held, or that appear to have some considerable argument in their favor. . . .

Reasons for doubting whether enjoyment, fame, virtue, or wealth is the whole good

To judge by men's mode of living, the mass of mankind think that good and happiness consist in pleasure, and consequently are content with a life of mere enjoyment. There are in fact three principal modes of life—the one just mentioned, the life of active citizenship, and the life of contemplation. The masses, being utterly servile, obviously prefer the life of mere cattle; and indeed they have some reason for this, inasmuch as many men of high station share the tastes of Sardanapalus.[2] The better people, on the other hand, and men of action, give the highest value to honor, since honor may be said to be the object aimed at in a public career. Nevertheless, it would seem that honor is a more superficial thing than the good which we are in search of, because honor seems to depend more on the people who render it than on the person who receives it, whereas we dimly feel that good must be something inherent in oneself and inalienable. Moreover, men's object in pursuing honor appears to be to convince themselves of their own worth; at all events they seek to be honored by persons of insight and by people who are well acquainted with them, and to be honored for their merit. It therefore seems that at all events in the opinions of these men goodness is more valuable than honor, and probably one may suppose that it has a better claim than honor to be deemed the end at which the life of politics aims. But even virtue appears to lack completeness as an end, inasmuch as it seems to be possible to possess it while one is asleep or living a life of perpetual inactivity, and moreover one can be virtuous and yet suffer extreme sorrow and misfortune; but nobody except for the sake of maintaining a paradox would call a man happy in those circumstances.

However, enough has been said on this topic, which has indeed been sufficiently discussed in popular treatises.

The third life is the life of contemplation, which we shall consider later.

The life of money-making is a cramped way of living, and clearly wealth is not the good we are in search of, as it is only valuable as a means to something else. Consequently a stronger case might be made for the objects previously specified, because they are valued for their own sake; but even they appear to be inadequate, although a great deal of discussion has been devoted to them. . . .

Reaffirmation that the good is the ultimate and self-sufficient object of desire and that "happiness" is the good

What then is the precise nature of the practicable good which we are investigating? It appears to be one thing in one occupation or profession and another in another: the object pursued in medicine is different from that of military science, and similarly in regard to the other activities. What definition of the term "good" then is applicable to all of them? Perhaps "the object for the sake of attaining which all the subsidiary activities are undertaken." The object pursued in the practice of medicine is health, in a military career victory, in architecture a building—one thing in one pursuit and another in another, but in every occupation and every pursuit it is the end aimed at, since it is for the sake of this that the subsidiary activities in all these pursuits are undertaken. Consequently if there is some one thing which is the end and aim of all practical activities whatsoever, that thing, or if there are several, those things, will constitute the practicable good.

Our argument has therefore come round again by a different route to the point reached before. We must endeavor to render it yet clearer.

Now the objects at which our actions aim are manifestly several, and some of these objects, for instance money, and instruments in general, we adopt as means to the attainment of something else. This shows that not all the objects we pursue are final ends. But the greatest good manifestly is a final end. Consequently if there is only one thing which is final, that will be the object for which we are now seeking, or if there are several, it will be that one among them which possesses the most complete finality.

Now a thing that is pursued for its own sake we pronounce to be more final than one pursued as a means to some other thing, and a thing that is never desired for the sake of something else we call more final than those which are desired for the sake of something else as well as for their own sake. In fact the absolutely final is something that is always desired on its own account and never as a means for obtaining something else. Now this description appears to apply in the highest degree to happiness, since we always desire happiness for its own sake and never on account of something else; whereas honor and pleasure and intelligence and each of the virtues, though we do indeed desire them on their own account as well, for we should desire each of them even if it produced no external result, we also desire for the sake of happiness, because we believe that they will bring it to us, whereas nobody desires happiness for the sake of those things, not for anything else but itself.

The same result seems to follow from a consideration of the subject of self-sufficiency, which is felt to be a necessary attribute of the final good. The term self-sufficient denotes not merely being sufficient for oneself alone, as if one lived the life of a hermit, but also being sufficient for the needs of one's parents and children and wife, and one's friends and fellow-countrymen in general, inasmuch as man is by nature a social being.

Yet we are bound to assume some limit in these relationships, since if one extends the connection to include one's children's children and friends' friends, it will go on *ad infinitum.* But that is a matter which must be deferred for later consideration. Let us define self-sufficiency as the quality which makes life to be desirable and lacking in nothing even when considered by itself; and this quality we assume to belong to happiness. Moreover, when we pronounce happiness to be the most desirable of all things, we do not mean that it stands as one in a list of good things—were it so, it would obviously be more desirable in combination with even the smallest of the other goods, inasmuch as that addition would increase the total of good, and of two good things the larger must always be the more desirable.

Thus it appears that happiness is something final and complete in itself, as being the aim and end of all practical activities whatever.

For a more specific conception of the kind of "happiness" which is the good, we do well to examine whether nature intended man for anything, as it intended the eye for sight. What is distinctive of man is reason, so the happiness which is the good must be the exercise of reason in living.

Possibly, however, the student may feel that the statement that happiness is the greatest good is a mere truism, and he may want a clearer explanation of what the precise nature of happiness is. This may perhaps be achieved by ascertaining what is the proper function of man. In the case of flute players or sculptors or other artists, and generally of all persons who have a particular work to perform, it is felt that their good and their well-being are found in that work. It may be supposed that this similarly holds good in the case of a human being, if we may assume that there is some work which constitutes the proper function of a human being as such. Can it then be the case that whereas a carpenter and a shoemaker have definite functions or businesses to perform, a man as such has none, and is not designed by nature to perform any function? Should we not rather assume that, just as the eye and hand and foot and every part of the body manifestly have functions assigned to them, so also there is a function that belongs to a man, over and above all the special functions that belong to his members? If so, what precisely will that function be? It is clear that the mere activity of living is shared by man even with the vegetable kingdom, whereas we are looking for some function that belongs specially to man. We must therefore set aside the vital activity of nutrition and growth. Next perhaps comes the life of the senses; but this also is manifestly shared by the horse and the ox and all the animals. There remains therefore what may be designated the practical life of the rational faculty.

But the term "rational" life has two meanings: it denotes both the mere possession of reason, and its active exercise. Let us take it that we here mean the latter, as that appears to be the more proper signification of the term. Granted then that the special function of man is the active exercise of the mind's faculties in accordance with rational principle, or at all events not in detachment from rational principle, and that the function of anything, for example, a harper, is generally the same as the function of a good specimen of that thing, for example a good harper (the specification of the function merely being augmented in the latter case with the statement of excellence—a harper is a man who plays the harp, a good harper one who plays the harp well)—granted, I say, the truth of these assumptions, it follows that the good of man consists in the active exercise of the faculties in conformity with excellence or virtue, or if there are several virtues, in conformity with the best and most perfect among them.

Notes

1. Plato and the Academy.
2. A mythical Assyrian king; two versions of his epitaph are recorded, one containing the words "Eat, drink, play, since all else is not worth that snap of the fingers," the other ending "I have what I ate, and the delightful deeds of wantonness and love in which I shared; but all my wealth is vanished."

Professional Ethics

How can computing professionals apply ethical decision making to their work? Because of the pervasiveness and power of information technology, many ethical dilemmas emerge in the field of computing.

This section examines the ways in which these dilemmas can be negotiated. For further study of computering ethics, you may also visit the Brookings Computer Ethics Institute website, www.brook.edu/its/cei/cei_hp.htm.

4

ACM Code of Ethics and Professional Conduct

On October 16, 1992, the Executive Council of the Association for Computing Machinery voted to adopt the following revised Code of Ethics. The Code contains twenty-four imperatives that define the personal responsibilities of computing professionals. ACM also sponsors a special-interest group on computing ethics (SIGCAS). See www.acm.org.

Association for Computing Machinery (ACM)

Commitment to ethical professional conduct is expected of every voting, associate, and student member of ACM. This Code, consisting of 24 imperatives formulated as statements of personal responsibility, identifies the elements of such a commitment.

It contains many, but not all, issues professionals are likely to face. Section 1 outlines fundamental ethical considerations, while Section 2 addresses additional, more specific considerations of professional conduct. Statements in Section 3 pertain more specifically to individuals who have a leadership role, whether in the workplace or in a volunteer capacity, for example with organizations such as ACM. Principles involving compliance with this Code are given in Section 4.

The Code is supplemented by a set of Guidelines, which provide explanation to assist members in dealing with the various issues contained in the Code. It is expected that the Guidelines will be changed more frequently than the Code.

The Code and its supplemented Guidelines are intended to serve as a basis for ethical decision making in the conduct of professional work. Secondarily, they may serve as a basis for judging the merit of a formal complaint pertaining to violation of professional ethical standards.

It should be noted that although computing is not mentioned in the moral imperatives section, the Code is concerned with how these fundamental imperatives apply to one's conduct as a computing professional. These imperatives are expressed in a general form to emphasize that ethical principles which apply to computer ethics are derived from more general ethical principles.

It is understood that some words and phrases in a code of ethics are subject to varying interpretations, and that any ethical principle may conflict with other ethical principles in specific situations. Questions related to ethical conflicts can best be answered by thoughtful consideration of fundamental principles, rather than reliance on detailed regulations.

1. General Moral Imperatives

As an ACM member I will . . .

1.1 Contribute to society and human well-being

This principle concerning the quality of life of all people affirms an obligation to protect fundamental human rights and to respect the diversity of all cultures. An essential aim of computing professionals is to minimize negative consequences of computing systems, including threats to health and safety. When designing or implementing systems, computing professionals must attempt to ensure that the products of their efforts will be used in socially responsible ways, will meet social needs, and will avoid harmful effects to health and welfare.

In addition to a safe social environment, human well-being includes a safe natural environment. Therefore, computing professionals who design and develop systems must be alert to, and make others aware of, any potential damage to the local or global environment.

1.2 Avoid harm to others

"Harm" means injury or negative consequences, such as undesirable loss of information, loss of property, property damage, or unwanted environmental impacts. This principle prohibits use of computing technology in ways that result in harm to any of the following: users, the general public, employees, employers. Harmful actions include intentional destruction or modification of files and programs leading to serious loss of resources or unnecessary expenditure of human resources such as the time and effort required to purge systems of computer viruses.

Well-intended actions, including those that accomplish assigned duties, may lead to harm unexpectedly. In such an event the responsible person or persons are obligated to undo or mitigate the negative consequences as much as possible. One way to avoid unintentional harm is to carefully consider potential impacts on all those affected by decisions made during design and implementation.

To minimize the possibility of indirectly harming others, computing professionals must minimize malfunctions by following generally accepted standards for system design and testing. Furthermore, it is often necessary to assess the social consequences of systems to project the likelihood of any serious harm to others. If system features are misrepresented to users, coworkers, or supervisors, the individual computing professional is responsible for any resulting injury.

In the work environment the computing professional has the additional obligation to report any signs of system dangers that might result in serious personal or social damage. If one's superiors do not act to curtail or mitigate such dangers, it may be necessary to "blow the whistle" to help correct the problem or reduce the risk. However, capricious or misguided reporting of violations can, itself, be harmful. Before reporting violations, all relevant aspects of the incident must be thoroughly assessed. In particular, the assessment of risk and responsibility must be credible. It is suggested that advice be sought from other computing professionals. (See principle 2.5 regarding thorough evaluations.)

1.3 Be honest and trustworthy

Honesty is an essential component of trust. Without trust an organization cannot function effectively. The honest computing professional will not make deliberately false or deceptive claims about a system or system design, but will instead provide full disclosure of all pertinent system limitations and problems.

A computer professional has a duty to be honest about his or her own qualifications, and about any circumstances that might lead to conflicts of interest.

Membership in volunteer organizations such as ACM may at times place individuals in situations where their statements or actions could be interpreted as carrying the "weight" of a larger group of professionals. An ACM member will exercise care to not misrepresent ACM or positions and policies of ACM or any ACM units.

1.4 Be fair and take action not to discriminate

The values of equality, tolerance, respect for others, and the principles of equal justice govern this imperative. Discrimination on the basis of race, sex, religion, age, disability, national origin, or other such factors is an explicit violation of ACM policy and will not be tolerated.

Inequities between different groups of people may result from the use or misuse of information and technology. In a fair society, all individuals would have equal opportunity to participate in, or benefit from, the use of computer resources regardless of race, sex, religion, age, disability, national origin or other such similar factors. However, these ideals do not justify unauthorized use of computer resources nor do they provide an adequate basis for violation of any other ethical imperatives of this code.

1.5 Honor property rights including copyrights and patents

Violation of copyrights, patents, trade secrets and the terms of license agreements is prohibited by law in most circumstances. Even when software is not so protected, such violations are contrary to professional behavior. Copies of software should be made only with proper authorization. Unauthorized duplication of materials must not be condoned.

1.6 Give proper credit for intellectual property

Computing professionals are obligated to protect the integrity of intellectual property. Specifically, one must not take credit for other's ideas or work, even in cases where the work has not been explicitly protected, for example by copyright or patent.

1.7 Respect the privacy of others

Computing and communication technology enables the collection and exchange of personal information on a scale unprecedented in the history of civilization. Thus there is increased potential for violating the privacy of individuals and groups. It is the responsibility of professionals to maintain the privacy and integrity of data describing individuals. This includes taking precautions to ensure the accuracy of data, as well as protecting it from unauthorized access or accidental disclosure to inappropriate individuals. Furthermore, procedures must be established to allow individuals to review their records and correct inaccuracies.

This imperative implies that only the necessary amount of personal information be collected in a system, that retention and disposal periods for that information be clearly defined and enforced, and that personal information gathered for a specific purpose not be used for other purposes without consent of the individual(s). These principles apply to electronic communications, including electronic mail, and prohibit procedures that capture or monitor electronic user data, including messages, without the permission of users or *bona fide* authorization related to system operation and maintenance. User data observed during the normal duties of system operation and maintenance must be treated with strictest confidentiality, except in cases where it is evidence for the violation of law, organizational regulations, or this Code. In these cases, the nature or contents of that information must be disclosed only to proper authorities.

1.8 Honor confidentiality

The principle of honesty extends to issues of confidentiality of information whenever one has made an explicit promise to honor confidentiality or, implicitly, when private information not directly related to the performance of one's duties becomes available. The ethical concern is to respect all obligations of confidentiality to employers, clients, and users unless discharged from such obligations by requirements of the law or other principles of this Code.

2. More Specific Professional Responsibilities

As an ACM computing professional I will . . .

2.1 Strive to achieve the highest quality, effectiveness and dignity in both the process and products of professional work

Excellence is perhaps the most important obligation of a professional. The computing professional must strive to achieve quality and to be cognizant of the serious negative consequences that may result from poor quality in a system.

2.2 Acquire and maintain professional competence

Excellence depends on individuals who take responsibility for acquiring and maintaining professional competence. A professional must participate in setting standards for appropriate levels of competence, and strive to achieve those standards. Upgrading technical knowledge and competence can be achieved in several ways: doing independent study; attending seminars, conferences, or courses; and being involved in professional organizations.

2.3 Know and respect existing laws pertaining to professional work

ACM members must obey existing local, state, province, national, and international laws unless there is a compelling ethical basis not to do so. Policies and procedures of the organizations in which one participates must also be obeyed. But compliance must be balanced with the recognition that sometimes existing laws and rules may be immoral or inappropriate and, therefore, must be challenged.

Violation of a law or regulation may be ethical when that law or rule has inadequate moral basis or when it conflicts with another law judged to be more important. If one decides to violate a law or rule because it is viewed as unethical, or for any other reason, one must fully accept responsibility for one's actions and for the consequences.

2.4 Accept and provide appropriate professional review

Quality professional work, especially in the computing profession, depends on professional reviewing and critiquing. Whenever appropriate, individual members should seek and utilize peer review as well as provide critical review of the work of others.

2.5 Give comprehensive and thorough evaluations of computer systems and their impacts, including analysis of possible risks

Computer professionals must strive to be perceptive, thorough, and objective when evaluating, recommending, and presenting system descriptions and alternatives. Computer professionals are in a position of special trust, and therefore have a special responsibility to provide objective, credible evaluations to employers, clients, users, and the public. When providing evaluations the professional must also identify any relevant conflicts of interest, as stated in imperative 1.3.

As noted in the discussion of principle 1.2 on avoiding harm, any signs of danger from systems must be reported to those who have opportunity and/or responsibility to resolve them. See the guidelines for imperative 1.2 for more details concerning harm, including the reporting of professional violations.

2.6 Honor contracts, agreements, and assigned responsibilities

Honoring one's commitments is a matter of integrity and honesty. For the computer professional this includes ensuring that system elements perform as intended. Also, when one contracts for work with another party, one has an obligation to keep that party properly informed about progress toward completing that work.

A computing professional has a responsibility to request a change in any assignment that he or she feels cannot be completed as defined. Only after serious consideration and with full disclosure of risk and concerns to the employer or client, should one accept the assignment. The major underlying principle here is the obligation to accept personal accountability for professional work. On some occasions other ethical principles may take greater priority.

A judgment that a specific assignment should not be performed may not be accepted. Having clearly identified one's concerns and reasons for that judgment, but failing to procure a change in that assignment, one may yet be obligated, by contract or by law, to proceed as directed. The computing professional's ethical judgment should be the final guide in deciding whether or not to proceed. Regardless of the decision, one must accept the responsibility for the consequences. However, performing assignments "against one's own judgment" does not relieve the professional of responsibility for any negative consequences.

2.7 Improve public understanding of computing and its consequences

Computing professionals have a responsibility to share technical knowledge with the public by encouraging understanding of computing, including the impacts of computer systems and their limitations. This imperative implies an obligation to counter any false views related to computing.

2.8 Access computing and communication resources only when authorized to do so

Theft or destruction of tangible and electronic property is prohibited by imperative 1.2—"Avoid harm to others." Trespassing and unauthorized use of a computer or communication system is addressed by this imperative. Trespassing includes accessing communication networks and computer systems, or accounts and/or files associated with those systems, without explicit authorization to do so. Individuals and organizations have the right to restrict access to their systems so long as they do not violate the discrimination principle (see 1.4).

No one should enter or use another's computing system, software, or data files without permission. One must always have appropriate approval before using system resources, including .rm57 communication ports, file space, other system peripherals, and computer time.

3. Organizational Leadership Imperatives

As an ACM member and an organizational leader, I will . . .

3.1 Articulate social responsibilities of members of an organizational unit and encourage full acceptance of those responsibilities

Because organizations of all kinds have impacts on the public, they must accept responsibilities to society. Organizational procedures and attitudes oriented toward quality and the welfare of society will reduce harm to members of the public, thereby serving public interest and fulfilling social responsibility. Therefore, organizational leaders must encourage full participation in meeting social responsibilities as well as quality performance.

3.2 Manage personnel and resources to design and build information systems that enhance the quality of working life

Organizational leaders are responsible for ensuring that computer systems enhance, not degrade, the quality of working life. When implementing a computer system, organizations must consider the personal and professional development, physical safety, and human dignity of all workers. Appropriate human-computer ergonomic standards should be considered in system design and in the workplace.

3.3 Acknowledge and support proper and authorized uses of an organization's computing and communications resources

Because computer systems can become tools to harm as well as to benefit an organization, the leadership has the responsibility to clearly define appropriate and inappropriate uses of organizational computing resources. While the number and scope of such rules should be minimal, they should be fully enforced when established.

3.4 Ensure that users and those who will be affected by a system have their needs clearly articulated during the assessment and design of requirements. Later the system must be validated to meet requirements.

Current system users, potential users and other persons whose lives may be affected by a system must have their needs assessed and incorporated in the statement of requirements. System validation should ensure compliance with those requirements.

3.5 Articulate and support policies that protect the dignity of users and others affected by a computing system

Designing or implementing systems that deliberately or inadvertently demean individuals or groups is ethically unacceptable. Computer professionals who are in decision-making positions should verify that systems are designed and implemented to protect personal privacy and enhance personal dignity.

3.6 Create opportunities for members of the organizations to learn the principles and limitations of computer systems

This complements the imperative on public understanding (2.7). Educational opportunities are essential to facilitate optimal participation of all organizational members. Opportunities must be available to all members to help them improve their knowledge and skills in computing, including courses that familiarize them with the consequences and limitations of particular types of systems. In particular, professionals must be made aware of the dangers of building systems around oversimplified models, the improbability of anticipating and designing for every possible operating condition, and other issues related to the complexity of this profession.

4. Compliance with the Code

As an ACM member I will . . .

4.1 Uphold and promote the principles of this Code

The future of the computing profession depends on both technical and ethical excellence. Not only is it important for ACM computing professionals to adhere to the principles expressed in this Code, each member should encourage and support adherence by other members.

4.2 Treat violations of this code as inconsistent with membership in the ACM

Adherence of professionals to a code of ethics is largely a voluntary matter. However, if a member does not follow this code by engaging in gross misconduct, membership in ACM may be terminated.

5

Using the ACM Code

The following article examines the twenty-four imperatives of the ACM Code of Ethics and demonstrates how they apply to individual decision making. The authors discuss intellectual property, privacy, fairness, conflicts of interest, and other ethical questions through nine hypothetical dilemmas. Imperatives from the ACM Code are related to each scenario to provide examples of how the Code can be applied.

Ronald E. Anderson, Deborah G. Johnson, Donald Gotterbarn, and Judith Perrolle

Historically, professional associations have viewed codes of ethics as mechanisms to establish their status as a profession or as a means to regulate their membership and thereby convince the public that they deserve to be self-regulating. Self-regulation depends on ways to deter unethical behavior of the members, and a code, combined with an ethics review board, was seen as the solution. Codes of ethics have tended to list possible violations and threaten sanctions for such violations. ACM's first code, the Code of Professional Conduct, was adopted in 1972 and followed this model. The latest ACM code, the Code of Ethics and Professional Conduct, was adopted in 1992 and takes a new direction.

ACM and many other societies have had difficulties implementing an ethics review system and came to realize that self-regulation depends mostly on the consensus and commitment of its members to ethical behavior. Now the most important rationale for a code of ethics is an embodiment of a set of commitments of that association's members. Sometimes these commitments are expressed as rules and sometimes as ideals, but the essential social function is to clarify and formally state those ethical requirements that are important to the group as a professional association. The new ACM Code of Ethics and Professional Conduct follows this philosophy.

Recent codes of ethics emphasize socialization or education rather than enforced compliance. A code can work toward the collective good even though it may be a mere distillation of collective experience and reflection. A major benefit of an educationally oriented code is its contribution to the group by clarifying the professionals' responsibility to society.

A code of ethics holds the profession accountable to the public. This tends to yield a major payoff in terms of public trust. In Frankel's words, "To the extent that a code confers benefits on clients, it will help persuade the public that professionals are deserving of its confidence and respect, and of increased social and economic rewards" [8].

The final and most important function of a code of ethics is its role as an aid to individual decision making. In the interest of facilitating better ethical decision making, we have developed a set of nine classes that describe situations calling for ethical decision making. These cases address in turn the topics of intellectual property, privacy, confidentiality, professional quality, fairness or discrimination, liability, software risks, conflicts of interest, and unauthorized access to computer systems.

Within each case we begin with a scenario to illustrate a typical ethical decision point and then lay out the different imperatives (principles) of the new Code of Ethics that pertain to that decision. There are 24 principles in the Code and each analysis calls on at least two or three different principles to evaluate the relevant ethical concerns. Each of the principles is relevant to at least one scenario, and some principles apply to several situations. The purpose of these case analyses is to provide examples of practical applications of the new ACM Code of Ethics.

Case 1: Intellectual Property

Jean, a statistical database programmer, is trying to write a large statistical program needed by her company. Programmers in this company are encouraged to write about their work and to publish their algorithms in professional journals. After months of tedious programming, Jean has found herself stuck on several parts of the program. Her manager, not recognizing the complexity of the problem, wants the job completed within the next few days. Not knowing how to solve the problems, Jean remembers that a coworker had given her source listings from his current work and from an early version of a commercial software package developed at another company. On studying these programs, she sees two areas of code which could be directly incorporated into her own program. She uses segments of code from both her coworker and the commercial software, but does not tell anyone or mention it in the documentation. She completes the project and turns it in a day ahead of time. (Adapted from a scenario by Dave Colantonio and Deborah Johnson.)

The Code addresses questions of intellectual property most explicitly in imperative 1.6: "Give proper credit for intellectual property. . . . Specifically, one must not take credit for other's ideas or work. . . ." This ethical requirement extends the property rights principle (1.5) that explicitly mentions copyrights, patents, trade secrets and license agreements. These restrictions are grounded in integrity (1.3) and in the need to comply with existing laws (2.3).

Jean violated professional ethics in two areas: failure to give credit for another's work and using code from a commercial package that presumably was copyrighted or in another way protected by law. Suppose that Jean only looked at her coworker's source code for ideas and then completely wrote her own program; would she still have an obligation to give credit? Our answer is yes, she should have acknowledged credit to her coworker in the documentation. There is a matter of professional discretion here, because if the use of another's intellectual material is truly trivial, then there probably is no need to give formal credit.

Jean's use of commercial software code was not appropriate because she should have checked to determine whether or not her company was authorized to use the source code before using it. Even though it is generally desirable to share and exchange intellectual materials, using bootlegged software is definitely a violation of the Code.

Those interested in additional discussions on this subject should refer to the numerous articles by Pamela Samuelson on intellectual property in *Communications*. Also recommended are [2, 7, 17].

Case 2: Privacy

Three years ago Diane started her own consulting business. She has been so successful that she now has several people working for her and many clients. Their consulting work included advising on how to network microcomputers, designing database management systems, and advising about security.

Presently she is designing a database management system for the personnel office of a medium-sized company. Diane has involved the client in the design process, informing the CEO, the director of computing, and the director of personnel about the progress of the system. It is now time to make decisions about the kind and degree of security to build into the system. Diane has described several options to the client. Because the system is going to cost more than they planned, the client has decided to opt for a less secure system. She believes the information they will be storing is extremely sensitive. It will include performance evaluations, medical records for filing insurance claims, salaries, and so forth.

With weak security, employees working on microcomputers may be able to figure out ways to get access to this data, not to mention the possibilities for on-line access from hackers. Diane feels strongly that the system should be much more secure. She has tried to explain the risks, but the CEO, director of computing and director of personnel all agree that less security will do. What should she do? Should she refuse to build the system as they request? (Adapted from [14]).

In the Code of Ethics, principle number 1.7 deals with privacy and 1.8 with confidentiality. They are integrally related but the privacy principle here is the most explicit. The Guidelines of the Code say that computer professionals are obligated to preserve the integrity of data about individuals "from unauthorized access or accidental disclosure to inappropriate individuals." The Code also specifies that organizational leaders have obligations to "verify that systems are designed and implemented to protect personal privacy and enhance personal dignity" (3.5), and to assess the needs of all those affected by a system (3.4).

The company officials have an obligation to protect the privacy of their employees, and therefore should not accept inadequate security. Diane's first obligation is to attempt to educate the company officials, which is implied by imperative 2.7 to promote "public understanding of computing and its consequences." If that fails, then Diane needs to consider her contractual obligations as noted under imperative 2.6 on honoring assigned responsibilities. We do not know the details of Diane's contract, but she may have to choose between her contract and her obligation to honor privacy and confidentiality.

Additional perspectives and discussion on the privacy obligations of computer professionals can be found in [5. 6. 14, 23]. We also recommend proceedings of the latest conference on Computers, Freedom and Privacy [13].

Case 3: Confidentiality

Max works in a large state department of alcoholism and drug abuse. The agency administers programs for individuals with alcohol and drug problems, and maintains a huge database of information on the clients who use their services. Some of the data files contain the names and current addresses of clients.

Max has been asked to take a look at the track records of the treatment programs. He is to put together a report that contains the number of clients seen in each program each month for the past five years, length of each client's treatment, number of clients who return after completion of a program, criminal histories of clients, and so on. In order to put together this report, Max has been given access to all files in the agency's mainframe computer. After assembling the data into a new file that includes the client names, he downloads it to the computer in his office.

Under pressure to get the report finished by the deadline, Max decides he will have to work at home over the weekend in order to finish on time. He copies the information onto several disks and takes them home. After finishing the report he leaves the disks at home and forgets about them (adapted from [14]).

This scenario resembles the previous one that dealt with privacy considerations. However, it raises several additional issues. From the Code of Ethics, principle 1.7 on privacy and 1.8 on confidentiality apply. Imperative 2.8 on constraining access to authorized situations is also central to a computer user's decisions in this type of situation. Additionally, the Code specifies that organizational leaders have obligations to "verify that systems are designed and implemented to protect personal privacy and enhance personal dignity," (3.5) and it also states that they should specify appropriate and authorized uses of an organization's resources (3.3).

The government agency should have had policies and procedures that protected the identity of its clients. Max's relatives and friends might accidentally discover the files and inappropriately use the information to harm the reputation of the clients. The files that Max worked with for his report did not need to have any names or other information in the records that made it possible to easily identify individuals. The agency should have removed the identifying information from the files it allowed Max to use. If that procedure had been followed, it would not have mattered that Max copied the file to his computer. Thus the organizational context created many ethical issues for Max, but unfortunately he was not attentive to these ethical issues ahead of time.

Further reading on this subject can be found in [12, 15, 20]. Discussions of computer-related procedures to maintain the confidentiality of data from specific sources also are available from other professional associations such as the American Medical Association and the American Statistical Association.

Case 4: Quality in Professional Work

A computer company is writing the first stage of a more efficient accounting system that will be used by the government. This system will save taxpayers a considerable amount of money every year. A computer professional, who is asked to design the accounting system, assigns different parts of the system to her staff. One person is responsible for developing the reports; another is responsible for the internal processing; and a third for the user interface. The manager is shown the system and agrees that it can do everything in the requirements. The system is installed, but the staff finds the interface so difficult to use that their complaints are heard by upper-level management. Because of these complaints, upper-level management will not invest any more money in the development of the new accounting system and they go back to their original, more expensive system (adapted from [10]).

The Code of Ethics advocates that computer professionals "strive to achieve the highest quality in both process and products" (2.1). Imperative 3.4 elaborates that users and those affected by a system have their needs clearly articulated.

We presume that in this case the failure to deliver a quality product is directly attributable to a failure to follow a quality process. It is likely that most of the problems with this interface would have been discovered in a review process, either with peers or with users, which is promoted by imperative 2.4. When harm results, in this case to taxpayers, the failure to implement a quality process becomes a clear violation of ethical behavior.

For recent discussion of ethics cases that deal with software quality, see [11].

Case 5: Fairness and Discrimination

In determining requirements for an information system to be used in an employment agency, the client explains that, when displaying applicants whose qualifications appear to match those required for a particular job, the names of white applicants are to be displayed ahead of those of nonwhite applicants, and names of male applicants are to be displayed ahead of those of female applicants (adapted from Donald Gotterbarn and Lionel Diemel).

According to the general moral imperative on fairness, an ACM member will be "fair and take action not to discriminate." In this case the system designer is being asked to build a system that, it appears, will be used to favor white males and discriminate against nonwhites and females. It would seem that the system designer should not simply do what he or she is told but should point out the problematic nature of what is being requested and ask the client why this is being done. Making this inquiry is consistent with 2.3 (to respect existing laws) and 2.5 (to give thorough evaluations) and 4.1 (to uphold and promote the Code of Ethics).

If the client concludes that he or she plans to use the information to favor white males, then the computer professional should refuse to build the system as proposed. To go ahead and build the system would be a violation not only of 1.4 (fairness), but of 2.3 (respecting existing laws) and would be inconsistent with 1.1 (human well-being) and 1.2 (avoiding harm).

For further discussion of the topic of bias see [9, 16, 21].

Case 6: Liability for Unreliability

A software development company has just produced a new software package that incorporates the new tax laws and figures taxes for both individuals and small businesses. The president of the company knows that the program has a number of bugs. He also believes the first firm to put this kind of software on the market is likely to capture the largest market share. The company widely advertises the program. When the company actually ships a disk, it includes a disclaimer of responsibility for errors resulting from the use of the program. The company expects it will receive a number of complaints, queries , and suggestions for modification.

The company plans to use these to make changes and eventually issue updated, improved, and debugged versions. The president argues that this is general industry policy and that anyone who buys version 1.0 of a program knows this and will take proper precautions. Because of bugs, a number of users filed incorrect tax returns and were penalized by the IRS (adapted from scenario V.7 in [18]).

The software company, the president in particular, violated several tenets of the ACM code of ethics. Since he was aware of bugs in the product, he did not strive to achieve the highest quality as called for by 2.1. In failing to inform consumers about bugs in the system, principle 2.5 was also violated.

In this instance the risks to users are great in that they have to pay penalties for mistakes in their income tax which are the result of the program. Companies by law can make disclaimers only when they are "in good conscience." The disclaimer here might not meet this legal test, in which case imperative 2.3 would be violated. As a leader in his organization the president is also violating 3.1, for he is not encouraging his staff to accept their social responsibilities.

Issues of software liability have been discussed by [19, 22].

Case 7: Software Risks

A small software company is working on an integrated inventory control system for a very large national shoe manufacturer. The system will gather sales information daily from shoe stores nationwide. This information will be used by the accounting, shipping, and ordering departments to control all of the functions of this large corporation. The inventory functions are critical to the smooth operation of this system.

Jane, a quality assurance engineer with the software company, suspects that the inventory functions of the system are not sufficiently tested, although they have passed all their contracted tests. She is being pressured by her employers to sign off on the software. Legally she is only required to perform those tests which had been agreed to in the original contract. However, her considerable experience in software testing has led her to be concerned over risks of the system. Her employers say they will go out of business if they do not deliver the software on time. Jane contends if the inventory subsystem fails, it will significantly harm their client and its employees. If the potential failure were to threaten lives, it would be clear to Jane that she should refuse to sign off. But since the degree of threatened harm is less, Jane is faced by a difficult moral decision (adapted from [10]).

In the Code of Ethics, imperative 1.2 stresses the responsibility of the computing professional to avoid harm to others. In addition, principle 1.1 requires concern for human well-being; 1.3 mandates professional integrity, and 2.1 defines quality as an ethical responsibility. These principles may conflict with the agreements and commitments of an employee to the employer and client.

The ethical imperatives of the Code imply that Jane should not deliver a system she believes to be inferior, nor should she mislead the client about the quality of the product (1.3). She should continue to test, but she has been told that her company will go out of business if she does not sign off on the system now. At the very least the client should be informed about her reservations.

For additional discussion of software risks, [3, 22] are suggested.

Case 8: Conflicts of Interest

A software consultant is negotiating a contract with a local community to design their traffic control system. He recommends they select the TCS system out of several available systems on the market. The consultant fails to mention that he is a major stockholder of the company producing TCS software.

According to the Guidelines, imperative 2.5 means that computer professionals must "strive to be perceptive, thorough and objective when evaluating, recommending, and presenting system descriptions and alternatives." It also says that imperative 1.3 implies a computer professional must be honest about "any circumstances that might lead to conflicts of interest." Because of the special skills held by computing professionals it is their responsibility to ensure that their clients are fully aware of their options and that professional recommendations are not modified for personal gain.

Additional discussion on conflict of interest appears in [1, 25].

Case 9: Unauthorized Access

Joe is working on a project for his computer science course. The instructor has allotted a fixed amount of computer time for this project. Joe has run out of time, but he has not yet finished the project. The instructor cannot be reached. Last year Joe worked as a student programmer for the campus computer center and is quite familiar with procedures to increase time allocations to accounts. Using what he learned last year, he is able to access the master account. Then he gives himself additional time and finishes his project.

The imperative to honor property rights (1.5) has been violated. This general, moral imperative leads to imperative 2.8, which specifies that ACM members should "access communication resources only when authorized to do so." In violating 2.8 Joe also is violating the imperative to "know and respect existing laws" (2.3). As a student member of the ACM he must follow the Code of Ethics even though he may not consider himself a computing professional.

For additional reading see [4, 24]. The most current material on this subject is likely to be found in [13].

Conclusion

These nine cases illustrate the broad range of issues a computer scientist may encounter in professional practice. While the ACM Code does not precisely prescribe what an individual must do in the situations described, it does identify some decisions as unacceptable. Often in ethical decision making many factors have to be balanced. In such situations computer professionals have to choose among conflicting principles adhering to the *spirit* of the Code as much as to the *letter.*

The ACM Code organizes ethical principles into the four categories: general moral imperatives, more specific professional responsibilities, organizational leadership imperatives, and compliance. Some may find it helpful to sort out the ethical issues involved in other ways. For example, the context of practice is relevant. Those in industry may encounter different issues from those in government or education. Those who are employed in large corporations may experience different tensions than those who work in small firms or who are self-employed. But whether working in private practice or in large organizations, computer professionals must balance responsibilities to employers, to clients, to other professionals, and to society, and these responsibilities can come into conflict. Our range of cases illustrates how one can use the general principles of the Code to deal with these diverse types of situations.

The reader may wonder why we did not have a whistle-blowing case. In a prototypical scenario, a professional has to take action which threatens the employer after concluding that the safety or well-being of some other group must take priority. Three of our cases—5, 6, 7—dealt with whistle-blowing indirectly. In all three cases, the computing professional served an outside client rather than an employer. This adds other dimensions to whistle-blowing. In Case 5, suppose the system designer learns that his client plans to use the database to discriminate and he refuses to design the system. Later he finds that a friend of his designed the system as the client wanted. He would then have to decide whether to "blow the whistle" on his ex-client. These and similar types of situations are indeed important, if not common, for computer professionals. (For more prototypical situations see discussion of the Bart case and [19] on SDI.)

In all of the cases presented, we portrayed individuals acting in constrained situations. Ethical decisions depend on one's institutional context. These environments can facilitate or constrain ethical behavior. Leadership roles can set the tone and create work environments in which computer professionals can express their ethical concerns. It is significant that leadership responsibilities were demonstrated in nearly all of our nine cases. In some instances, the problem could be resolved by following the imperatives in the Code that apply to leaders. In other cases, the problem was created by a lack of ethical leadership; and the individual professional had to make a personal decision on how to proceed.

Several ethical topics were not specifically interpreted in either the Guidelines or in our cases. For instance, specific requirements of integrity for research in computing and computer science were not detailed. Nor were specific suggestions offered for maintaining professional development. These should be among the tasks of the ACM leadership to address with future additions to the Guidelines.

Other ethical issues, such as software copyright violation, were addressed but not with sufficient detail relative to their salience to the field of computing. These issues, as well as new issues not yet imagined, will confront the field of computing in the future. Not only will the Guidelines need to be updated, but there will be a need for writing and interpreting more cases typical of the ethical decisions of computing professionals. Those with special ethical computing situations are encouraged to share them with us and with others in order to foster more discussion and attention to exemplary ethical decision-making.

References

1. Bayles, M. D. *Professional Ethics*. Wadsworth, Belmont, Calif., 1981.
2. Bynum, T. W., Maner, W. and Fodor, J., Eds. *Software Ownership and Intellectual Property Rights*. Research Center on Computing and Society, Southern Connecticut State University, New Haven, Conn. 06515, 1992.
3. Clark, D. *Computers at Risk: Safe Computing in the Information Age*. National Research Council, National Academy Press, Washington, D.C., 1990.
4. Denning, P. J., Ed. *Computers under Attack: Intruders, Worms and Viruses*. Addison-Wesley, Inc., Reading, Mass., 1990.
5. Dunlop, C. and Kling, R., Eds. *Computerization and Controversy: Value Conflicts and Social Choices*. Academic Press, New York, N.Y., 1991.
6. Flaherty, D. *Protecting Privacy in Surveillance Societies*. University of North Carolina Press, Chapel Hill, N.C., 1989.

7. Forester, T. Software theft and the problem of intellectual property rights. *Comput. Soc. 20,* 1 (Mar. 1990), 2–11.

8. Frankel, M. S. Professional Codes: Why, How, and with What Impact? *J. Bus. Ethics 8* (2 and 3) (1989), 109–116.

9. Frenlel, K. A. Women and computing. *Commun. ACM 33,* 11 (Nov., 1990), 34–46.

10. Gotterbarn, D. Computer ethics: Responsibility regained. *National Forum* (Summer 1991).

11. Gotterbarn, D. Editor's corner. *J. Syst. Soft. 17* (Jan. 1992), 5–6.

12. Guynes, C. S. Protecting statistical databases: A Matter of privacy. *Comput. Soc. 19,* 1 (Mar. 1989), 15–23.

13. IEEE Computer Society Press. *Proceedings of the Second Conference on Computers, Freedom and Privacy.* (Los Alamitos, Calif.), IEEE Computer Society Press, 1992.

14. Johnson, D. G. *Computer Ethics,* Second Ed. Prentice Hall, Englewood Cliffs, N.J., 1993.

15. Laudon, K. C. *Dossier Society: Value Choices in the Design of National Information Systems.* Columbia University Press, New York, N.Y., 1986.

16. Martin, C. D. and Murche-Beyma, E., Eds. In *Search of Gender Free Paradigms for Computer Science Education.* International Society for Technology in Education, Eugene, Ore., 1992.

17. National Research Council. *Intellectual Property Issues in Software.* National Academy of Sciences, Washington, D.C., 1991.

18. Parker, D., Swope, S. and Baker, B. Ethical conflicts in information and computer science. *Technology and Business.* Wellesley, Mass. QED Information Sciences, 1990.

19. Parnas, D L. SDI: A violation of professional responsibility. *Abacus 4,* 2 (Winter 1987), 46–52.

20. Perrolle, J. A. *Computers and Social Change: Information, Property, and Power.* Wadsworth , Belmont, Calif., 1987.

21. Perrolle, J. Conservations and trust in computer interfaces. In *Computer and Controversy.* Dunlop and Kling, Eds., 1991.

22. Pressman, R. S. and Herron, R. *Software Shock: The Danger and the Opportunity.* Dorsett House, 1991.

23. Salpeter, J. Are you obeying copyright law? *Technol. Learning 12,* 8 (1992), 12–23.

24. Spafford, G. Are computer hacker break-ins ethical? *J. Syst. Softw. 17* (Jan. 1992).

25. Stevenson, J. T. *Engineering Ethics: Practices and Principles.* Canadian Scholars Press, Toronto, 1987.

Note: A more extensive list of references for each of the nine specific cases, as well as general discussions of professional ethics, can be obtained by writing Ronald E. Anderson, 909 Social Sciences Bldg., University of Minnesota, Minneapolis, MN 55455. Both the ACM Code of Ethics and the bibliography are available on the Internet from acm.org using anonymous ftp or mailserve. The files are under the SIGCAS Forum and called code—of—ethics.txt and ethics—biblio.txt.

———— 6 ————————————————————

Can We Find a Single Ethical Code?

Robert N. Barger argues that an individual's ethical judgments are strongly influenced by his or her philosophical worldview. As an example, he shows the influence of the worldviews of idealism and pragmatism on computer ethics. He also shows how different worldviews may give different solutions to computing dilemmas.

Robert N. Barger

Several years ago, Josephine C. Barger and I conducted research on a random sample of 347 students at a midwestern regional/comprehensive university. These students had academic majors representative of all six colleges in the University. Through the use of SPSSX discriminant analysis, Duncan multiple analysis, and SPSSX univariate analysis, we found (Barger & Barger, 1989) that there were distinguishable philosophies among the students. In other words, separate philosophical viewpoints (to be described below) were both real and measurable.

The Major Metaphysical Positions and Their Resultant Ethics

The philosophies which were empirically evidenced in our research were the traditional systematic philosophies of Idealism, Realism, Pragmatism, and Existentialism. Idealism and Realism might be characterized as absolute or objective philosophies. Pragmatism and Existentialism might be characterized as relative or subjective philosophies.

Idealism

The metaphysical position of the philosophy of Idealism is that reality is basically spirit rather than matter. For the Idealist, the idea is more real than the thing, since the thing only reflects or represents the idea. The world of spirit or idea is static and absolute. Socrates and Plato are perhaps the best known ancient representatives of this view, while Immanuel Kant and Thomas Hill Green are more modern Idealists.

Once the metaphysical view that reality is found in the idea is assumed, the ethical position that goodness is to be found in the ideal (that is, in perfection) automatically follows. Goodness is found on the immaterial level, that is, in the perfect concept, or notion, or idea, of something. Thus, perfect goodness is never to be found in the material world. Evil, for the Idealist, consists of the absence or distortion of the ideal. Since ideals can never change (because they are a priori and absolute), moral imperatives concerning them do not admit of exceptions. That is, these imperatives are stated in terms of "always" or "never." For example: "Always tell the truth" or (put negatively) "Never tell a lie." Since truth is the knowledge of ideal reality and a lie is a distortion of that reality, truth must always be told and lying can never be justified.

Realism

The person with a Realistic world view believes that reality is basically matter, rather than spirit. For the Realist, the thing is more real than the idea. Whatever exists is therefore primarily material, natural, and physical. As such, reality exists in some quantity and therefore can be measured. It exists independently of any mind and is governed by the laws of nature, primary among which are the laws of cause and effect. The universe, according to the Realist, is one of natural design and order. Aristotle was an early representative of this view. B. F. Skinner, the behavioral psychologist, is a more current representative.

The result ethical position that flows from a Realist metaphysics is one that views the baseline of value as that which is natural (that is, that which is in conformity with nature). Nature is good. One need not look beyond nature to some immaterial ideal for a standard of right and wrong. Rather, goodness will be found by living in harmony with nature. Evil, for the Realist, is a departure from this natural norm either in the direction of excess or defect (i.e., having, or doing, too much or too little of something which is naturally good).

Pragmatism

For the Pragmatist, metaphysics is not so simple a matter as it is for the Idealist and Realist. Reality is neither an idea nor is it matter. It would be a mistake to view reality as either a spiritual or physical "something." Rather, the Pragmatist believes that reality is a process. It is a dynamic coming-to-be rather than a static fixed being. It is change, happening, activity, interaction . . . in short, it is experience. Reality is more like a verb than a noun. It is flux and flow where the concentration is not so much on the things as on the relationship between the things. Since everything changes—indeed, the Pragmatist would say that change is everything—nothing can have any permanent essence or identity. An ancient Greek Pragmatist used to say in this regard: "You can't step in the same river twice." For the Pragmatist, everything is essentially relative. The only constant is change. The only absolute is that there are no absolutes! The Americans Charles Sanders Pierce, William James, and John Dewey are representatives of this view.

The ethical result of the Pragmatic metaphysical position demands that value claims must be tested and proven in practice. This is so because meaning is inherent in the consequences of actions. In the Pragmatist's view, things are value-neutral in themselves. There is nothing that is always good, nor is there anything that is always bad. The value of anything is determined solely in terms of its usefulness in achieving some end. In answer to the question, "Is that good?," a Pragmatist would probably reply, "Good for what?" Thus, the Pragmatist believes that the end justifies the means. That is, if an act is useful for achieving some laudable end or goal, then it becomes good. To state this another way, a means gets its positive value from being an efficient route to the achievement of a laudable end (a laudable end is one that brings about the greatest good for the greatest number of people). Thus, a means is not valued for its own sake, but only in relation to its usefulness for achieving some laudable end. Results or consequences are the ultimate measure of goodness for a Pragmatist, since the usefulness of a means to an end can only be judged after the fact by its effect on the end. Thus, for the Pragmatist, there can be no assurance that something is good . . . until it is tried. Even then, it is only held tentatively as good since a thing is good only as long as it continues to work. There can, however, be a dispute about which means are more effective for achieving an end. Indeed, there can be a dispute about which ends should, in fact, be pursued. Thus, the Pragmatist looks for guidance from the group. The reasons for this are metaphysical: reality is experience, but it is the experience of the whole. For the Pragmatist, the whole is greater than the sum of its parts. This means that the whole is more valuable than any of its parts. In the field of value judgments, the group's wisdom is more highly esteemed than the wisdom of any individual within the group.

Existentialism

The Existentialist joins with the Pragmatist in rejecting the belief that reality is a priori and fixed. But instead of believing that reality is a process whose meaning is defined primarily by the controlling group, Existentialist metaphysics holds that reality must be defined by each autonomous individual. The Existentialist notions of subjectivity and phenomenological self emphasize that the meaning or surdity of an otherwise "absurd" universe is individually determined. Any meaning that gets into the world must be put in it by the individual, and that meaning or value will hold only for that individual. Thus each person's world, as well as each person's own identity, is the product of that person's own choice. Thus, each person can be defined as the sum of that person's choice. A person's world is what that person chooses it to be. Thus, reality is different for each individual. We each live in our own world and we are who we choose to be. Søren Kierkegaard and Jean-Paul Sartre are frequently associated with this view.

Like the Existentialist position on reality, its ethical position is that the individual must create his/her own value. There is no escape from the necessity of creating values. Just as the world is defined by the choices regarding reality that an individual makes, so the individual must express her or his own preferences. In making choices, or defining values, the individual becomes responsible for those choices. The individual cannot deflect praise or blame for those choices onto others. If the choices were freely made, then responsibility for them must be accepted. While groups might influence what choices an individual makes, there is a zone of freedom within each individual that cannot be conditioned or predetermined. While emphasizing a highly individualized choice of values, an Existentialist is not necessarily a non-conformist, but if an Existentialist does conform to the values of a group it will be because that person has freely chosen to do so—not because they have been pressured to do so by the group.

The Problem of Consistency

The above outline of philosophical views might appear to oversimplify the basis for ethical decision-making. I would readily agree that ethical decision-making in real time is a much more difficult process than might appear from the above summaries. For instance, our research (Barger & Barger, 1989) found that while most of the students we surveyed had a predominant leaning toward one of the four philosophies described above, they also had lesser learnings toward some of the other three philosophies. In other words, nobody is 100% an Idealist (. . . or Realist, or Pragmatist, or Existentialist).

This means that simply knowing a person's dominant philosophical outlook will not allow assured prediction of how he or she might act in response to a given ethical situation. This is true for two reasons: 1) the one just stated, that strong sympathies with other philosophical views besides one's dominant view might end up controlling action in this or that particular situation; and, 2) the fact that people do not always conscientiously act in a manner consistent with their beliefs. That is, they might fail to follow through with what they believe is the right thing to do in a particular situation. . . .

Divergent Solutions to Selected Computing Dilemmas

I offer some divergent solutions to three ethical dilemmas having to do with piracy, privacy, and power in computing. The divergence of these solutions is the result of their different metaphysical and ethical viewpoints. For reasons of brevity, I will present what I call an "absolutist" type of solution which is characteristic of the Idealist and Realist views, and what I call a "relativist" solution which is characteristic of the Pragmatist and Existentialist views.

Here is the piracy dilemma (i.e., a dilemma concerning wrongful appropriation of computing resources). Suppose I use my account on one of my university's mainframe computers for something that has no direct relation to University business. This use could be anything from sending an e-mail message to a friend, to conducting a full-blown private business on the computer (billing, payroll, inventory, etc.). The absolutest solution to this dilemma would probably be that the above-described activities are unethical—whether only the e-mail message is involved, or the larger-scale business activities (although the absolutist would recognize a difference between the two in the amount of wrong being done). On the other hand, a relativist might say that the latter activities were wrong because they tied up too much memory and slowed down the machine's operation, but the e-mail message wasn't wrong because it had no significant effect on operations.

Next consider a dilemma having to do with privacy. I use my account to acquire the cumulative grade point average of a student who is in a class which I instruct. I obtained the password for this restricted information from someone in the Records Office who erroneously thought that I was the student's advisor. The absolutist solution to this dilemma would probably be that I acted wrongly, since the only person who is entitled to this information is the student and his or her advisor. The relativist would probably ask why I wanted the information. If I said that I wanted it to be sure that my grading of the student was consistent with the student's overall academic performance record, the relativist might agree that such use was acceptable.

Finally, let us look at a dilemma concerning power. I am a university professor and if I want computer account, all I have to do is request one. But if I am a student at my university, I must obtain faculty sponsorship in order to receive an account. An absolutist (because of a proclivity for hierarchical thinking) might not have a problem with this situation. A relativist, on the other hand, might question what makes the two situations essentially different (e.g., are faculty assumed to have more need for computers than students? are students more likely to cause problems than faculty? is this a hold-over from the days of "in loco parentis"?).

Conclusion

The skeletal cases I have just presented are not meant to suggest that ethical solutions to computing dilemmas can be easily generated. Indeed, just the opposite is true. In the present world of computing, where ethical dilemmas are becoming ever more complex, the hope of finding a single normative code which would contain standards with which everyone would agree seems dim. That does not mean, however, that such an effort is futile. . . .

References

Barger, Robert N., & Barger, Josephine C. (1989). Do Pragmatists Choose Business While Idealists Choose Education? Charleston: Eastern Illinois University. (ERIC Document Reproduction Service No. ED 317 904).

Halverson, William H. (1981). Introduction to Philosophy (4th ed.). New York: Random House.

Wittgenstein, Ludwig. (1961). Tractatus Logico-philosophicus. (D. F. Pears & B. F. McGuinness, Trans.) London: Routledge & Kegan Paul, Ltd. (Original work published 1921).

——— 7 ———

The Morality of Whistle-Blowing

Computer scientists, like other professionals , may find a conflict between their other loyalties and their obligation to protect the public's health, privacy, and general welfare. In this reading, Sissela Bok analyzes the conflicting pressures n professionals and offers guidance about when they should "blow the whistle." For further study of computing and social responsibility, you may also visit the website of Computing Professionals for Social Responsibility at www.cpsr.org.

Sissela Bok

"Whistle-blower" is a label for those who . . . make revelations meant to call attention to negligence, abuses, or dangers that threaten the public interest. They sound an alarm based on their expertise or inside knowledge, often from within the very organization in which they work. With as much resonance as they can muster, they strive to breach secrecy, or else arouse an apathetic public to dangers everyone knows about but does not fully acknowledge.[1] . . . Most [whistle-blowers know] that their alarms pose a threat to anyone who benefits from the ongoing practice and that their own careers and livelihood may be at risk. The lawyer who breaches confidentiality in reporting bribery by corporate clients knows the risk, as does the nurse who reports on slovenly patient care in a hospital, the engineer who discloses safety defects in the braking systems of a fleet of new rapid-transit vehicles, or the industrial worker who speaks out about hazardous chemicals seeping into a playground near the factory dump.

. . . . .

Would-be whistle-blowers also face conflicting pressures from without. In many professions, the prevailing ethic requires above all else loyalty to colleagues and to clients; yet the formal codes of professional ethics stress responsibility to the public in cases of conflict with such loyalties. Thus the largest professional engineering society asks members to speak out against abuses threatening the safety, health, and welfare of the public.[2] A number of business firms have codes making similar requirements; and the United States Code of Ethics for government servants asks them to "expose corruption wherever uncovered" and to "put loyalty to the highest moral principles and to country above loyalty to persons, party, or Government department."[3] Regardless of such exhortations, would-be whistle-blowers have reason to fear the results of carrying out the duty to reveal corruption and neglect. However strong this duty may seem in principle, they know that in practice, retaliation is likely. They fear for their careers and for their ability to support themselves and their families.

. . . . .

Blowing the Whistle

The alarm of the whistle-blower is meant to disrupt the status quo: to pierce the background noise, perhaps the false harmony, or the imposed silence of "business as usual." Three elements, each jarring, and triply jarring when conjoined, lend acts of whistle-blowing special urgency and bitterness: dissent, breach of loyalty, and accusation.[4]

Like all *dissent*, first of all, whistle-blowing makes public a disagreement with an authority or a majority view. But whereas dissent can arise from all forms of disagreement with, say, religious dogma or government policy or court decisions, whistle-blowing has the narrower aim of casting light on negligence or abuse, of alerting the public to a risk and of assigning responsibility for that risk.

It is important, in this respect, to see the shadings between the revelations of neglect and abuse which are central to whistle-blowing, and dissent on grounds of policy. In practice, however, the two often come together.

Coercive regimes or employers may regard dissent of any form as evidence of abuse or of corruption that calls for public exposure. And in all societies, persons may blow the whistle on abuses in order to signal policy dissent. Thus Daniel Ellsberg, in making his revelations about government deceit and manipulation in the Pentagon Papers, obviously aimed not only to expose misconduct and assign responsibility but also to influence the nation's policy toward Southeast Asia.

In the second place, the message of the whistle-blower is seen as a *breach of loyalty* because it comes from within. The whistle-blower, though he is neither referee nor coach, blows the whistle on his own team. His insider's position carries with it certain obligations to colleagues and clients. He may have signed a promise of confidentiality or a loyalty oath. When he steps out of routine channels to level accusations, he is going against these obligations. Loyalty to colleagues and to clients comes to be pitted against concern for the public interest and for those who may be injured unless someone speaks out. Because the whistle-blower criticizes from within, his act differs from muckraking and other forms of exposure by outsiders. Their acts may arouse anger, but not the sense of betrayal that whistle-blowers so often encounter.

The conflict is strongest for those who take their responsibilities to the public seriously, yet have close bonds of collegiality and of duty to clients as well. They know the price of betrayal. They know, too, how organizations protect and enlarge the area of what is concealed, as failures multiply and vested interests encroach. And they are aware that they violate, by speaking out, not only loyalty but usually hierarchy as well.

It is the third element of *accusation,* of calling a "foul" from within, that arouses the strongest reactions on the part of the hierarchy. The charge may be one of unethical or unlawful conduct on the part of colleagues or superiors. Explicitly or implicitly, it singles out specific groups or persons as responsible: as those who knew or should have known what was wrong and what the dangers were, and who had the capacity to make different choices. If no one could be held thus responsible—as in the case of an impending avalanche or a volcanic eruption—the warning would not constitute whistle-blowing.

. . . . .

Not only immediately but also specificity is needed for the whistle-blower to assign responsibility. A concrete risk must be at issue rather than a vague foreboding or a somber prediction. The act of whistle-blowing differs in this respect from the lamentation or the dire prophecy.

Such immediate and specific threats would normally be acted upon by those at risk. But the whistle-blower assumes that his message will alert listeners to a threat of which they are ignorant, or whose significance they have not grasped. It may have been kept secret by members within the organization, or by all who are familiar with it. Or it may be an "open secret," seemingly in need only of being pointed out in order to have its effect. In either case, because of the elements of dissent, breach of loyalty, and accusation, the tension between concealing and revealing is great. It may be intensified by an urge to throw off the sense of complicity that comes from sharing secrets one believes to be unjustly concealed, and to achieve peace of mind by setting the record straight at last. Sometimes a desire for publicity enters in, or a hope for revenge for past slights or injustices. Colleagues of the whistle-blower often suspect just such motives; they may regard him as a crank, publicity-hungry, eager for scandal and discord, or driven to indiscretion by his personal biases and shortcomings.[5]

On the continuum of more or less justifiable acts of whistle-blowing, the whistle-blower tends to see more such acts as justified and even necessary than his colleagues. Bias can affect each side in drawing the line, so that each takes only some of the factors into account—the more so if the action comes at the end of a long buildup of acrimony and suspicion.

The Leak

Both leaking and whistle-blowing can be used to challenge corrupt or cumbersome systems of secrecy—in government as in the professions, the sciences, and business. Both may convey urgently needed warnings, but they may also peddle false information and vicious personal attacks. How, then, can one distinguish the many acts of revelation from within that are genuinely in the public interest from all the petty, biased, or lurid tales that pervade our querulous and gossip-ridden societies? Can we draw distinctions between different messages, different methods and motivations?

We clearly can, in a number of cases. Whistle-blowing and leaks may be starkly inappropriate when used in malice or in error, or when they lay bare legitimately private matters such as those having to do with political belief or sexual life. They may, just as clearly, offer the only way to shed light on an ongoing practice such as fraudulent scientific research or intimidation of political adversaries; and they may be the last resort for alerting the public to a possible disaster. Consider, for example, the action taken by three engineers to alert the public to defects in the braking mechanisms of the Bay Area Rapid Transit System (BART):

> The San Francisco Bay Area Rapid Transit System opened in 1972. It was heralded as the first major breakthrough toward a safe, reliable, and sophisticated method of mass transportation. A public agency had been set up in 1952 to plan and carry out the project; and the task of developing its major new component, a fully automatic train control system, was allocated to Westinghouse.
>
> In 1969, three of the engineers who worked on this system became increasingly concerned over its safety. They spotted problems independently, and spoke

to their supervisors, but to no avail. They later said they might well have given up their effort to go farther had they not found out about one another. They made numerous efforts to speak to BART's management. But those in charge were already troubled by costs that had exceeded all projections, and by numerous unforseen delays. They were not disposed to investigate the charges that the control system might be unsafe. Each appeal by the three engineers failed.

Finally, the engineers interested a member of BART's board of trustees, who brought the matter up at a board meeting. Once again, the effort failed. But in March 1973, the three were fired once the complaint had been traced to them. When they wrote to ask why they had been dismissed, they received no answer.

Meanwhile, the BART system had begun to roll. The control system worked erratically, and at times dangerously. A month after the opening, one train overshot the last station and crashed into a parking lot for commuters. Claiming that some bugs still had to be worked out, BART began to use old-fashioned flagmen in order to avoid collisions.

The three engineers had turned, in 1972, to the California Society of Professional Engineers for support. The Society, after investigating the complaint, agreed with their views, and reported to the California State legislature. It too had launched an investigation, and arrived at conclusions quite critical of BART's management.

The engineers filed a damage suit against BART in 1974, but settled out of court in 1975. They had difficulties finding new employment, and suffered considerable financial and emotional hardship in spite of their public vindication.[6]

The three engineers were acting in accordance with the law and with engineering codes of ethics in calling attention to the defects in the train control system. Because of their expertise, they had a special responsibility to alert the company, and if need be its board of directors and the public, to the risks that concerned them. If we take such a clear-cut case of legitimate whistle-blowing as a benchmark, and reflect on what it is about it that weighs so heavily in favor of disclosure, we can then examine more complex cases in which speaking out in public is not so clearly the right choice or the only choice.

Individual Moral Choice

What questions might individuals consider, as they wonder whether to sound an alarm? How might they articulate the problem they see, and weigh its seriousness before deciding whether or not to reveal it? Can they make sure that their choice is the right one? And what about the choices confronting journalists or others asked to serve as intermediaries?

In thinking about these questions, it helps to keep in mind the three elements mentioned earlier: dissent, breach of loyalty, and accusation. They impose certain requirements: of judgment and accuracy in dissent, of exploring alternative ways to cope with improprieties that minimize the breach of loyalty, and of fairness in accusation. The judgment expressed by whistle-blowers concerns a problem that should matter to the public. Certain outrages are so blatant, and certain dangers so great, that all who are in a position to warn of them have a *prima facie* obligation to do so. Conversely, other problems are so minor that to blow the whistle would be a disproportionate response. And still others are so hard to pin down that whistle-blowing is premature. In between lie a great many of the problems troubling whistle-blowers. Consider, for example, the following situation:

> An attorney for a large company manufacturing medical supplies begins to suspect that some of the machinery sold by the company to hospitals for use in kidney dialysis is unsafe, and that management has made attempts to influence federal regulatory personnel to overlook these deficiencies.
>
> The attorney brings these matters up with a junior executive, who assures her that he will look into the matter, and convey them to the chief executive if necessary. When she questions him a few weeks later, however, he tells her that all the problems have been taken care of, but offers no evidence, and seems irritated at her desire to learn exactly where the issues stand. She does not know how much further she can press her concern without jeopardizing her position in the firm.

The lawyer in this case has reason to be troubled, but does not yet possess sufficient evidence to blow the whistle. She is far from being as sure of her case as . . . the engineers in the BART case, whose professional expertise allowed them to evaluate the risks of the faulty braking system . . . The engineers would be justified in assuming that they had an obligation to draw attention to the dangers they saw, and that anyone who shared their knowledge would be wrong to remain silent or to suppress evidence of the danger. But if the attorney blew the whistle about her company's sales of machinery to hospitals merely on the basis of her suspicions, she would be doing so prematurely. At the same time, the risks to hospital patients from the machinery, should she prove correct in her suspicions, are sufficiently great so that she has good reason to seek help in looking into the problem, to feel complicitous if she chooses to do nothing, and to take action if she verifies her suspicions.

Her difficulty is shared by many who suspect, without being sure, that their companies are concealing the defective or dangerous nature of their products—automobiles that are firetraps, for instance, or canned foods with carcinogenic additives. They may sense that merely to acknowledge that they don't know for sure is too often a weak excuse for inaction, but recognize also that the destructive power of adverse publicity can be great. If the warning turns out to have been inaccurate, it may take a long time to undo the damage to individuals and organizations. As a result, potential whistle-blowers must first try to specify the degree to which there is genuine impropriety, and consider how imminent and how serious the threat is which they perceive.

If the facts turn out to warrant disclosure, and if the would-be-whistle-blower has decided to act upon them in spite of the possibilities of reprisal, then how can the second element—breach of loyalty—be overcome or minimized? Here, as in the Pentagon Papers case, the problem is one of which set of loyalties to uphold. Several professional codes of ethics, such as those of engineers and public servants, facilitate such a choice at least in theory, by requiring that loyalty to the public interest should override allegiance to colleagues, employers, or clients whenever there is a genuine conflict. Accordingly, those who have assumed a professional responsibility to serve the public interest—as had . . . the engineers in the BART case—have a special obligation not to remain silent about dangers to the public.

Before deciding whether to speak out publicly, however, it is important for [whistle-blowers] to consider whether the existing avenues for change within the organizations have been sufficiently explored. By turning first to insiders for help, one can often uphold both sets of loyalties and settle the problem without going outside the organization. The engineers in the BART case clearly tried to resolve the problem they saw in this manner, and only reluctantly allowed it to come to public attention as a last resort.

· · · · ·

It *is* disloyal to colleagues and employers, as well as a waste of time for the public, to sound the loudest alarm first. Whistle-blowers has to remain a last alternative because of its destructive side effects. It must be chosen only when other alternatives have been considered and rejected. They may be rejected if they simply do not apply to the problem at hand, or when there is not time to go through routine channels, or when the institution is so corrupt or coercive that steps will be taken to silence the whistle-blower should he try the regular channels first.

What weight should an oath or a promise of silence have in the conflict of loyalties? There is no doubt that one sworn to silence is under a stronger obligation because of the oath he has taken, unless it was obtained under duress or through deceit, or else binds him to something in itself wrong or unlawful. In taking an oath, one assumes specific obligations beyond those assumed in accepting employment. But even such an oath can be overridden when the public interest at issue is sufficiently strong. The fact that one has promised silence is no excuse for complicity in covering up a crime or violating the public trust.

The third element in whistle-blowing—accusation—is strongest whenever efforts to correct a problem without going outside the organization have failed, or seem likely to fail. Such an outcome is especially likely whenever those in charge take part in the questionable practices, or have too much at stake in maintaining them.

. . . . .

Given these difficulties, it is especially important to seek more general means of weighing the arguments for and against whistle-blowing; to take them up in public debate and in teaching; and to consider changes in organizations, law, and work practices that could reduce the need for individuals to choose between blowing and "swallowing" the whistle.[7]

Notes

1. I draw, for this chapter, on my earlier essays on whistle-blowing: "Whistle-blowing and Professional Responsibilities," in Daniel Callahan and Sissela Bok, eds., *Ethics Teaching in Higher Education* (New York: Plenum Press, 1980), pp. 277–95 (reprinted, "Blowing the Whistle," in Joel Fleishman, Lance Liebman, and Mark Moore, eds., *Public Duties: The Moral Obligations of Officials* (Cambridge, Mass.: Harvard University Press, 1981), pp. 204–21.
2. Institute of Electrical and Electronics Engineers, Code of Ethics for Engineers, art, 4, *IEEE Spectrum* 12 (February 1975): 65.
3. Code of Ethics for Government Service, passed by the U.S. House of Representatives in the 85th Congress, 1958, and applying to all government employees and officeholders.
4. Consider the differences and the overlap between whistle-blowing and civil disobedience with respect to these three elements. First, whistle-blowing resembles civil disobedience in its openness and its intent to act in the public interest. But the dissent in whistle-blowing, unlike that in civil disobedience, usually does not represent a breach of law; it is, on the contrary, protected by the right of free speech and often encouraged in codes of ethics and other statements of principle. Second, whistle-blowing violates loyalty, since it dissents from within and breaches secrecy, whereas civil disobedience need not and can as easily challenge from without. Whistle-blowing, finally, accuses specific individuals, whereas civil disobedience need not. A combination of the two occurs, for instance, when former CIA agents public books to alert the public about what they regard as unlawful and dangerous practices, and in so doing openly violate, and thereby test, the oath of secrecy that they have sworn.
5. Judith P. Swazey and Stephen R. Scheer suggest that when whistle-blowers expose fraud in clinical research, colleagues respond *more* negatively to the whistle-blowers who report the fraudulent research than to the person whose conduct has been reported. See "The Whistleblower as a Deviant Professional: Professional Norms and Responses to Fraud in Clinical Research," Workshop on Whistleblowing in Biomedical Research, Washington, D.C., September 1981.
6. See Robert J. Baum and Albert Flores, eds., *Ethical Problems in Engineering* (Troy, N.Y.: Center for the Study of the Human Dimension of Science and Technology, 1978), pp. 227–47.
7. Alal Westin discusses "swallowing" the whistle in *Whistle Blowing!*, pp. 10–13. For a discussion of debate concerning whistle-blowing, see Rosemary Chalk, "The Miner's Canary," Bulletin of the Atomic Scientists 38 (February 1982): pp. 16–22.

——— 8 —————————————————————————

The Ethics of Systems Design

The authors assert that people who use or design computer systems are morally responsible for any resulting harm. They discuss existing computer practices that increase the tendency for users and designers to feel little responsibility for harmful outcomes. To correct this problem the authors suggest alternative approaches to computer system design.

Batya Friedman and Peter H. Kahn, Jr.

Societal interest in responsible computing perhaps most often arises in response to harmful consequences that can result from computing. For instance, consider the frustration and economic loss incurred by individuals and businesses whose computer systems have been infected by . . . computer viruses. Or consider the physical suffering and death of the cancer patients who were overradiated by Therac-25, or of civilians accidentally bombed in the Persian Gulf war by "smart" missiles gone astray. Largely in reaction to events like these, we have in recent years seen a surge of interest in preventing or at least minimizing such harmful consequences. But if responsible computing is to be understood as something more than a form of damage control, how are we to understand the term? Moreover, how can responsible computing be promoted within the computing community?

Design to Support Human Agency and Responsible Computing

[W]e propose that responsible computing often depends on humans' clear understanding that humans are capable of being moral agents and that computational systems are not. However . . . this understanding can be distorted in one of two ways. In the first type of distortion, the computational system diminishes or undermines the human user's sense of his or her own moral agency. In such systems, human users are placed into largely mechanical roles, either mentally or physically, and frequently have little understanding of the larger purpose or meaning of their individual actions. To the extent that humans experience a diminished sense of agency, human dignity is eroded and individuals may consider themselves to be largely unaccountable for the consequences of their computer use. Conversely, in the second type of distortion the computational system masquerades as an agent by projecting intentions, desires, and volition. To the extent that humans inappropriately attribute agency to such systems, humans may well consider the computational systems, at least in part, to be morally responsible for the effects of computer-mediated or computer-controlled actions.

Accordingly, to support humans' responsible use of computational systems, system design should strive to minimize both types of distortion. That is, system design should seek to protect the moral agency of humans and to discourage in humans a perception of moral agency in the computational system. How might design practices achieve these goals? Given that little research exists that addresses this question directly, we seek to provide some initial sketches by examining three types of computer practices.

Anthropomorphizing the Computational System

Anthropomorphic metaphors can be found in some of the definitions and goals for interface design. For example, some interfaces are designed to "use the process of human-human communication as a model for human-computer interaction" ([1], p. 86), to "interact with the user similar to the way one human would interact with another" ([1], p. 87), or to be "intelligent" where intelligence is based on a model of human intelligence. When such anthropomorphic metaphors become embedded in the design of a system, the system can fall prey to the second type of distortion by projecting human agency onto the computational system.

Moreover, even in unsophisticated designs of this type, there is some evidence that people do attribute agency to the computational system. For example, Weizenbaum [2] reported that some adults interacted with his computer program DOCTOR with great emotional depth and intimacy, "conversing with the computer as if it were a person" (p. 7). In a similar vein, some of the children Turkle [3] interviewed about their experiences with an interactive computer game called Merlin that played Tic-Tac-Toe attributed psychological (mental) characteristics to Merlin. For example, children sometimes accused Merlin of cheating, an accusation that includes a belief that the computer has both the intention and desire to deceive. In another example, Rumelhart and Norman [4] attempted to teach novices to use an editing program by telling the novices that the system was like a secretary. The novices drew on this human analogy to attribute aspects of a secretary's intelligence to the editing system and assumed (incorrectly) that the system would be able to understand whether they intended a particular string of characters to count as text or as commands.

While these examples of human attribution of agency to computational systems have largely benign consequences, this may not always be the case. Consider Jenkins' [5] human factors experiment that simulated a nuclear power plant failure. In the experiment, nuclear power plant operators had access to an expert system to aid them in responding to the plant failure. Although previously instructed on the expert system's limitations, . . . the "operators expected that the expert system implemented in the computer 'knew' about the failures of the cooling system without being told. The system [however] was neither designed nor functioned as an automatic fault recognition system" (p. 258). Jenkins attributed this overestimation of the system's capabilities to the power plant operators' expectations for the expert system to know certain information, presumably the type of information that any responsible human expert would know or attempt to find out in that situation.

Because nonanthropomorphic design does not encourage people to attribute agency to the computational system, such designs can better support responsible computing. To clarify what such design looks like in practice, consider the possibilities for interface design. Without ever impersonating human agency, interface design can appropriate pursue such goals as learnability, ease and pleasure of use, clarity, and quick recovery from errors. In addition, nonanthropomorphic interface design can employ such techniques as novel pointing devices, nonanthropomorphic analogies, speech input and output, and menu selection. Or consider the characteristics of another plausible technique: direct manipulation. According to Jacob [6], direct manipulation refers to a user interface in which the user "seems to operate directly *on* the objects in the computer rather than carrying on a dialogue *about* them" (p. 166). For example, the Xerox Star desktop manager adapted for systems such as the Apple Macintosh uses images of standard office objects (e.g., files, folders, and trash cans) and tasks to represent corresponding objects and functions in the editing system [7]. In this environment, disposing of a computer file is achieved by moving the image of the file onto the image of the trash can, akin to disposing of a paper file by physically placing the file in a trash can. There is no ambiguity in this direct manipulation interface as to who is doing the acting (the human user) and what the user is acting upon (objects in the computational system). The defining characteristics of direct manipulation suggest that this technique would not lead to projecting human agency onto the system. This is because direct manipulation involves physical action on an object as opposed to social interaction with an other as an undenying metaphor. Additionally, direct manipulation seeks to have the human user directly manipulate computational objects, thereby virtually eliminating the possibility for the human user to perceive the computer interface as an intermediary agent.

Nonanthropomorphic design considerations fit within a larger vision for interface design that is already part of the field. For example, Shneiderman

[8] draws on Weizenbaum [2] to advocate design that "sharpen[s] the boundaries between people and computers . . . [for] human-human communication is a poor model for human-computer interaction" (p. 434). More recently, Shneiderman [9] writes that "when an interactive system is well designed, it almost disappears, enabling the users to concentrate on their work or pleasure" (p. 169). Winograd and Flores [10] similarly advocate the design of nonanthropomorphic computer tools that provide a transparent interaction between the user and the resulting action. "The transparency of interaction is of utmost importance in the design of tools, including computer systems, but it is not best achieved by attempting to mimic human faculties" (p. 194). When a transparent interaction is achieved, the user is freed from the details of using the tool to focus on the task at hand. The shared vision here is for the interface to "disappear," not to intercede in the guise of another "agent" between human users and the computational system.

Delegating Decision Making to Computational Systems

When delegating decision making to computational systems, both types of distortions can occur. The discussion that follows examines these distortions in the context of the APACHE system [11, 12]. More generally, however, similar analyses could be applied to other computer-based models and knowledge-based systems such as MYCIN [13] or the Authorizer's Assistant used by the American Express Corporation [14].

APACHE is a computer-based model [designed to determine] when to withdraw life support systems from patients in intensive care units. Consider the nature of the human-computer relationship if APACHE, used as a closed-loop system, determines that life support systems should be withdrawn from a patient, and then turns off the life support systems. In ending the patient's life the APACHE system projects a view of itself to the medical personnel and the patient's family as a purposeful decision maker (the second type of distortion). Simultaneously, the system allows the attending physician and critical care staff to distance or numb themselves from the decision making process about when to end another human's life (the first type of distortion).

Now, in actuality, at least some of the researchers developing APACHE did not recommend its use as a closed-loop system, but as a consultation system, one that recommends a course of action to a human user who may or may not choose to follow the recommendation [11]. These researchers wrote: "Computer predictions should never dictate clinical decisions, as very often there are many factors other than physiologic data to be considered when a decision to withdraw therapy is made" (p. 1096). Thus, used as a consultation system, APACHE [would function] as a tool to aid the critical care staff with making difficult decisions about the withdrawal of therapy. Framed in this manner, the consultation system approach seems to avoid the distortions of human agency described above: the consultation system does not mimic purposeful action or inappropriately distance the medical staff from making decisions about human life and death.

In practice, however, the situation can be more complicated. Most human activity, including the decision by medical personnel to withdraw life support systems, occurs in a web of human relationships. In some circumstances, because a computational system is embedded in a complex social structure human users may experience a diminished sense of moral agency. Let us imagine, for instance, that APACHE is used as a consultation system. With increasing use and continued good performance by APACHE, it is likely that the medical personnel using APACHE would develop increased trust in APACHE's recommendations. Over time, these recommendations would carry increasingly greater authority within the medical community. Within this social context, it may become the practice for critical care staff to act on APACHE's recommendations somewhat automatically, and increasingly difficult for even an experienced physician to challenge the "authority" of APACHE's recommendation, since to challenge APACHE would be to challenge the medical community. But at this point the open-loop consultation system through the social context has become, in effect, a closed-loop system wherein computer prediction dictates clinical decisions.

Such potential effects point to the need to design computational systems with an eye toward the larger social context, including long-term effects that may not become apparent until the technology is well situated in the social environment. Participatory design methods offer one such means [15, 16]. Future users, who are experienced in their respective fields, are substantively involved in the design process. As noted at a recent conference [17], Thoresen worked with hospital nurses to design a computer-based record-keeping system. In the design process, nurses helped to define on a macro level what institutional problems the technology would seek to solve, and on a micro level how such technological solutions would be implemented. From the perspective of human agency, such participatory design lays the groundwork for users to see themselves as responsible for shaping the system's design and use.

Delegating Instruction to Computational Systems

Instructional technology programs that deliver systematically designed computer-based courseware to students can suffer from the first type of distortion—computer use that erodes the human user's sense of his or her own agency. Often absent from this type of instructional technology is a meaningful notion of the student's responsibility for learning. Johnsen and Taylor [18] have discussed this problem in a paper aptly titled "At cross-purpose: instructional technology and the erosion of personal responsibility." According to Johnsen and Taylor, instructional technology "define[s] responsibility operationally in the context of means/ends rationality. The singular responsibility for a student's education becomes identified with the success of the program" (p. 9). They further point to the logical conclusion of this educational view for students, parents, teachers, and government: failure to educate comes to mean that the instructional technology failed to teach, not that students failed to learn.

As an example of this type of instructional technology, consider how the GREATERP intelligent tutoring system (described in [19]) for novice programmers in LISP handles students' errors. When GREATERP determined that the student entered "incorrect" information, the tutor interrupted the student's progress toward the student's proposed solution (viable or not) and forced the student to backtrack to the intelligent tutor's "correct" solution. Thus GREATERP assumed responsibility not only for student learning but also for preventing student errors along the way and for the process of achieving a solution. In so doing, this intelligent tutoring system—and other comparable instructional technology programs—can undermine the student's sense of his or her own agency and responsibility for the educational endeavor.

In contrast, other educational uses of computing promote students' sense of agency and active decision making. For example, just as consultation systems can to some degree place responsibility for decision making on the human user, so educational uses of computer applications software (e.g., word processors, spreadsheets, data bases, microcomputer-based labs) can place responsibility for learning on the student. With computer applications students determine when the applications would be useful and for what purposes, and evaluate the results of their use. Moreover, the social organization of school computer use can contribute to students' understanding of responsible computing. As with participatory design, consider the value of student participation in creating the policies that govern their own school computer use. For example, as discussed in an article by Friedman [20], students can determine the privacy policy for their own electronic mail at school. To establish such a privacy policy, "students must draw on their fundamental understandings of privacy rights to develop specific policies for this new situation. In turn, circumstances like these provide opportunities for students not only to develop morally but to make decisions about a socially and computationally powerful technology, and thus to mitigate a belief held by many people that one is controlled by rather than in control of technology." Through such experiences, students can learn that humans determine how computer technology is used and that humans bear responsibility for the results of that use.

Conclusion

We argued initially that humans, but not computers (as they can be conceived today in material and structure), are or could be moral agents. Based on this view, we identified two broad approaches by which computer system design can promote responsible computer use. Each approach seeks to minimize a potential distortion between human agency and computer activity. First, computational systems should be designed in ways that do not denigrate the human user to machine-like status. Second, computational systems should be designed in ways that do not impersonate human agency by attempting to mimic intentional states. Both approaches seek to promote the human user's autonomous decision making in ways that are responsive to and informed by community and culture.

What we have provided, of course, are only broad approaches and design sketches. But if we are correct that human agency is central to most endeavors that seek to understand and promote responsible computing, then increased attention should be given to how the human user perceives specific types of human-computer interactions, and how human agency is constrained, promoted, or otherwise affected by the larger social environment. In such investigations, it is likely that research methods can draw substantively on existing methods employed in the social-cognitive and moral-developmental psychological fields. Methods might include 1) semistructured hypothetical interviews with participants about centrally relevant problems [21–25]; 2) naturalistic and structured observations [26–28]; and 3) semistructured interviews based on observations of the participant's practice [29–31]. Of note, some anthropologists [32] and psychologists [33] working in the area of human factors have with some success incorporated aspects of these methods into their design practices.

A final word needs to be said about the role of moral psychology in the field of computer system design. As increasingly sophisticated computational systems have become embedded in social lives and societal practices, increasing pressure has been placed on the computing field to go beyond purely technical considerations and to promote responsible computing. In response, there has been, understandably, a desire to know the "right" answer to ethical problems that arise, where "right" is understood to mean something like "philosophically justified or grounded." We argue that there is an important place for philosophical analyses in the field. But philosophy seldom tells us how or why problems relevant to a philosophical position involving computing occur in practice, let alone what can most effectively resolve them. Such issues require empirical data that deal substantively with the psychological reality of humans. Thus, by linking our technical pursuits with both philosophical inquiry and moral-psychological research, responsible computing can be enhanced as a shared vision and practice within the computing community.

References

1. R. E. Eberts and C. G. Eberts, Four approaches to human computer interaction, in *Intelligent Interfaces: Theory, Research and Design* (P. A. Hancock and M. H. Chignell, eds.), Elsevier Science Publishers, New York, 1989.
2. J. Weizenbaum, *Computer Power and Human Reason,* W. H. Freeman & Company, New York, 1976.
3. S. Turkle, *The Second Self: Computers and the Human Spirit,* Simon & Schuster, New York, 1984.
4. D. E. Rumelhart and D. A. Norman, Analogical processes in learning, in *Cognitive Skills and Their Acquisition* (J. R. Anderson, ed.), Lawrence Erlbaum Associates, Hillsdale, NJ, 1981.
5. J. P. Jenkins, An application of an expert system to problem solving in process control displays, in *Human-Computer Interaction* (G. Salvendy, ed.), Elsevier Science Publishers, New York, 1984.
6. R. J. K. Jacob, Direct manipulation in the intelligent interface, in *Intelligent Interfaces: Theory, Research and Design* (P. A. Hancock and M. H. Chignell, eds.), Elsevier Science Publishers, New York, 1989.
7. D. C. Smith, C. Irby, R. Kimball, W. Verplank, and E. Marslem, Designing the user interface, *Byte* 7, 242–282 (1982).
8. B. Shneiderman, *Designing the User Interface: Strategies for Effective Human-Computer Interaction,* Addison-Wesley Publishing Company, Reading, Massachusetts, 1987.
9. B. Shneiderman, Designing the user interface, in *Computers in the Human Context: Information Technology, Productivity and People* (T. Forester, ed.), The MIT Press, Cambridge, Massachusetts, 1989.
10. T. Winograd and F. Flores, *Understanding Computers and Cognition: A New Foundation for Design,* Addison-Wesley Publishing Company, Reading, Massachusetts, 1986.
11. R. W. S. Chang, B. Lee, S. Jacobs, and B. Lee, Accuracy of decisions to withdraw therapy in critically ill patients: clinical judgment versus a computer model, *Crit. Care Med.* 17, 1091–1097 (1989).
12. J. E. Zimmerman, ed., APACHE III study design: analytic plan for evaluation of severity and outcome, *Crit. Care Med.* 17 (Part 2 Suppl), S169–S221 (1989).
13. E. H. Shortliffe, Medical consultation systems: designing for doctors, in *Designing for Human-Computer Communication* (M. E. Sime and M. J. Coombs, eds.), Academic Press, New York, 1983.
14. C. L. Harris *et al.,* Office automation: making it pay off, in *Computers in the Human Context: Information Technology, Productivity, and People* (T. Forester, ed.), The MIT Press, Cambridge, Massachusetts, 1989.
15. P. Ehn, *Work-oriented Design of Computer Artifacts,* Lawrence Erlbaum Associates, Hillsdale, New Jersey, 1989.

16. J. Greenbaum and M. Kyng, eds., *Design at Work: Cooperative Design of Computer Systems,* Lawrence Erlbaum Associates, Hillsdale, New Jersey, 1990.

17. A. Namioka and D. Schuler, eds., *Proceedings from the Conference on Participatory Design 1990,* Computer Professionals for Social Responsibility, Palo Alto, California, 1990.

18. J. B. Johnsen and W. D. Taylor, At cross-purpose: instructional technology and the erosion of personal responsibility, paper presented at the annual meeting of the American Educational Research Association, New Orleans, April 1988.

19. R. Kass, Student modeling in intelligent tutoring systems—implications for user modeling, in *User Models in Dialog Systems* (A. Kobsa and W. Wahlster, eds.), Springer-Verlag, New York, 1989.

20. B. Friedman, Social and moral development through computer use: a constructivist approach, *J. Res. Comput. Educ.* 23: 560–567 (1991).

21. W. Damon, *The Social World of the Child,* Jossey-Bass, San Francisco, 1977.

22. L. Kohlberg, Stage and sequence: the cognitive-developmental approach to socialization, in *Handbook of Socialization Theory and Research* (D. A. Goslin, ed.), Rand-McNally, Chicago, 1969.

23. J. Piaget, *The Child's Conception of the World,* Routledge & Kegan Paul, London, 1929.

24. J. Piaget, *The Moral Judgment of the Child,* Routledge & Kegan Paul, London, 1932.

25. E. Turiel, *The Development of Social Knowledge: Morality and Convention,* Cambridge University Press, Cambridge, England, 1983.

26. R. DeVries and A. Goncu, Interpersonal relations in four-year dyads from constructivist and Montesorri programs, *J. Appl. Dev. Psychol.* 8, 481–501 (1987).

27. B. Friedman, Societal issues and school practices: An ethnographic investigation of the social context of school computer use, paper presented at the annual meeting of the American Educational Research Association, Boston, April 1990 (ERIC Document Reproduction Service No. ED 321 740).

28. L. P. Nucci and M. Nucci, Children's responses to moral and social conventional transgressions in free-play settings, *Child Dev.* 53, 1337–1342 (1982).

29. R. DeVries, Children's conceptions of shadow phenomena, *Gen. Soc. Gen. Psychol. Monographs* 112, 479–530 (1986).

30. L. P. Nucci and E. Turiel, Social interactions and the development of social concepts in preschool children, *Child Dev.* 49, 400–407 (1978).

31. G. B. Saxe, *Culture and Cognitive Development: Studies in Mathematical Understanding,* Lawrence Erlbaum Press, Hillsdale, New Jersey, 1990.

32. L. A. Suchman, *Plans and Situated Actions: The Problem of Human-Machine Communication,* Cambridge University Press, Cambridge, England, 1987.

33. C. Allen and R. Pea, Reciprocal evolution of research, work practices and technology, in *Proceedings from the Conference on Participatory Design 1990* (A. Namioka and D. Schuler, eds.), Computer Professionals for Social Responsibility, Palo Alto, 1990.

——— 9 ———————————————————————

Are Hacker Break-ins Ethical?

Eugene H. Spafford argues that we should judge the actions of hackers, not the rationalizations they offer. He rejects arguments that hackers actually enhance long-run security, that student hacking is merely a way to harmlessly learn about computer functioning, and that information should be free. (See also Stallman, "The GNU Manifesto.")

Eugene H. Spafford

Introduction

. . . . The continuing evolution of our technological base and our increasing reliance on computers for critical tasks suggest that future hacking incidents may well have more serious consequences than those we have seen to date. With human nature as varied and extreme as it is, and with the technology as available as it is, we must expect to experience more of these incidents.

In this article, I will introduce a few of the major issues that these past incidents have raised, and present some arguments related to them. For clarification, I have separated several issues that often have been combined when debated; it is possible that most people agree on some of these points once they are viewed as individual issues.

What Is Ethical?

Webster's Collegiate Dictionary defines ethics as "the discipline dealing with what is good and bad and with moral duty and obligation." More simply, it is the study of what is right to do in a given situation—what we ought to do. Alternatively, it is sometimes described as the study of what is good and how to achieve that good. To suggest whether an act is right or wrong we need to agree on an ethical system that is easy to understand and apply as we consider the ethics of computer break-ins.

Philosophers have been trying for thousands of years to define right and wrong, and I will not make yet another attempt at such a definition. Instead, I will suggest that we make the simplifying assumption that we can judge the ethical nature of an act by applying a deontological assessment: regardless of the effect, is the act itself ethical? Would we view that act as sensible and proper if everyone were to engage in it? Although this may be too simplistic a model (and it can certainly be argued that other ethical philosophies may also be applied), it is a good first approximation for purposes of discussion. If you are unfamiliar with any other formal ethical evaluation method, try applying this assessment to the points I raise later in this article. If the results are obviously unpleasant or dangerous in the large, then they should be considered unethical as individual acts.

Note that this philosophy assumes that right is determined by actions, not results. Some ethical philosophies assume that the ends justify the means; our society does not operate by such a philosophy, although many individuals do. As a society, we profess to believe that "it isn't whether you win or lose, it's how you play the game." This is why we are concerned with issues of due process and civil rights, even for those espousing repugnant views and committing heinous acts. The process is important no matter the outcome, although the outcome may help to resolve a choice between two almost equal courses of action.

Philosophies that consider the results of an act as the ultimate measure of good are often impossible to apply because of the difficulty in understanding exactly what results from any arbitrary activity. Consider an extreme example: the government orders 100 cigarette smokers, chosen at random, to be beheaded on live nationwide television. The result might well be that many hundreds of thousands of other smokers would quit cold turkey, thus prolonging their lives. It might also prevent hundreds of thousands of people from ever starting to smoke, thus improving the health and longevity of the general populace. The health of millions of other people would improve because they would no longer be subjected to secondary smoke, and the overall impact on the environment would be favorable as tons of air and ground pollutants would no longer be released by smokers or tobacco companies.

Yet, despite the great good this might hold for society, everyone, except for a few extremists, would condemn such an act as immoral. We would likely object even if only one person were executed. It would not matter what the law might be on such an issue; we would not feel that the act was morally correct, nor would we view the ends as justifying the means.

Note that we would be unable to judge the morality of such an action by evaluating the results, because we would not know the full scope of those results. Such an act might have effects, favorable or otherwise, on issues of law, public health, tobacco use, and daytime TV shows for decades or centuries to follow. A system of ethics that considered primarily only the results of our actions would not allow us to evaluate our current activities at the time when we would need such guidance; if we are unable to discern the appropriate course of action prior to its commission, then our system of ethics is of little or no value to us. To obtain ethical guidance, we must base our actions primarily on evaluations of the actions and not on the possible results.

More to the point here, if we attempt to judge the morality of a computer break-in based on the sum total of all future effects, we would be unable to make such a judgment, either for a specific incident or for the general class of acts. In part, this is because it is so difficult to determine the long-term effects of various actions and to discern their causes. We cannot know, for instance, if increased security awareness and restrictions are better for society in the long term, or whether these additional restrictions will result in greater costs and annoyance when using computer systems. We also do not know how many of these changes are directly traceable to incidents of computer break-ins.

One other point should be made here: it is undoubtedly possible to imagine scenarios where a computer break-in would be considered to be the preferable course of action. For instance, if vital medical data were on a computer and necessary to save someone's life in an emergency, but the authorized users of the system could not be located, breaking into the system might well be considered the right thing to do. However, that action does not make the break-in ethical. Rather, such situations occur when greater wrong would undoubtedly occur if the unethical act were not committed. Similar reasoning applies to situations such as killing in self defense. In the following discussion, I will assume that such conflicts are not the root cause of the break-ins; such situations should very rarely present themselves.

Motivations

Individuals who break into computer systems or who write vandalware usually use one of several rationalizations for their actions. (See, for example, [12] and the discussion in [13].) Most of these individuals would never think to walk down a street, trying every door to find one unlocked, then search through the drawers of the furniture inside. Yet these same people seem to give no second thought to making repeated attempts at guessing passwords to accounts they do not own, and once into a system, browsing through the files on disk.

These computer burglars often give the same reasons for their actions in an attempt to rationalize their activities as morally justified. I present and refute some of the most commonly used ones: motives involving theft and revenge are not uncommon, and their moral nature is simple to discern, so I shall not include them here.

The Hacker Ethic

Many hackers argue that they follow an ethic that both guides their behavior and justifies their break-ins. This hacker ethic states, in part, that all information should be free [11]. This view holds that information belongs to everyone and there should be no boundaries or restraints to prevent anyone from examining information. Richard Stallman states much the same thing in his GNU Manifesto [14]. He and others have stated in various forums that if information is free, it logically follows that there should be no such thing as intellectual property, and no need for security.

What are the implications and consequences of such a philosophy? First and foremost, it raises some disturbing questions of privacy. If all information is (or should be) free, then privacy is no longer a possibility. For information to be free to everyone and for individuals to no longer be able to claim it as property means that anyone may access the information if they please. Furthermore, as it is no longer property of any individual, anyone can alter the information. Items such as bank balances, medical records, credit histories, employment records, and defense information all cease to be controlled. If someone controls information and controls who may access it, the information is obviously not free. But without that control, we would no longer be able to trust the accuracy of the information.

In a perfect world, this lack of privacy and control might not be cause for concern. However, if all information were to be freely available and modifiable, imagine how much damage and chaos would be caused in our real world! Our whole society is based on information whose accuracy must be assured. This includes information held by banks and other financial institutions, credit bureaus, medical agencies and professionals, government agencies such as the IRS, law enforcement agencies, and educational institutions. Clearly, treating all their information as "free" would be unethical in any world where there might be careless and unethical individuals.

Economic arguments can be made against this philosophy, too, in addition to the overwhelming need for privacy and control of information accuracy. Information is not universally free. It is held as property because of privacy concerns, and because it is often collected and developed at great expense. Development of a new algorithm or program or collection of a specialized data base may involve the expenditure of vast sums of time and effort. To claim that it is free or should be free to express a naive and unrealistic view of the world. To use this to justify computer break-ins is clearly unethical. Although not all information currently treated as private or controlled as proprietary needs such protection, that does not justify unauthorized access to it or to any other data.

The Security Arguments

These arguments are the most common ones offered within the computer community. One argument is that . . . break-ins illustrate security problems to a community that will otherwise not note the problems.

In the INTERNET WORM hacking case over a decade ago, for example, one of the first issues to be discussed widely in Internet mailing lists dealt with the intent of the perpetrator—exactly why the worm program had been written and released. Explanations put forth by members of the community ranged from simple accident to the actions of a sociopath. Many said that the WORM was designed to reveal security defects to a community that would not otherwise pay attention. This was not supported by the testimony of the author during his trial, nor is it supported by past experience of system administrators.

The WORM author, Robert T. Morris, appears to have been well known at some universities and major companies, and his talents were generally respected. Had he merely explained the problems or offered a demonstration to these people, he would have been listened to with considerable attention. The month before he released the WORM program on the Internet, he discovered and disclosed a bug in the file transfer program *ftp;* news of the flaw spread rapidly, and an official fix was announced and available within a matter of weeks. The argument that no one would listen to his report of security weaknesses is clearly fallacious.

In the more general case, this security argument is also without merit. Although some system administrators might have been complacent about the security of their systems before the WORM incident, most computer vendors, managers of government computer installations, and system administrators at major colleges and universities have been attentive to reports of security problems. People wishing to report a problem with the security of a system need not exploit it to report it. By way of analogy, one does not set fire to the neighborhood shopping center to bring attention to a fire hazard in one of the stores, and then try to justify the act by claiming that firemen would otherwise never listen to reports of hazards.

The most general argument that some people make is that the individuals who break into systems are performing a service by exposing security flaws, and thus should be encouraged or even rewarded. This argument is severely flawed in several ways. First, it assumes that there is some compelling need to force users to install security fixes on their systems, and thus computer burglars are justified in "breaking and entering" activities. Taken to extremes, it suggests that it would be perfectly acceptable to engage in such activities on a continuing basis, so long as they might expose security flaws. This completely loses sight of the purpose of the computers in the first place—to serve as tools and resources, not as exercises in security. The same reasoning would imply that vigilantes have the right to attempt to break into the homes in my neighborhood on a continuing basis to demonstrate that they are susceptible to burglars.

Another flaw with this argument is that it completely ignores the technical and economic factors that prevent many sites from upgrading or correcting their software. Not every site has the resources to install new system software or to correct existing software. At many sites, the systems are run as turnkey systems—employed as tools and maintained by the vendor. The owners and users of these machines simply do not have the ability to correct or maintain their systems independently, and they are unable to afford custom software support from their vendors. To break into such systems, with or without damage, is effectively to trespass into places of business; to do so in a vigilante effort to force the owners to upgrade their security structure is presumptuous and reprehensible. A burglary is not justified, morally or legally, by an argument that the victim has poor locks and was therefore "asking for it."

A related argument has been made that vendors are responsible for the maintenance of their software, and that such security breaches should immediately require vendors to issue corrections to their customers, past and present. The claim is made that without highly-visible break-ins, vendors will not produce or distribute necessary fixes to software. This attitude is naive, and is neither economically feasible nor technically workable. Certainly, vendors should bear some responsibility for the adequacy of their software [15], but they should not be responsible for fixing every possible flaw in every possible configuration.

Many sites customize their software or otherwise run systems incompatible with the latest vendor releases. For a vendor to be able to provide quick response to security problems, it would be necessary for each customer to run completely standardized software and hardware mixes to ensure the correctness of vendor-supplied updates. Not only would this be considerably less attractive for many customers and contrary to their usual practice, but the increased cost of such "instant" fix distribution would add to the price of such a system and greatly increase the cost borne by the customer. It is unreasonable to expect the user community to sacrifice flexibility and pay a much higher cost per unit simply for faster corrections to the occasional security breach, assuming it is possible for the manufacturer to find those customers and supply them with fixes in a timely manner— something unlikely in a market where machines and software are often repackaged, traded, and resold.

The case of the INTERNET WORM is a good example of the security argument and its flaws. It further stands as a good example of the conflict between ends and means valuation of ethics. Various people have argued that the WORM's author did us a favor by exposing security flaws. At Mr. Morris's trial on Federal charges stemming from the incident, the defense attorneys also argued that their client should not be punished because of the good the WORM did in exposing those flaws. Others, including the prosecuting attorneys, argued that the act itself was wrong no matter what the outcome. Their contention has been that the result does not justify the act itself, nor does the defense's argument encompass all the consequences of the incident. . . .

The Idle System Argument

Another argument put forth by system hackers is that they are simply making use of idle machines. They argue that because some systems are not used at a level near their capacity, the hacker is somehow entitled to use them.

This argument is also flawed. First of all, these systems are usually not in service to provide a general-purpose user environment. Instead, they are in use in commerce, medicine, public safety, research, and government functions. Unused capacity is present for future needs and sudden surges of activity, not for the support of outside individuals. Imagine if large numbers of people without a computer were to take advantage of a system with idle processor capacity: the system would quickly be overloaded and severely degraded or unavailable for the rightful owners. Once on the system, it would be difficult (or impossible) to oust these individuals if sudden extra capacity were needed by the rightful owners. Even the largest machines available today would not provide sufficient capacity to accommodate such activity on any large scale.

I am unable to think of any other item that someone may buy and maintain, only to have others claim a right to use it when it is idle. For instance, the thought of someone walking up to my expensive car and driving off in it simply because it is not currently being used is ludicrous. Likewise, because I am away at work, it is not proper to hold a party at my house because it is otherwise not being used. The related positions that unused computing capacity is a shared resource, and that my privately-developed software belongs to everyone, are equally silly (and unethical) positions.

The Student Hacker Argument

Some trespassers claims that they are doing no harm and changing nothing—they are simply learning about how computer systems operate. They argue that computers are expensive, and that they are merely furthering their education in a cost-effective manner. Some authors of computer viruses claim that their creations are intended to be harmless, and that they are simply learning how to write complex programs.

There are many problems with these arguments. First, as an educator, I claim that writing vandalware or breaking into a computer and looking at the files has almost nothing to do with computer education. Proper education in computer science and engineering involves intensive exposure to fundamental aspects of theory, abstraction, and design techniques. Browsing through a system does not expose someone to the broad scope of theory and practice in computing, nor does it provide the critical feedback so important to a good education [16, 17]; neither does writing a virus or worm program and releasing it into an unsupervised environment provide any proper educational experience. By analogy, stealing cars and joyriding does not provide one with an education in mechanical engineering, nor does pouring sugar in the gas tank.

Furthermore, individuals "learning" about a system cannot know how everything operates and what results from their activities. Many systems have been damaged accidentally by ignorant (or careless) intruders; most of the damage from computer viruses . . . appears to be caused by unexpected interactions and program faults. Damage to medical systems, factory control, financial information, and other computer systems could have drastic and far-ranging effects that have nothing to do with education, and could certainly not be considered harmless.

A related refutation of the claim has to do with knowledge of the extent of the intrusion. If I am the person responsible for the security of a critical computer system, I cannot assume that *any* intrusion is motivated solely by curiosity and that nothing has been harmed. If I know that the system has been compromised, I must fear the worst and perform a complete system check for damages and changes. I cannot take the word of the intruder, for any intruder who actually caused damage would seek to hide it by claiming that he or she was "just looking." To regain confidence in the correct behavior of my system, I must expend considerable energy to examine and verify every aspect of it.

Apply our universal approach to this situation and imagine if this "educational" behavior was widespread and commonplace. The result would be that we would spend all our time verifying our systems and never be able to trust the results fully. Clearly, this is not good, and thus we must conclude that these "educational" motivations are also unethical.

The Social Protector Argument

One last argument, more often heard in Europe than the United States, is that hackers break into systems to watch for instances of data abuse and to help keep "Big Brother" at bay. In this sense, the hackers are protectors rather that criminals. Again, this assumes that the ends justify the means. It also assumes that the hackers are actually able to achieve some good end.

Undeniably, there is some misuse of personal data by corporations and by the government. The increasing use of computer-based record systems and networks may lead to further abuses. However, it is not clear that breaking into these systems will aid in righting the wrongs. If anything, it may cause those agencies to become even more secretive and use the break-ins as an excuse for more restricted access. Break-ins and vandalism have not resulted in new open-records law, but they have resulted in the introduction and passage of new criminal statutes. Not only has such activity failed to deter "Big Brother," but it has also resulted in significant segments of the public urging more laws and more aggressive law enforcement—the direct opposite of the supposed goal.

It is also not clear that these hackers are the individuals we want "protecting" us. We need to have the designers and users of the systems—trained computer professionals—concerned about our rights and aware of the dangers involved with the inappropriate use of computer monitoring and record keeping. The threat is a relatively new one, as computers and networks have become widely used only in the last few decades. It will take some time for awareness of the dangers to spread throughout the profession. Clandestine efforts to breach the security of computer systems do nothing to raise the consciousness of the appropriate individuals. Worse, they associate that commendable goal (heightened concern) with criminal activity (computer break-ins), thus discouraging proactive behavior by the individuals in the best positions to act in our favor. Perhaps it is in this sense that computer break-ins and vandalism are most unethical and damaging.

Conclusion

I have argued here that computer break-ins, even when no obvious damage results, are unethical. This must be the considered conclusion even if the result is an improvement in security, because the activity itself is disruptive and immoral. The results of the act should be considered separately from the act itself, especially when we consider how difficult it is to understand all the effects resulting from such an act.

Of course, I have not discussed every possible reason for a break-in. There might well be an instance where a break-in might be necessary to save a life or to preserve national security. In such cases, to perform one wrong act to prevent a greater wrong may be the right thing to do. It is beyond the scope or intent of this paper to discuss such cases, especially as no known hacker break-ins have been motivated by such instances.

Historically, computer professionals as a group have not been overly concerned with questions of ethics and propriety as they relate to computers. Individuals and some organizations have tried to address these issues, but the whole computing community needs to be involved to address the problems in any comprehensive manner. Too often, we view computers simply as machines and algorithms, and we do not perceive the serious ethical questions inherent in their use.

However, when we consider that these machines influence the quality of life of millions of individuals, both directly and indirectly, we understand that there are broader issues. Computers are used to design, analyze, support, and control applications that protect and guide the lives and finances of people. Our use (and misuse) of computing systems may have effects beyond our wildest imagining. Thus, we must reconsider our attitudes about acts demonstrating a lack of respect for the rights and privacy of other people's computers and data.

We must also consider what our attitudes will be towards future security problems. In particular, we should consider the effect of widely publishing the source code for worms, viruses, and other threats to security. Although we need a process for rapidly disseminating corrections and security information as they become known, we should realize that widespread publication of details will imperil sites where users are unwilling or unable to install updates and fixes.[1] Publication should serve a useful purpose; endangering the security of other people's machines or attempting to force them into making changes they are unable to make or afford is not ethical.

Finally, we must decide these issues of ethics as a community of professionals and then present them to society as a whole. No matter what laws are passed, and no matter how good security measures might become, they will not be enough for us to have completely secure systems. We also need to develop and act according to some shared ethical values. The members of society need to be educated so that they understand the importance of respecting the privacy and ownership of data. If locks and laws were all that kept people from robbing houses, there would be many more burglars than there are now; the shared mores about the sanctity of personal property are an important influence in the prevention of burglary. It is our duty as informed professionals to help extend those mores into the realm of computers.

Note

1. To anticipate the oft-used comment that the "bad guys" already have such information: not every computer burglar knows or will know *every* system weakness—unless we provide them with detailed analyses.

References

1. E. H. Spafford, Is a computer break-in ever ethical? *Info. Tech Quart.* IX, 9–14 (1990).
2. D. Seeley, A tour of the worm, In *Proceedings of the Winter 1989 Usenix Conference,* The Usenix Association, Berkeley, CA, 1989.
3. E. H. Spafford, The internet worm: crisis and aftermath. *Commun. ACM* 32, 678–698 (1989).
4. E. H. Spafford, An analysis of the internet work. In *Proceedings of the 2nd European Software Engineering Conference* (C. Ghezzi and J. A. McDermid, eds.), Springer-Verlag, Berlin, Germany, 1989, pp. 446–468.
5. C. Stoll, *Cuckoo's Egg,* Doubleday, New York, 1989.
6. John Schwartz, The hacker dragnet, *Newsweek* 65, (April, 1990).

7. E. H. Spafford, K. A. Heaphy, and D. J. Ferbrache, *Computer Viruses: Dealing with Electronic Vandalism and Programmed Threats,* ADAPSO, Arlington, Virginia, 1989.
8. L. Hoffman, ed., *Rogue Programs: Viruses, Worms, and Trojan Horses,* Van Nostrand Reinhold, New York, 1990.
9. D. J. Stang, *Computer Viruses,* 2nd ed., National Computer Security Association, Washington, DC, 1990.
10. P. J. Denning, ed., *Computers Under Attack: Intruders, Worms, and Viruses.* ACM Books/Addison-Wesley, Reading, Massachusetts, 1991.
11. B. J. Baird, L. L. Baird, Jr., and R. P. Ranauro, The moral cracker? *Comp. Sec.* 6, 471–478 (1987).
12. W. Landreth, *Out of the Inner Circle: a Hacker's Guide to Computer Security,* Microsoft Press, New York, 1984.
13. Adelaide, J. P. Barlow, R. J. Bluefire, R. Brand C. Stoll, D. Hughes, F. Drake, E. J. Homeboy, E. Goldstein, H. Roberts, J. Gasperini (JIMG), J. Carroll (JRC), L. Felsenstein, T. Mandel, R. Horvitz (RH), R. Stallman (RMS), G. Tenney, Acid Phreak, and Phiber Optik, Is computer hacking a crime? *Harper's Magazine* 280, 45–57 (March 1990).
14. R. Stallman, The GNU Manifesto, in *GNU EMacs Manual,* Free Software Foundation, Cambridge, MA, 1986, pp. 239–248.
15. M. D. McIlroy, Unsafe at any price, *Info. Techn. Quart.* IX, 21–23 (1990).
16. P. J. Denning, D. E. Comer, D. Gries, M. C. Mulder, A. Tucker, A. J. Turner, and P. R. Young, Computing as a discipline, *Commun. ACM* 32, 9–23 (1989).
17. A. B. Tucker, B. H. Barnes, R. M. Aiken, K. Barker, K. B. Bruce, J. T. Cain, S. E. Conry, G. L. Engel, R. G. Epstein, D. K. Lidtke, M. C. Mulder, J. B. Rogers, E. H. Spafford, and A. J. Turner, *Computing Curricula 1991,* IEEE Society Press, Piscataway, NJ, 1991.

— 10

Using Computers as Means, Not Ends

Herbert and Stuart Dreyfus forcefully sound the alarm against the "computer-type rationality" that pervades technological society. Human thought, they argue, is holistic in nature and inseparable from emotions, skills, and one's situation in the world. The Dreyfuses condemn the "false optimism and unrealistic expectations" of computer advocates, regarding computer intelligence as

From Herbert L. and Stuart E. Dreyfus, *Mind Over Machine,* pp. xi–xiv, 31–36, 202–6. The Free Press, 1986. Reprinted by permission.

an outgrowth of the overemphasis on reason that can be traced back to Greek philosophy. (See also Aristotle, "The Best Action Is the One That Exercises the Mind's Faculties.")

Herbert L. Dreyfus and Stuart E. Dreyfus with Tom Athanasiou

Despite what you may have read in magazines and newspapers, regardless of what your congressman was told when he voted on the Strategic Computing Plan, twenty-five years of artificial intelligence research has lived up to very few of its promises and has failed to yield any evidence that it ever will. The time has come to ask what has gone wrong and what we can reasonably expect from computer intelligence. How closely can computers processing facts and making inferences approach human intelligence? How can we profitably use the intelligence that can be given to them? What are the risks of enthusiastic and ambitious attempts to redefine our intelligence in their terms, of delegating to computers key decision-making powers, of adapting ourselves to the educational and business practices attuned to mechanized reason?

In short, we want to put the debate about the computer in perspective by clearing the air of false optimism and unrealistic expectations. The debate about what computers should do is properly about social values and institutional forms. But before we can profitably discuss what computers *should* do we have to be clear about what they *can* do. Our bottom line is that computers as reasoning machines can't match human intuition and expertise, so in determining what computers should do we have to contrast their capacities with the more generous gifts possessed by the human mind.

. . . . .

Computers are certainly more precise and more predictable than we, but precision and predictability are not what human intelligence is about. Human beings have other strengths, and here we do not mean just the shifting moods and subtle empathy usually ceded to humanity by even the most hard-line technologists. Human emotional life remains unique, to be sure, but what is more important is our ability to recognize, to synthesize, to intuit.

. . . . .

The acquisition of medical diagnosis skill using X-ray film has recently been studied. After a few years of training, radiologists seem to form diagnostic hypotheses and draw conclusions from sets of relevant features as described in our third stage of skill acquisition, competence. [The first two stages are novice and advanced beginner—Eds.] But do experts perform in that way? Our skill acquisition model suggests that after enough experience with the films of patients with a particular condition, the pattern of dark and light regions associated with that condition is stored in memory, and when a similar pattern is seen, the memory is triggered and the diagnosis comes to mind. There would be no decomposition of the patterns on the film into features, and no need for rules associating conditions with features. If you doubt that a dark and light pattern could look to the specialist like a collapsed lung lobe without need for detection of features and application of rules, imagine a patient with a glass chest. Even a novice doctor would see at a glance that a lung lobe was collapsed. Why should it be surprising that with enough experience an X-ray might look as familiar and informative to the expert as the actul chest looks to the novice doctor and that the expert should be able to "see" an abnormality through the X-ray as the novice doctor would see it through glass?

. . . . .

With enough experience in a variety of situations, all seen from the same perspective or with the same goal in mind but requiring different tactical decisions, the mind of the proficient performer seems to group together situations sharing not only the same goal or perspective but also the same decision, action, or tactic. At this point not only is a situation, when seen as similar to a prior one, understood, but the associated decision, action, or tactic simultaneously comes to mind.

An immense library of distinguishable situations is built up on the basis of experience. A chess master, it has been estimated, can recognize roughly 50,000 types of positions, and the same can probably be said of automobile driving. We doubtless store many more typical situations in our memories than words in our vocabularies. Consequently, such situations of reference bear no names and, in fact, seem to defy complete verbal description.

With expertise comes fluid performance. We seldom "choose our words" or "place our feet"—we simply talk and walk. The skilled outfielder doesn't take the time to figure out where a ball is going. Unlike the novice, he simply runs to the right spot.

. . . . .

The grandmaster chess player can recognize a large repertoire of types of position for which the desirable tactic or move immediately becomes obvious. Excellent chess players can play at the rate of five to ten seconds a move and even faster without serious degradation in performance. At that speed they must depend almost entirely on intuition and hardly at all on analysis and comparing alternatives.

. . . . .

The moral of [this discussion] is: there is more to intelligence than calculative rationality. Although irrational behavior—that is, behavior contrary to logic or reason—should generally be avoided, it does not follow that behaving rationally should be regarded as the ultimate goal. A vast area exists between irrational and rational that might be called *arational*. The word rational, deriving from the Latin word *ratio,* meaning to reckon or calculate, has come to be equivalent to calculative thought and so carries with it the connotation of "combining component parts to obtain a whole"; arational behavior, then, refers to action without conscious analytic decomposition and recombination. *Competent performance is rational; proficiency is transitional; experts act arationally.*

. . . . .

Socrates stands at the beginning of our tradition as the hero of critical, objective thought. There is something to be said for his sort of detached calculative rationality, but we have seen that it should be appealed to only by a beginner or an expert who, having left his domain of experience, can no longer trust his instincts. Nietzsche, who wrote at what he considered the end of our Western philosophical tradition, had a view of Socratic rationality similar to our own. For Nietzsche, Socrates was not the hero of our culture but its first degenerate, because Socrates had lost the ability of the nobles to trust intuition. "Honest men do not carry their reasons exposed in this fashion," Nietzsche maintained.

Of course, Socrates' "rationality" was not a personal sickness. Athenian society was coping with monumental changes, not the least of which was the transformation of Athens into an imperial power. Deliberative reflection no doubt served as a device for evaluating the continued relevance of traditional ways. But Socrates seems to have overreacted and tried to call all traditional wisdom into question. As Nietzsche saw it, Socrates was symptomatic of a whole culture that, having lost its intuitive sense, desperately sought rules and principles to guide its actions:

> Rationality was at the time divined as a *saviour;* neither Socrates nor his "invalids" were free to be rational or not, as they wished—it was *de rigueur,* it was their *last* expedient. The fanaticism with which the whole of Greek thought throws itself at rationality betrays a state of emergency: one was in peril, one had only *one* choice: either to perish or—be *absurdly rational.*[1]

Aristotle, living a generation after Socrates, occupied an ambiguous position as the opponent of Socrates and Plato. He realized that even if, as Socrates and Plato had believed, people were continuously following rules, they needed wisdom or judgment in order to apply those rules to particular cases. But Aristotle nonetheless seems to have thought that before one could act, one had to deduce one's actions from one's desires and beliefs. The basis of action was, for Aristotle, the practical syllogism: If I desire S and I believe that A will bring about S, then I should do A. Both Aristotle's sense of the importance of judgment and his problem-solving view of intelligence were compatible with his definition of man as *zoion logon echon,* the animal equipped with *logos,* for when Aristotle thought of man as an animal equipped with *logos,* the word *logos* could still mean speaking, or the grasping of whole situations, as well as logical thought. But when *logos* was translated into Latin as *ratio,* meaning "reckoning," its field of meaning was decisively narrowed. It was a fateful turn for our Western tradition: man, the logical animal, was now he who counted, he who measured.

All that was necessary to complete the degeneration of reason into calculation was to equate concepts with collections of objective features, e.g., house = object, shelter, for man; man = thing, living, thinking. By the time Hobbes wrote, around 1600, it was possible to claim not only that reasoning meant reckoning, but that reckoning was nothing more than "the addition of parcels." Four centuries later we so consider reckoning our essence that, trying to create machines in our own images, we see only the problem of creating machines that can make millions of inferences per second.

We have gone father than Aristotle and Hobbes could have imagined, generalizing Aristotle's model of intelligence to all skills, even physical skills, so that even the animal part of man, which Aristotle understood as animated, that is, self-moving, is thought to function by unconscious calculation. At Wright State University Dr. Roger Glaser and Dr. Jerrold Petrofsky have performed ground-breaking research using computer-controlled electrical impulses to exercise the paralyzed limbs of spinal-cord-injured individuals. Yet that amazing therapy is surrounded by heated debate. Dr. Petrofsky, who apparently believes that man's animality is rational, has begun to make extraordinary claims, predicting that the new techniques will eventually lead to computer-controlled free walking for the paralyzed—a strikingly literal example of the first-step fallacy that has buttressed faith in AI [artificial intelligence] for years. He has begun to search for facts about muscle condition, limb position, and terrain that can be combined by rule to produce flexible walking. In a conversation with us, Dr. Glaser opposed that optimism as unrealistic and as cruelly raising false hopes: "We have no idea how the subconscious process that replaces the conscious step-by-step procedure used by beginners works," he said. "We might walk by using sophisticated subconscious rules, but how can we find them? Or walking might involve some process of direct pattern recognition followed by a learned response."

We sometimes work out solutions to problems in our heads, but we rarely "figure out" how to move our bodies. Thus thinking looks like a better candidate for computerization than walking. And if thinking *is* reckoning, then it is reasonable to expect that, as futurists have been telling us for years, the computer as logic machine is the next stage of evolution, which will someday not only excel us but replace us.

That is an appalling vision of the future. Yet there is no disputing computers have fundamentally and permanently transformed our relationship to our technologies. Soon we shall live in a world of extraordinarily rich, subtle, and powerful tools. Will they remain our servants, helping us to our human ends? Or will they outstrip our humanity, and cast us aside?

To the already anxious swirl of modern life a final element of anxiety has been added, fear of absolescence. And anxiety drives us in several desperate directions. Luddites reappear, warning not against the improper uses of computers, but against computers in general, offering, as Jerry Mander did in the "computer-as-poison" issue of the *Whole Earth Review,* six sweeping reasons for ding away with computers altogether. Mystics emerge too, and warn that technology is cutting us off from our intuitive capacity to commune directly with other minds and with nature. Finally, romantics rebel against rationality as they did in the days of Goethe and return to his old slogan, "Feeling is everything."

From out point of view the problem with those reactions is not that they are wrongheaded but that they are misdirected. The enemies of technology focus valuable attention on the fact that computers are no panaceas, but such opposition can at best slow their proliferation. A real victory over the improper application of advanced technology—a victory of mind over machine—can come only with recognition that technology has many proper as well as improper uses and with a widely cultivated ability to tell the difference. Computers are perhaps the most powerful, and certainly the most flexible, devices we have yet built. They have many positive, indeed many wonderful uses. The question is not how to eliminate them but how to make the most of their powers.

Likewise, nostalgia for what is being lost is a healthy reaction to the glorification of the "hacker culture." The back-to-nature mystics, however, confuse the supposed dangers of technological devices with the real danger of the technological mentality. In opposing computers they miss the real problem: total dependence upon calculative thinking and a loss of respect for the less formalizable powers of the mind. They fail to see that computers properly used need not alienate us from our everyday experience-based intuition or whatever other intuitive powers we may possess.

Of the computer opponents only the romantics are on the right track. They oppose not technology but technological rationality. But by rejecting *all* rationality, they fail to see that calculative rationality is appropriate for beginners and in novel situations and that deliberative rationality is not opposed to intuition but based upon it. Put in its proper place rational deliberation sharpens intuition.

The question is whether we are going to accept the view of man as an information processing device, or whether we are still enough in touch with our pre-Platonic essence to realize the limits of the computer metaphor. With our mechanical contrivances now able to solve certain problems more effectively than we can, we are being forced to rethink some very old and by now very basic elements of our self-image. It is our hope that the rethinking will lead to a new definition of what we are, one that values our capacity for involved intuition more than our ability to be rational animals.

What we do now will determine what sort of society and what sort of human beings we are to become. We can make such a decision wisely only if we have some understanding of what sort of human beings we already are. If we think of ourselves only as repositories of factual knowledge and of information processing procedures, then we understand ourselves as someday to be surpassed by bigger and faster machines running bigger and more sophisticated programs. Those who embrace that limited conception of intelligence welcome the change with enthusiasm.[2]

Should we become servants of expert systems and, demanding of our experts their rules and facts, become careless of the intuitive powers that fall outside our stunted vision, we will in one generation lose our professional expertise and confirm those expectations. Our children brought up on Logo and our *competent* specialists crammed with procedures will indeed be inferior to the systems they have been trained to imitate.

But fortunately there are other possibilities. We can use computers to track the vast array of facts and law-governed relationships of our modern technological world, yet continue to nurture the human expertise that inference engines cannot share by encouraging learners to pass from rule following to experience-based intuition. If we do so, our experts will be empowered by their computer aids to make better use of their wisdom in grappling with the still unresolved problems of technological society.

The chips are down; the choice is being made right now. And at all levels of society computer-type rationality is winning out. Experts are an endangered species. If we fail to put logic machines in their proper place, as aids to human beings with expert intuition, then we shall end up servants supplying data to our competent machines. Should calculative rationality triumph, no one will notice that something is missing, but now, while we still know what expert judgment is, let us use that expert judgment to preserve it.

Notes

1. Nietzsche, *Twilight of the Idols,* Aphorism #10 (Penguin Classics, 1968), p. 33 (italics in original).
2. As Roger Schank wrote: "Ultimately, AI will be assimilated into every other dis-

cipline. . . . The ability to create better and better knowledge systems will allow people in every field to develop new ideas and to find new approaches to their oldest problems. AI will encourage a renaissance in practically every area that it touches." Roger Schank, *The Cognitive Computer* (Addison-Wesley, 1984), pp. 221–22.

II

Historical and Cultural Contexts

Are computers and other technologies best understood as increasingly powerful machines born of human inventiveness, or are they the results of historical contingencies and other cultural factors? The following readings argue that technologies are not "neutral" machines but, rather, complex systems that emphasize certain values over others. As you study this section, consider whether you think technologies are value-free inventions or whether they are tools that reinforce particular values and ways of thinking.

11

Technology Is a Tool of the Powerful

Philip Bereano argues that political, cultural, and economic forces determine how new technologies are used
and abused. He is particularly concerned about how
power differences in our society are linked to the use of
computers and other technologies.

Philip Bereano

Most of us have been brought up to believe that the term "technology" refers
to physical artifacts, like a typewriter or a heating system. But that view is
not sufficiently helpful in analyzing technologies in terms of their social, political, cultural, and economic ramifications. I prefer to define "technologies" as the things *and* the institutional (the social, political, cultural, and
economic) mechanisms which produce them and are affected by them.

Human beings have been involved in producing technologies and using
and exploiting them for a long time. But now many of the effects and ramifications are much more massive than they were in the past and, in certain
ways, not readily reversible. New terms such as "postindustrial society" or
"technotronic society" are attempts to indicate that there is something
qualitatively different about what is currently going on.

Emmanuel Mesthane of Harvard's former technology and society program wrote:

> New technology creates new opportunities for men and societies and it also gen-
> erates new problems for them. It has both positive and negative effects and it
> usually has the two at the same time and in virtue of each other.

In certain aspects I think this observation is pretty shrewd, but I fundamentally disagree with his position that technology is neutral. David Dick-

From Philip Bereano, "Technology and Human Freedom" pp. 132–43, *Science for the People*,
November/December 1984. Reprinted by permission.

son has called this the "use/abuse" model of technology. For example, I have a pen in my pocket which I can use to sign someone's death warrant or to write the Declaration of Independence. The uses and abuses of the pen are many, but the pen itself is neutral. Although this might be true about some very simple technologies such as ballpoint pens, I maintain that it is not true about most of the substantial and important technological phenomena which we find in our civilization.

The notion that technology is neutral is very important to the corporate ideology in America. This free enterprise model says that the problems associated with technology are what the economists call "externalities"—the unexpected, unintended side effects of things. The factory which is manufacturing something that we all want may be polluting the air or the water, but pollution is a side effect and is not intentional. Until society creates air pollution laws which internalize these external factors, such side effects will continue.

Because technologies are the result of human interventions into the otherwise natural progression of activities, they themselves are imbued with intentions or purposes. Current technologies, however, are not intended to equally benefit all segments of society. We are not all equally involved. Our society is a class society in which different people have different access to wealth, in power, to decision making, to responsibility, to education, et cetera. We live in a society in which such access is differentiated on the basis of gender, of color, and so on. Because technologies are intentional or purposeful interventions into the environment, those people with more power can determine the kinds of technological interventions which occur. Because of their size, their scale, their requirements for capital investments and for knowledge, modern technologies are powerful interventions into the natural order. They tend to be the mechanisms by which previously powerful groups extend, manifest, and further exacerbate their power. These technologies are not neutral; they are social and political phenomena.

The Appearance of Choice

These social and political aspects of technologies are often hidden behind the appearance of decentralized "choice." On the surface, modern technology offers society many choices, many sources of information.

Television, for example, appears to be a great decentralized resource, with 60 to 70 percent of Americans using TV as their primary source of news. Yet as a technological system, television is one of the most highly centralized phenomena that we have. It is literally true that a very small number of people are able to determine what *is* and what *is not* news; how material classified as news shall be presented and how not; whether it will get thirty seconds or fifteen seconds or no time at all.

Census data are also available in a decentralized way to many people.

Any person can walk into the library and get access to the computer print-out. But the census itself is not really decentralized. The actual forming of the data pool, the decisions as to what questions will be asked and how they will be formulated are very centralized. These centralized decisions reflect the power differentials which exist in our society. Census takers ask how many bathtubs there are in a household (of interest to the American Porcelain Institute) but they don't ask questions which are of particular interest to me or to you. This appearance of access to information and of choice also occurs in the transportation system.

As David Dickson has said about the automobile, they give you tremendous numbers of choices: color, white or black wall tires, digital or sweep-hand clock. But the important decisions, like what kind of propulsion system it's going to have, you don't have any choice about. The fact is there have been propulsion systems, such as electric or steam, that have been technologically feasible for over half a century. Yet they do not in any real sense exist for people. In fact, it is not practical to have electric cars today because technologies are not individual components but systems. The automotive system is designed for gas combustion cars. We would need to have a totally different kind of support network—completely different service stations—if a hundred million electric cars were on the road. This happened to a small degree with an increase in diesel cars. One's ability to get fuel, top service, and knowledgeable mechanics changed dramatically. Without the whole technological infrastructure, which is as much a part of the technology as the artifact of the car, you cannot have an electric car. It is not a real choice. But I *can* have a car with whitewalls if I want. Dickson claims that this is a very common manifestation of modern technology. One's choices only appear to be decentralized.

Control and Understanding of Technology

We live in a society which styles itself to be democratic. How are we to reconcile the fact that the technological values of efficiency, expediency, and high-powered knowledge and science, tend to involve a relatively small number of people? Academics, government, and corporate officials routinely make important decisions that have impacts upon all of us, but over which most of us have relatively little control. And it is not only control. I think that our society is historically unique because for the first time the overwhelming majority of people do not even pretend to understand how their life-support systems operate. What actually happens when you flip the light switch on the wall? In many earlier societies, whether we may now ridicule their beliefs or not, people thought they understood how things important to them and to their culture worked and why. The reason this is important is that what technology has really produced—and I think this also has relevance for human freedom—is a very profound sense of alienation. I mean it in the Marxian sense, not in the pop-psychology or pop-sociology sense of alienation. Alienation is the sense that something is going on which is "other," apart from what I am. Most people have a very pervasive, inchoate, unrealized alienation in their day-to-day life.

The workplace is a good example of a situation where most of the technology that people use they are powerless to make choices about. Each week thousands and thousands of women are told that they are going to become word processors and that their typewriter is going to be replaced by a word processor. They have absolutely no control over the phenomenon. And that phenomenon is more than just getting a new high-powered machine to do what they used to do. Technology, in this case, is not just a machine. It is a whole social milieu and involves a very important redefinition of roles and functions. A woman who did typing and filing, answered the phone and interacted with people, also had a certain measure of control over the arrangement, flow and pacing of the various activities. In this example, she is now being transformed into a person who will sit eight hours a day in front of a cathode ray tube and "word process." She will do so whether or not it hurts her eyes or her overall health. This person's job is being substantially degraded; the whole notion of control, the sense of autonomy, no matter how limited it might have been under the earlier situation, is being taken away, all under the guise of a new technology.

Most of us learned that, in the Industrial Revolution, people invented productive machines and then gathered workers together to use them in factories. But actually the factory was a social system which *preceded* many of the new technological mechanisms. It was designed for the social goal of controlling the workers, regulating and rationalizing production (at the very least because the entrepreneur did not know how to make cloth and wanted to control the operation of those who did).

There are two objectives a capitalist has: productivity, and control of the workers. Only one of them has been generally presented as being the reason for all these changes. We can see that today in the arguments being made for things like word processing are these neutral-sounding "increased productivity" arguments. When corporations advertise in the general press—the *New York Times, Atlantic* or *Harper's*—they talk about productivity in such a way that the readers will not conclude that these people are actually scheming to further control workers.

For example, high tech industries offer a limited range of jobs in which average pay levels are low. Most of these industries, largely un-unionized, have lots of low-paying, boring, repetitive, unskilled jobs and a very few flashy engineering positions. Yet, when the promoters of high tech talk about the need to increase productivity in this society, they want people to view that position as neutral, good, and progressive. So they say things like, "progress is our most important product." But they do not talk about how the industry will affect the workers and their workplace. We have all been subjected to a tremendous barrage of attempts to sell us computers. Such efforts inevitably engender in us a fear that our children will be technologically inadequate if they are not "computer literate." But most people do not need computers. They are not writing books, analyzing large masses of data with correlation and regression statistics. What are the companies telling these people? They are telling these people that a computer will help manage their finances, which, for most people, means balancing a checkbook. This is a third-grade skill: the addition and subtraction of whole numbers. The mistakes made are mostly entry mistakes which computers will not avoid. The computer is a two thousand-dollar abacus.

I believe that most computer users of the future will be word processors and not highly educated high tech people. There will be some of the latter but there will be ten unskilled laborers plugged into a computer for every one creative person who is working on a novel and wants to be able to justify the margins as the work progresses.

Another area in which I have done research is household technology—or kitchen technology, for instance. Without painting any kind of conspiracy theory, the overwhelming decisions about household technology, their development, their deployment, have been made by men who do not use, have never used, and do not want to use these technologies. Here again, there is a tremendous dichotomy between the people who are making those kinds of choices and, at least demographically speaking, a totally different group of users.

Utopian Visions Versus Decreased Possibilities

There are writers such as Cullenbach, LeGuin, and Bookchin who offer a political, utopian vision of a different kind of society and a different way to organize the "good life" socially. They would use technological systems very differently from those which are currently manifest around us. They would be much more conductive to the fulfillment of human values by a large number of people, increase human autonomy and decrease alienation, put more of a premium on altruism and less on selfishness and privatism. I think they are structured on a set of values preferable to those I see imbedded in the dominant technology around us.

But utopian means "nowhere." You cannot wake up one morning and find that liberation has occurred. It is a very long and intricate kind of process to raise the consciousness of people so that they can develop that kind of autonomy. When people criticize Marcuse, for example, they say he is elitist because he claims he knows better what people want than they themselves. The point these critics miss, however, is that Marcuse is quite firm about the fact that humans have the potential for autonomous decision making. But he also realizes that in this highly industrialized society, most people have had that sense of their power and their ability systematically stripped from them, not only through their socialization (so that the ideologies they believe tend to disempower them), but through the realities in which they find themselves, which give them relatively little freedom of movement.

I will conclude with a quotation by Lewis Mumford. Mumford was very romantic about technology and values, with the result that he is not terribly helpful to us. But in this quotation I think he shows tremendous insight. He is talking about automation, but it is really about technology in the larger sense. He states:

> It has a colossal qualitative defect that springs directly from its quantitative virtues. It increases probability and it decreases possibility.

In other words, there is something wrong about the qualitative aspects of technological phenomena, something, he says, which springs directly from "their qualitative virtues." That is to say, the power that technology has in the quantitative sense reduces quality. One of the things that modern technology claims to do, for example, is to make available to masses of people experiences which were once reserved for the few, such as the opportunity to have tomatoes in January. In the early part of this century you had to be someone like Andrew Carnegie to have a tomato in January. Now anyone can have a tomato in January just by going to the supermarket. But the quantitative virtue—the ability to produce week after week millions of tomatoes—has altered, must alter, the quality of the tomatoes you can buy. The tomatoes we get at Safeway are intentionally not the same as the tomatoes that Carnegie ate, because the tomatoes he ate were grown in Cuba or Mexico and specially transported, or grown in special hothouses. But you cannot do a million of those a week. In order to have the mass phenomenon of tomatoes in January, the technological adventure had to change the essense of what the tomato is. And the mass phenomenon means that certain technological events become very probable, and alternative possibilities are decreased (e.g., the internal combustion engine overwhelms the electric car).

Since technologies are systems of hardware *and* social institutions, the phenomenon is linked increasingly to concentrations of power—a threat to our existence as a truly free people.

References

Mumford, Lewis. 1964. Automation of knowledge. *Vital Speeches of the Day,* May 1: 442.

Mesthane, Emmanuel. 1976. Social change. In *Technology as a social and political phenomenon,* Philip Bereano, New York: John Wiley & Sons, p. 69.

Dickson, David. 1974. *The Politics of Alternative Technology.* New York: Universe Books.

12

A History of the Personal Computer

Robert Pool examines the development of the personal computer and finds that it was as much the result of "coincidence and serendipity" as engineering. A fascinating look at the early Apple computers and the IBM PC, this selection argues that the personal computer standard grew out of a momentum rooted in business practices, not purely technological choice.

Robert Pool

In general, writers tend to present the development of any technology as a progression of technical innovations: A led to B, which allowed C to happen, then D and E opened the door to F, and so on. It is, on the surface, a sensible approach. Edison's first commercial lighting network could not have opened without the light bulb and many other devices having been developed first. Today's electrical power systems in turn rely on a host of more recent technical advances, such as transformers that turn the high-voltage current of transmission wires into the low-voltage current used in businesses and homes. Clearly, any technology depends critically on the ideas and innovations of inventors and engineers.

But there is more—much more—to the story of a technology than this. Look closely at the history of any invention and you'll find coincidence and serendipity and things that happen for no reason at all but which affect everything that comes after. In the personal computer industry, for instance, it's well known that the Microsoft Corporation's dominating influence on software got its start by pure chance. When IBM decided to create its personal computer, the PC, the group in charge of its development first approached a computer called Digital Research about providing the PC's operating system. When Digital Research put IBM off, the group interviewed Bill Gates and his still-small company, Microsoft. Recognizing what a tremendous opportunity it was, Gates did everything he could to convince IBM that Microsoft would be the right choice, but the ultimate selection of Microsoft came down at least in part to a personal connection: IBM chairman John Opel had served on the board of the United Way with Gates's

From *Beyond Engineering: How Society Shapes Technology* by Robert Pool, copyright © 1977 by Robert Pool. Used by permission of Oxford University Press, Inc.

mother and thought it would be nice to do business with "Mary Gates's boy's company." The operating system that Microsoft developed, MS-DOS, became the industry standard—not so much on its own merits as because it was part of the IBM PC package—and Gates was on his way to becoming a multibillionaire.

Besides such random but formative events, the development of any technology has much else that doesn't fit into the neat logical progression of the textbook. There are the wrong turns and blind alleys that in retrospect seem hardly worth mentioning but that at the time played a large role in engineers' thinking. There are the quirks and biases that can influence individuals' opinions as much as any rational arguments. There are the external circumstances that constrain and shape the inventors and their inventions. And there are the details of how a society adopts a technology and adapts to its own needs.

To truly understand why a technology developed as it did, we must look past the ideas and engineering choices and put them in some sort of context. Who were the inventors? What were their strengths and weaknesses, and how did they interact with their peers and rivals? What was going on in the world outside the laboratory? Did the government weigh in? The media? What sorts of organizations did the inventors work in? To examine the complex interaction of contingencies that lead to the development of any technology, let us further consider the personal computer. The Apple I looked even less like a computer than did the first Altair. Designed by Steven Wozniak about a year after the Altair appeared, it was simply a circuit board with a microprocessor, memory chips, and interfaces that could be connected to a keyboard and television monitor. There was no case, no power supply. It did, however, have a programming language, BASIC, which allowed the user to instruct the computer much more easily than was possible with the first Altairs.

Wozniak, a young computer whiz working for Hewlett-Packard, hadn't thought of his machine as a commercial product. It was simply an intellectual challenge—a game, really—to test his programming and design skills. He had chosen the MOS Technology 6502 chip, a knockoff of Motorola's 6800 chip, as the microprocessor for his computer not because it was better than other available chips, but because it was much cheaper. The better-known 6800 cost $175, but Wozniak could get the 6502 for $25. In April 1976 he brought his first computer to a meeting of the Homebrew Computer Club, a band of San Francisco-area computer enthusiasts, and provided copies of the design to anyone who was interested.

But where Wozniak saw an intellectual challenge, his friend and fellow computer enthusiast Steven Jobs saw a chance to make some money. In the year since the introduction of the Altair, personal computers had become increasingly popular, although still just among a small group of hobbyists and computer buffs. Several companies had begun to offer personal computers for sale through the mail, clubs like Homebrew were springing up, and even a few retail stores were starting to sell personal computers. In January 1976, Jobs had suggested to Wozniak that they make and sell printed circuit boards based on Wozniak's design, and, after some hesitation, Wozniak agreed. Their initial idea was to sell only the circuit boards and let the customer get the chips and electronic components and install them on the boards in order to create a working computer. Jobs thought they might be able to sell about a hundred of the circuit boards for $50 apiece.

But plans changed quickly in July 1976. Paul Terrell, owner of one of the first computer stores and a frequenter of the Homebrew Club, liked Wozniak's machine—which Wozniak and Jobs had decided to call the Apple—and offered to buy fifty of them to sell in his shop. But, Terrell said, he wasn't interested in just the circuit boards. He wanted fully assembled computers. Suddenly the two Apple entrepreneurs had to shift gears. They had raised $1,300 to pay for developing the circuit boards, Wozniak by selling an HP-65 calculator and Jobs by selling his Volkswagen bus, but now they needed about $25,000. With Terrell's order in hand, they were able to get credit for the parts, and they set to work assembling the computers in Jobs's parents' garage. They hired Jobs's sister, Patty, and an old friend, Dan Kottke, to plug the components into the circuit boards. The embryonic company supplied Terrell the fifty computers he'd ordered and eventually was able to sell about 150 more, both by mail and through various computer stores in the San Francisco Bay area. The Apple I was priced at $666.66, a number Jobs chose because he liked the looks of it.

With the Apple I under his belt, Wozniak began work on what would become the Apple II. He had several improvements in mind. The new machine would include a keyboard, power supply, and the BASIC programming language, all things that had to be tacked onto the Apple I by the user. Most strikingly, the Apple II would display color, something that no other personal computer could do. At the time, most computer designers believed it would take dozens of chips to create a color circuit, but Wozniak came up with a clever approach that cut the number of extra chips down to a handful. When hooked up to a color television, the Apple II provided an unmatched show.

Although Wozniak thought that he and Jobs might sell a few hundred of the computers, Jobs saw the Apple II as a chance to create a truly successful business, and he sought advice from people in the computer industry about how to do that. Jobs soon hooked up with Mike Markkula, a thirty-three-year-old veteran of the semiconductor business who had worked for both Fairchild and Intel. Markkula had retired in 1975, after becoming a vice president at Intel. A millionaire from his Intel stock options, he had been relaxing at home, but by October 1976, when he first met with Jobs and Wozniak, he was ready to ease back into the industry. At first he agreed only to give the two advice on how to organize Apple, but after a few months he offered to join them. For a $91,000 investment, he took one-third interest in the company, with Jobs and Wozniak splitting the remaining two-thirds.

Now everything was in place. Apple had a brilliant designer in Steve Wozniak; a person experienced in computer marketing, distribution, and finance in Mike Markkula; and an indefatigable driving force in Steve Jobs. The combination gave the company a leg up on the competition at a critical point in the development of the personal computer. *Fire in the Valley,* a history of the personal computer, describes the situation like this:

> Dozens of companies had come and gone [in the two years since the introduction of the Altair]. Most notably, MITS, the industry pioneer, was thrashing about. IMSAI, Processor Technology, and a few other companies were jockeying for control of the market even as they wobbled. All of these companies failed. In some cases, their failure stemmed from technical problems with the computers. Burt more serious was the lack of expertise in marketing, distributing, and selling the products. The corporate leaders were primarily engineers, not managers. They alienated their customers and dealers. . . .
>
> At the same time, the market was changing. Hobbyists had organized into clubs and users' groups that met regularly in garages, basements, and school auditoriums around the country. The number of people who wanted to own computers was growing. And the ranks of knowledgeable hobbyists who wanted a better computer were also growing. The manufacturers wanted that "better computer" too. But they all faced one seemingly insurmountable problem. They didn't have the money. The manufacturers were garage enterprises, growing, like MITS had since January of 1975, on prepaid mail orders. They needed investment capital, and there were strong arguments against giving it to them: the high failure rate among microcomputer companies, the lack of managerial experience among their leaders, and—the ultimate puzzle—the absence of IBM from the field. Investors had to ask: If this area has any promise, why hasn't IBM preempted it?

Because of Jobs's entrepreneurial instincts, Apple now had what its competitors lacked. Not only did it have a solid product, thanks to Wozniak's engineering skills, but it also had experienced management in Markkula and Mike Scott, a Markkula protege from Fairchild who was hired as Apple president. Just as important, it had money—Markkula, as part of joining the company, had agreed to underwrite a $250,000 loan from a bank. And soon it would have one of the best advertising and public relations minds in the industry. Jobs had courted Regis McKenna, already well known for shaping Intel's image, and although McKenna had initially turned Jobs down, he eventually changed his mind. It was McKenna's agency that came up with the playful Apple logo, an apple with broad horizontal stripes in various colors and a bite taken out of it. The logo was designed to appeal to a broader public than hobbyists and computer enthusiasts. And it was McKenna who took out a color ad in *Playboy,* a move that brought national attention not just to Apple but to the emerging personal computer industry as well.

In 1977 Apple began to grow quickly. By the end of the year it was profitable and was doubling its production of Apple IIs every three or four months. To finance the rapid growth, Markkula had convinced a venture capital firm to put up money in return for a share of the company. And Wozniak was creating one accessory after another: a printer card to hook up the Apple II to a printer, a communications card, and, most important, a disk drive. At the time, the only way to store relatively large amounts of data for a personal computer was on audio cassette tapes, which were slow and unreliable. Wozniak was the first to design a floppy disk drive for a personal computer. When it became available in June 1978, personal computer users for the first time had the option not only of storing large amounts of data but also of loading sophisticated software into their machines.

With that option, computer programmers began to write more useful software. The most important program for the Apple's success was VisiCalc, the first spreadsheet program. VisiCalc allowed a user to do financial calculations in a way never before possible. VisiCalc allowed a user to do financial calculations in a way never before possible, changing one or a few numbers and seeing immediately how all the other figures in a financial spreadsheet were affected. It appeared in October 1979 and was available for use only on an Apple for its first year, and its success drove much of the early popularity of the Apple II.

The defining moment for Apple came when Jobs visited Xerox PARC in the spring of 1979. Xerox's engineers showed Jobs the Alto with its brilliant graphics, mouse, icons, and windows, and Jobs was hooked. He quickly grasped the importance of the Alto's ease of use and how valuable that would be in a personal computer—the same lesson that the PARC engineers had failed to get across to the Xerox management for several years. Jobs decided that future Apple computers should have similar capabilities, and he hired away Larry Tesler, one of the scientists at Xerox who had worked on the Alto. It took several years to recreate Apple computers in the Alto's image, but by the early 1980s the company had done it. The Lisa, a relatively expensive computer aimed at business executives, was the first to offer the mouse-and-windows system that would become Apple's hallmark. It was released in 1983. Early the next year came the Macintosh, an inexpensive machine designed to attract a new group of users to personal computers. Although the effort to keep the price down had saddled the Mac with a small memory, and little software was available at first, the first inexpensive, user-friendly personal computer was an immediate hit. Later, Apple provided similar capabilities for the Apple II.

As Apple was developing its Lisa and Macintosh computers, it was awaiting the coming of the computer industry's 800-pound gorilla: IBM. For more than two decades IBM had been the dominant figure in the computer business, and no one doubted that, given the growing size of the personal computer market, IBM would soon weigh in.

Actually, the company had already weighed in, but in such an inept way that almost no one had noticed. In 1975, conscious of the hoopla surrounding the personal computer, IBM announced the 5100, its first personal computer. Unlike the Altair, however, the 5100 was much more "computer" than "personal." It was a full-featured machine with plenty of memory plus tape cartridges for data storage. It had a sophisticated operating system and could run programs written in either BASIC or APL, a programming language used primarily by scientists. And it weighed seventy pounds and cost many thousands of dollars. IBM had aimed the 5100 at scientists, a group the company had no experience in selling to and a group that studiously ignored IBM's offering. The 5100 was a major flop.

Undaunted, the same IBM development team that had produced the 5100 revamped it to appeal to the business market. But the new version, the 5110, was no more personal than the 5100. It sold for $8,000, far too much to be of interest to those who were intrigued by the Altair and the Apple, yet not enough to trigger the enthusiasm of IBM computer salesmen. Why try hard to sell a 5110, when traditional computers costing ten times as much could be sold with little more effort? The 5110 flopped too.

Despite the failures, IBM—and particularly its chairman, John Opel—remained interested in personal computers, and that interest grew with the steady expansion of the personal computer industry. So in 1980, when William Lowe, director of an IBM laboratory in Boca Raton, Florida, approached the company's senior management with a detailed proposal to develop an IBM personal computer, he quickly got a go-ahead. IBM would set up an independent business unit in Boca Raton, free of pressures from the rest of the company, to put the personal computer together—quickly. Lowe was given a year to bring it to market.

Because Apple and other firms had already defined what a personal computer should look like, and because IBM wanted to develop its own product fast, the IBM PC would be a computer unlike any the company had ever offered. Most of its components would be built not by IBM itself but by outside contractors. Its operating system—the language that gives instructions to the computer's processor—would be provided by someone outside the company, as would the software for the PC. More important, the computer would have an "open architecture" so that other companies could design and make components that would operate in it. And IBM would sell the personal computers through retail outlets instead of through its large in-house sales staff. All of these were major deviations from the normal IBM way of doing business.

The IBM Personal Computer, announced on August 12, 1981, made no attempt to be on the cutting edge. Its microprocessor, the Intel 8088 chip, was a fine choice for a personal computer and it made the IBM PC as good or better than any of the competition, but there were faster, more powerful chips available that IBM could have chosen. The computer used a cassette tape recorder for data storage (although a floppy disk drive was available as an option). The printer was a standard Epson model with an IBM label slapped on. Available software included VisiCalc and a word processor called EasyWriter, both originally developed for the Apple. The most surprising thing about the IBM computer was that there were no surprises—instead of special components, the machine was constructed from standard parts, and it ran standard software.

That was enough. IBM's reputation as the undisputed leader of the computer industry gave its personal computer instant credibility. Anyone who had been contemplating buying a personal computer was bound to at least consider the IBM PC. And for those who had questioned the value of personal computers, wondering if they were simply faddish toys, IBM's PC seemed proof that they were important and useful. IBM wouldn't sell something frivolous.

Almost overnight, the IBM PC became a standard for the personal computer industry. Companies rushed to develop components and peripheral devices for the PC. Software developers wrote programs to run on it. Some firms began to manufacture computers—IBM clones, they were called—that would perform similarly to the PC and be compatible with all its hardware and software. Meanwhile, many of the pioneering companies that had helped develop the personal computer industry found their sales drying up. All but a few went bankrupt. When the dust settled, only two companies remained with any real influence over the direction that the personal computer would take: Apple and IBM.

Today, those two standards define the personal computer. They have converged somewhat with time and may merge almost completely sometime in the future, but they still represent two very different visions of what a personal computer should be. The Apple is a people's computer, fashioned to be inviting and accessible even to those who have never used a computer before. Yet the technology underlying that friendly facade is aggressively state-of-the-art, with designs that win accolades and awards from the industry. The IBM is more businesslike, an accountant's machine instead of an artist's, and its structure and components are reliable but seldom inspiring.

The differences between the two computers reflect, more than anything else, the different business environments in which the two were developed. Apple began as a small start-up company with computers built by and for computer enthusiasts. "We didn't do three years of research and come up with this concept," Steve Jobs has said. "What we did was follow our own instincts and construct a computer that was what we wanted." That was possible only because Apple, as an embryonic, one-product firm, retained the flexibility and the recklessness of youth. Had Wozniak and Jobs been working for IBM, they would certainly have never produced anything like an Apple computer.

The same sort of difference between a small, new firm and a large, established one can be seen in how Apple and Xerox responded to the ideas coming out of PARC. Xerox, which had paid for the PARC research, could not appreciate its value. Despite the company's talk about developing an office of the future, Xerox found it almost impossible to step away from its established ways of seeing things and to envision radically new products. Even the PARC scientists were caught in a rut. Accustomed to thinking in terms of large, expensive office equipment and systems, they continued to focus on networks of linked computers even when the personal computer revolution was in full swing. At Apple, some resisted when Jobs came back from Xerox and pushed to put the Alto's features in the Lisa, which was already under development. But because Apple was still small and flexible enough to change direction, and because the aggressive Jobs wielded great influence, the Lisa—and later the Macintosh and Apple II—took on the trappings of the Alto. Years afterward, because of the popularity of the Apple operating system, IBM-type computers were provided with a similar operating system called Windows. Today, Windows is the dominant operating system for personal computers, and it can trace its ancestry back to those PARC scientists, whose company couldn't appreciate what they had done, and to Steve Jobs, who did.

Unlike Apple, IBM was already a huge company when it decided to become involved in personal computers, and the preexisting culture and concerns of the firm pushed its PC in a completely different direction from the Apple. IBM's customers were business people—always had been, and, as far as many in the computer were concerned, always would be. So the IBM PC was intended to be a serious business machine. Let Apple and others speak of bringing computer power to the people and depict their machines as tools of popular insurgency; IBM was part of the establishment, and its computers would reflect that. Indeed, eyebrows shot up inside the company and out when, shortly before the PC's release, IBM decided to include a computer game as part of its optional software.

But of greater influence than IBM's corporate culture was the company's decision to develop its PC in an independent business unit (IBU) that was well isolated from the rest of the company. Over the years IBM has established a number of these IBUs to develop and market products new to the company, on the theory that real innovation demands freedom and flexibility. Although they're funded by IBM and staffed by IBM employees, the IBUs have little else to do with the corporation. They set their direction internally with only general oversight from top IBM management, and they're free of many of the rules and policies governing the rest of the company.

It was this freedom that allowed the IBM PC to break so many of the usual rules for IBM products. Only an independent business unit could look outside IBM for most of the computer's hardware and software or decide to sell the computer through retail outlets. And the choice of an open architecture for the PC went against every instinct of the corporate IBM. For decades the company had protected its designs with patents and secrecy. Now it was, in essence, inviting other businesses to make components that could be added onto the IBM PC and to write software that would run on it—all without a license or permission.

Still, the independent business unit that developed the PC was a part of IBM, and it was constrained by the company's needs and goals if not by all its normal rules and policies. As industry observers James Chpolsky and Ted Leonsis have noted, IBM's standard strategy for emerging technologies was "noninvolvement until a market was established by the smaller and generally entrepreneurially driven companies in the industry—at which time IBM bullied its way in and, on the strength of its reputation for excellence and its superior manpower and resources, proceeded to dominate the market at the expense of the bit players who were often there at the beginning." This would be IBM's strategy for the personal computer: the independent business unit was intended to develop a product that would allow IBM to dominate the personal computing market.

Given this goal and the complexion of the existing market, the engineers and other specialists in the independent business unit found that many of their decisions were already made for them. IBM would not, for instance, be attempting to create a computer radically different from those already in the market. Instead the machine would be firmly in the mainstream of personal computer development. It would have a monitor, keyboard, and a box containing the processing unit. For output it could be hooked up to a separate printer, and for data storage and retrieval it would use a cassette recorder/player, with the option for a floppy disk drive. The IBM personal computer would adopt the best of what had already been developed, but it would not blaze new trails.

Because the personal computer business was growing so quickly and because other large companies were looking to jump in, IBM gave its independent business unit a year to get its product to market, and this, more than anything else, set the constraints that would shape the IBM PC. To get everything done in a year, the PC team had to subcontract much of the development work to companies outside IBM and to buy many of the computer's components off the shelf. Thus the main processor chip was the Intell 8088, the power supply was made by Zenith, the disk drives by the Tandon Corporation, and the printer came from Epson. The software, too, was farmed out, with Microsoft supplying both the basic operating system, PC-DOS, and a BASIC programming language, and other companies providing business software and the spreadsheet and word processing programs.

The most important consequence of the short development schedule was the decision to give the PC an open architecture. By doing this, the design team could lay out the basics of the computer and then have software development take place at the same time as the remaining hardware development. This saved time and allowed the PC to be created within a year, but it would also change the shape of the entire personal computing industry. Until that point, the Apple had been the closest thing to a standard that the industry had, but it had a closed architecture. No one but Apple and those companies licensed by Apple could make components or accessories for an Apple computer or write software for it, which gave Apple tight control over the direction its product would take. Other companies making personal computers did have open architectures, but they were generally incompatible with one another and none was accepted as a standard. The introduction of the IBM PC offered a standard that was open to everyone, and the industry blossomed. Because anyone with an idea and a little capital could create hardware or software that would work on an IBM—and also on the IBM clones that soon appeared—the personal computer began to evolve and improve far faster than would otherwise have been possible. Granted, that growth was often haphazard, but the rollicking, free-for-all market that IBM unleashed with its PC revolutionized the world. Since then, computing power and capabilities have risen dramatically sharply while costs have dropped even more significantly.

For its part, IBM seems to have had second thoughts about the wisdom of the open architecture. Yes, IBM-type computers now own more than 90 percent of the personal computer market, but IBM itself has only a small share of that. Indeed, IBM is no longer even the leading seller of IBM-type computers. In 1994, Compaq Computer Corporation claimed that title with 10.1 percent of all personal computer sales around the world, compared with only 8.7 percent for IBM. Since its introduction of the PC, IBM has offered other personal computer lines that aren't nearly so open in an attempt to reassert some control over its own products, but the industry is now far too large and diffuse for any one company, even IBM, to have much influence on it.

Ironically, following the success of the PC, IBM eventually decided against using independent business units to develop products. If IBM had made that decision before 1980, it might never have developed a successful personal computer, and it almost certainly would not have created a personal computer with an open architecture. In that case, the personal computer revolution would have proceeded much differently—and surely much more slowly.

. . . . .

The history of the personal computer reveals . . . a momentum with its roots in the business world. Technologies are pushed this way and that by the companies that develop them, market them, and buy and operate them, and the larger the company, the more influence business and organizational factors will exert over the development of a technology.

This is just one example of how non-technological factors shape and drive the development of technology. Given these factors, and their impact, it is impossible to describe technology as value-free. Every technology takes on the values of the culture and climate from which it emerges.

—— 13 ——————————————

Informing Ourselves to Death

Neil Postman argues that technology is never value-neutral. Technological change is always a Faustian bargain in which something is created but something else is destroyed. According to Postman, information technologies have created a data deluge that, while advantageous to large-scale operations like airlines and governments, is meaningless to the average person because "it has no relation to the solution of problems." Postman's is a cautious voice that implores us to balance enthusiasm for new technologies with sensitivity to their human costs.

Neil Postman

The great English playwright and social philosopher George Bernard Shaw once remarked that all professions are conspiracies against the common folk. He meant that those who belong to elite trades—physicians, lawyers, teachers, and scientists—protect their special status by creating vocabularies that are incomprehensible to the general public. This process prevents outsiders from understanding what the profession is doing and why—and protects the insiders from close examination and criticism. Professions, in other words, build forbidding walls of technical gobbledegook over which the prying and alien eye cannot see.

Unlike George Barnard Shaw, I raise no complaint against this, for I consider myself a professional teacher and appreciate technical gobbledegook as much as anyone. But I do not object if occasionally someone who does not know the secrets of my trade is allowed entry to the inner halls to express an untutored point of view. Such a person may sometimes give a refreshing opinion or, even better, see something in a way that the professionals have overlooked.

Perhaps I can do just this sort of thing for computer professionals. I do not know very much more about computer technology than the average person—which isn't very much. I have little understanding of what excites a computer programmer or scientist. So, I clearly qualify as an outsider.

But I think that what is needed is not merely an outsider but an outsider who has a point of view that might be useful to the insiders. I believe I know something about what technologies do to culture, and I know even more about what technologies undo in a culture. In fact, I might say, at the start, that what a technology undoes is a subject that computer experts apparently know very little about. I have heard many experts in computer technology speak about the advantages that computers will bring. With one exception—namely, Joseph Weizenbaum—I have never heard anyone speak seriously and comprehensively about the disadvantages of computer technology, which strikes me as odd, and makes me wonder if the profession is hiding something important. That is today, what seems to be lacking among computer experts is a sense of technological modesty.

After all, anyone who has studied the history of technology knows that technological change is always a Faustian bargain: Technology giveth and technology taketh away, and not always in equal measure. A new technology sometimes creates more than it destroys. Sometimes, it destroys more than it creates. But it is never one-sided.

The invention of the printing press is an excellent example. Printing fostered the modern idea of individuality but it destroyed the medieval sense of community and social integration. Printing created prose but made poetry into an exotic and elitist form of expression. Printing made modern science possible but transformed religious sensibility into an exercise in superstition. Printing assisted in the growth of the nation-state but, in so doing, made patriotism into a sordid if not a murderous emotion.

Another way of saying this is that a new technology tends to favor some groups of people and harms other groups. Schoolteachers, for example, will, in the long run, probably be made obsolete by television, as blacksmiths were made obsolete by the automobile, as balladeers were made obsolete by the printing press. Technological change, in other words, always results in winners and losers.

In the case of computer technology, there can be no disputing that the computer has increased the power of large-scale organizations like military establishments or airline companies or banks or tax collecting agencies. And it is equally clear that the computer is now indispensable to high-level researchers in physics and other natural sciences. But to what extent has computer technology been an advantage to the masses of people? To steel workers, vegetable store owners, teachers, automobile mechanics, musicians, bakers, brick layers, dentists and most of the rest into whose lives the computer now intrudes? These people have had their private matters made more accessible to powerful institutions. They are more easily tracked and controlled; they are subjected to more examinations, and are increasingly mystified by the decisions made about them. They are more often reduced to mere numerical objects. They are being buried by junk mail. They are easy targets for advertising agencies and political organizations. The schools teach their children to operate computerized systems instead of teaching things that are more valuable to children. In a word, almost nothing happens to the losers that they need, which is why they are losers.

It is to be expected that the winners—for example, most computer professionals—will encourage the losers to be enthusiastic about computer technology. That is the way of winners, and so they sometimes tell the losers that with personal computers the average person can balance a checkbook more neatly, keep better track of recipes, and make more logical shopping lists. They also tell them that they can vote at home, shop at home, get all the information they wish at home, and thus make community life unnecessary. They tell them that their lives will be conducted more efficiently, discreetly neglecting to say from whose point of view or what might be the costs of such efficiency.

Should the losers grow skeptical, the winners dazzle them with the wondrous feats of computers, many of which have only marginal relevance to the quality of the losers' lives but which are nonetheless impressive. Eventually, the losers succumb, in part because they believe that the specialized knowledge of the masters of a computer technology is a form of wisdom. The masters, of course, come to believe this as well. The result is that certain questions do not arise, such as, to whom will the computer give greater power and freedom, and whose power and freedom will be reduced?

Now, I have perhaps made all of this sound like a well-planned conspiracy, as if the winners know all too well what is being won and what lost. But this is not quite how it happens, for the winners do not always know what they are doing, and where it will all lead. The Benedictine monks who invented the mechanical clock in the 12th and 13th centuries believed that such a clock would provide a precise regularity to the seven periods of devotion they were required to observe during the course of the day. As a matter of fact, it did. But what the monks did not realize is that the clock is not merely a means of keeping track of the hours but also of synchronizing and controlling the actions of men. And so, by the middle of the 14th century, the clock had moved outside the walls of the monastery, and brought a new and precise regularity to the life of the workman and the merchant. The mechanical clock made possible the idea of regular production, regular working hours, and a standardized product. Without the clock, capitalism would have been quite impossible. And so, here is a great paradox: the clock was invented by men who wanted to devote themselves more rigorously to God; and it ended as the technology of greatest use to men who wished to devote themselves to the accumulation of money. Technology always has unforeseen consequences, and it is not always clear, at the beginning, who or what will win, and who or what will lose.

I might add, by way of another historical example, that Johannes Gutenberg was by all accounts a devoted Christian who would have been horrified to hear Martin Luther, the accursed heretic, declare that printing is "God's highest act of grace, whereby the business of the Gospel is driven forward." Gutenberg thought his invention would advance the cause of the Holy Roman See, whereas in fact, it turned out to bring a revolution which destroyed the monopoly of the Church.

We may well ask ourselves, then, is there something that the masters of computer technology think they are doing for us which they and we may have reason to regret? I believe there is, and it is suggested by my title, "Informing Ourselves to Death." In the space remaining, I will try to explain what is dangerous about the computer, and why. And I trust you will be open enough to consider what I have to say. Now, I think I can begin to get at this by telling you of a small experiment I have been conducting, on and off, for the past several years. There are some people who describe the experiment as an exercise in deceit and exploitation but I will rely on your sense of humor to pull me through.

Here's how it works: It is best done in the morning when I see a colleague who appears not to be in possession of a copy of *The New York Times*. "Did you read The Times this morning?," I ask. If the colleague says yes, there is no experiment that day. But if the answer is no, the experiment can proceed. "You ought to look at Page 23," I say. "There's a fascinating article about a study done at Harvard University." "Really? What's it about?" is the usual reply. My choices at this point are limited only by my imagination. But I might say something like this: "Well, they did this study to find out what foods are best to eat for losing weight, and it turns out that a normal diet supplemented by chocolate eclairs, eaten six times a day, is the best approach. It seems that there's some special nutrient in the eclairs—encomial dioxin—that actually uses up calories at an incredible rate."

Another possibility, which I like to use with colleagues who are known to be health conscious is this one: "I think you'll want to know about this," I say. "The neuro-physiologists at the University of Stuttgart have uncovered a connection between jogging and reduced intelligence. They tested more than 1200 people over a period of five years, and found that as the number of hours people jogged increased, there was a corresponding decrease in their intelligence. They don't know exactly why but there it is."

I'm sure, by now, you understand what my role is in the experiment: to report something that is quite ridiculous—one might say, beyond belief. Let me tell you, then, some of my results: Unless this is the second or third time I've tried this on the same person, most people will believe or at least not disbelieve what I have told them. Sometimes they say: "Really? Is that possible?" Sometimes they do a double-take, and reply, "Where'd you say that study was done?" And sometimes they say, "You know, I've heard something like that."

Now, there are several conclusions that might be drawn from these results, one of which was expressed by H. L. Mencken fifty years ago when he said, there is no idea so stupid that you can't find a professor who will believe it. This is more of an accusation than an explanation but in any case I have tried this experiment on nonprofessors and get roughly the same results. Another possible conclusion is one expressed by George Orwell—also about 50 years ago—when he remarked that the average person today is about as naive as was the average person in the Middle Ages. In the Middle Ages people believed in the authority of their religion, no matter what. Today, we believe in the authority of our science, no matter what.

But I think there is still another and more important conclusion to be drawn, related to Orwell's point but rather off at a right angle to it. I am referring to the fact that the world in which we live is very nearly incomprehensible to most of us. There is almost no fact—whether actual or imagined—that will surprise us for very long, since we have on comprehensive and consistent picture of the world which would make the fact appear as an unacceptable contradiction. We believe because there is no reason not to believe. No social, political, historical, metaphysical, logical or spiritual reason. We live in a world that, for the most part, makes no sense to us. Not even technical sense. . . .

Perhaps I can get a bit closer to the point I wish to make with an analogy: If you opened a brand-new deck of cards, and started turning the cards over, one by one, you would have a pretty good idea of what their order is. After you had gone from the ace of spades through the nine of spades, you would expect a ten of spades to come up next. And if a three of diamonds showed up instead, you would be surprised and wonder what kind of deck of cards this is. But if I gave you a deck that had been shuffled twenty times, and then asked you to turn the cards over, you would not expect any card in particular—a three of diamonds would be just as likely as a ten of spades. Having no basis for assuming a given order, you would have no reason to react with disbelief or even surprise to whatever card turns up.

The point is that, in a world without spiritual or intellectual order, nothing is unbelievable; nothing is predictable, and therefore, nothing comes as a particular surprise.

In fact, George Orwell was more than a little unfair to the average person in the Middle Ages. The belief system of the Middle Ages was rather like my brand-new deck of cards. There existed an ordered, comprehensible world-view, beginning with the idea that all knowledge and goodness come from God. What the priests had to say about the world was derived from the logic of their theology. There was nothing arbitrary about the things people were asked to believe, including the fact that the world itself was created at 9 AM on October 23 in the year 4004 B.C. That could be explained, and was, quite lucidly, to the satisfaction of anyone. So could the fact that 10,000 angels could dance on the head of a pin. It made quite good sense, if you believed that the Bible is the revealed word of God and that the universe is populated with angels. The medieval world was, to be sure, mysterious and filled with wonder, but it was not without a sense of order. Ordinary men and women might not clearly grasp how the harsh realities of their lives fit into the grand and benevolent design, but they had no doubt that there was such a design, and their priests were well able, by deduction from a handful of principles, to make it, if not rational, at least coherent.

The situation we are presently in is much different. And I should say, sadder and more confusing and certainly more mysterious. It is rather like the shuffled deck of cards I referred to. There is no consistent, integrated conception of the world which serves as the foundation on which our edifice of belief rests. And therefore, in a sense, we are more naive than those of the Middle Ages, and more frightened, for we can be made to believe almost anything.

Now, in a way, none of this is our fault. If I may turn the wisdom of Cassius on its head: the fault is not in ourselves but almost literally in the stars. When Galileo turned his telescope toward the heavens, and allowed Kepler to look as well, they found no enchantment or authorization in the stars, only geometric patterns and equations. God, it seemed, was less of a moral philosopher than a master mathematician. This discovery helped to give impetus to the development of physics but did nothing but harm to theology. Before Galileo and Kepler, it was possible to believe that the Earth was the stable center of the universe, and that God took a special interest in our affairs. Afterward, the Earth became a lonely wanderer in an obscure galaxy in a hidden corner of the universe, and we were left to wonder if God had any interest in us at all. The ordered, comprehensible world of the Middle Ages began to unravel because people no longer saw in the stars the face of a friend.

And something else, which once was our friend, turned against us, as well. I refer to information. There was a time when information was a resource that helped human beings to solve specific and urgent problems of their environment. It is true enough that in the Middle Ages, there was a scarcity of information but its very scarcity made it both important and usable. This began to change, as everyone knows, in the late 15th century when a goldsmith named Gutenberg, from Mainz, converted an old wine press into a printing machine, and in so doing, created what we now call an information explosion. Forty years after the invention of the press, there were printing machines in 110 cities in six different countries; 50 years after, more than eight million books had been printed, almost all of them filled with information that had previously not been available to the average person. Nothing could be more misleading than the idea that computer technology introduced the age of information. The printing press began that age, and we have not been free of it since.

But what started out as a liberating stream has turned into a deluge of chaos. Here is what we are faced with: In America, there are 260,000 billboards; 11,520 newspapers; 11,556 periodicals; 27,000 video outlets for renting tapes; 362 million tv sets; and over 400 million radios. There are 40,000 new book titles published every year (300,000 world-wide) and every day in America 41 million photographs are taken, and just for the record, over 60 billion pieces of advertising junk mail come into our mail boxes every year. Everything from telegraphy and photography in the 19th century to the silicon chip in the twentieth has amplified the din of information, until matters have reached such proportions today that for the average person, information no longer has any relation to the solution of problems.

The tie between information and action has been severed. Information is now a commodity that can be bought and sold, or used as a form of entertainment, or worn like a garment to enhance one's status. It comes indiscriminately, directed at no one in particular, disconnected from usefulness; we are glutted with information, drowning in information, have no control over it, don't know what to do with it.

And there are two reasons we do not know what to do with it. First, as I have said, we no longer have a coherent conception of ourselves, and our universe, and our relation to one another and our world. We no longer know, as the Middle Ages did, where we come from, and where we are going, or why. That is, we don't know what information is relevant, and what information is irrelevant to our lives. Second, we have directed all of our energies and intelligence to inventing machinery that does nothing but increase the supply of information. As a consequence, our defenses against information glut have broken down; our information immune system is inoperable. We don't know how to filter it out; we don't know how to reduce it; we don't know to use it. We suffer from a kind of cultural AIDS.

Now, into this situation comes the computer. The computer, as we know, has a quality of universality, not only because its uses are almost infinitely various but also because computers are commonly integrated into the structure of other machines. Therefore it would be fatuous of me to warn against every conceivable use of a computer. But there is no denying that the most prominent uses of computers have to do with information. When people talk about "information sciences," they are talking about computers—how to store information, how to retrieve information, how to organize information. The computer is an answer to the questions, how can I get more information, faster, and in a more usable form? These would appear to be reasonable questions. But now I should like to put some other questions to you that seem to me more reasonable. Did Iraq invade Kuwait because of a lack of information? If a hideous war should ensue between Iraq and the U.S., will it happen because of a lack of information? If children die of starvation in Ethiopia, does it occur because of a lack of information? Does racism in South Africa exist because of a lack of information? If criminals roam the streets of New York City, do they do so because of a lack of information?

Or, let us come down to a more personal level: If you and your spouse are unhappy together, and end your marriage in divorce, will it happen because of a lack of information? If your children misbehave and bring shame to your family, does it happen because of a lack of information? If someone in your family has a mental breakdown, will it happen because of a lack of information?

I believe you will have to concede that what ails us, what causes us the most misery and pain—at both cultural and personal levels—has nothing to do with the sort of information made accessible by computers. The computer and its information cannot answer any of the fundamental questions we need to address to make our lives more meaningful and humane. The computer cannot provide an organizing moral framework. It cannot tell us what questions are worth asking. It cannot provide a means of understanding why we are here or why we fight each other or why decency eludes us so often, especially when we need it the most. The computer is, in a sense, a magnificent toy that distracts us from facing what we most needed to confront—spiritual emptiness, knowledge of ourselves, usable conceptions of the past and future. Does one blame the computer for this? Of course not. It is, after all, only a machine. But it is presented to us, with trumpets blaring, as a technological messiah.

Through the computer, the heralds say, we will make education better, religion better, politics better, our minds better—best of all, ourselves better. This is, of course, nonsense, and only the young or the ignorant or the foolish could believe it. I said a moment ago that computers are not to blame for this. And that is true, at least in the sense that we do not blame an elephant for its huge appetite or a stone for being hard or a cloud for hiding the sun. That is their nature, and we expect nothing different from them. But the computer has a nature, as well. True, it is only a machine but a machine designed to manipulate and generate information. That is what computers do, and therefore they have an agenda and an unmistakable message.

The message is that through more and more information, more conveniently packaged, more swiftly delivered, we will find solutions to our problems. And so all the brilliant young men and women, believing this, create ingenious things for the computer to do, hoping that in this way, we will become wiser and more decent and more noble. And who can blame them? By becoming masters of this wondrous technology, they will acquire prestige and power and some will even become famous. In a world populated by people who believe that through more and more information, paradise is attainable, the computer scientist is king. But I maintain that all of this is a monumental and dangerous waste of human talent and energy. Imagine what might be accomplished if this talent and energy were turned to philosophy, to theology, to the arts, to imaginative literature or to education? Who knows what we could learn from such people—perhaps why there are wars, and hunger, and homelessness and mental illness and anger.

As things stand now, the geniuses of computer technology will give us Star Wars, and tell us that is the answer to nuclear war. They will give us artificial intelligence, and tell us that this is the way to self-knowledge. They will give us instantaneous global communication, and tell us this is the way to mutual understanding. They will give us Virtual Reality and tell us this is the answer to spiritual poverty. But that is only the way of the technician, the fact-monger, the information junkie, and the technological idiot.

Here is what Henry David Thoreau told us: "All our inventions are but improved means to an unimproved end." Here is what Goethe told us: "One should, each day, try to hear a little song, read a good poem, see a fine picture, and, if it is possible, speak a few reasonable words." And here is what Socrates told us: "The unexamined life is not worth living." And here is what the prophet Micah told us: "What does the Lord require of thee but to do justly, and to love mercy and to walk humbly with thy God?" And I can tell you—if I had the time (although you all know it well enough)—what Confucius, Isaiah, Jesus, Mohammed, the Buddha, Spinoza and Shakespeare told us. It is all the same: There is no escaping from ourselves. The human dilemma is as it has always been, and we solve nothing fundamental by cloaking ourselves in technological glory.

Even the humblest cartoon character knows this, and I shall close by quoting the wise old possum named Pogo, created by the cartoonist, Walt Kelley. I commend his words to all the technological utopians and messiahs present. "We have met the enemy," Pogo said, "and he is us."

— 14 —

Why the Future Doesn't Need Us

Bill Joy, cofounder and chief scientist of Sun Microsystems, argues that the technologies of the future (genetic engineering, nanotechnology, and robotics), made possible by powerful computers, may do uncontrollable harm. Without an appreciation for the uses to which technology has historically been put, Joy warns, we may be unwittingly building the machines that extremists in the future will use to wield enormous destructive power.

Bill Joy

From the moment I became involved in the creation of new technologies, their ethical dimensions have concerned me, but it was only in the autumn of 1998 that I became anxiously aware of how great are the dangers facing us in the 21st century. I can date the onset of my unease to the day I met Ray Kurzweil, the deservedly famous inventor of the first reading machine for the blind and many other amazing things.

Ray and I were both speakers at George Gilder's Telecosm conference, and I encountered him by chance in the bar of the hotel after both our sessions were over. I was sitting with John Searle, a Berkeley philosopher who studies consciousness. While we were talking, Ray approached and a conversation began, the subject of which haunts me to this day.

I had missed Ray's talk and the subsequent panel that Ray and John had been on, and they now picked right up where they'd left off, with Ray saying that the rate of improvement of technology was going to accelerate and that we were going to become robots or fuse with robots or something like

Excerpted from Bill Joy, "Why the Future Doesn't Need Us." *Wired,* Vol. 8, April 2000. Full text of the article available http://www.wired.com/wired/archive/8.04/joy.html.

that, and John countering that this couldn't happen, because the robots couldn't be conscious.

While I had heard such talk before, I had always felt sentient robots were in the realm of science fiction. But now, from someone I respected, I was hearing a strong argument that they were a near-term possibility. I was taken aback, especially given Ray's proven ability to imagine and create the future. I already knew that new technologies like genetic engineering and nanotechnology were giving us the power to remake the world, but a realistic and imminent scenario for intelligent robots surprised me.

It's easy to get jaded about such breakthroughs. We hear in the news almost every day of some kind of technological or scientific advance. Yet this was no ordinary prediction. In the hotel bar, Ray gave me a partial preprint of his then-forthcoming book *The Age of Spiritual Machines,* which outlined a utopia he foresaw—one in which humans gained near immortality by becoming one with robotic technology. On reading it, my sense of unease only intensified; I felt sure he had to be understating the dangers, understating the probability of a bad outcome along this path.

I found myself most troubled by a passage detailing a *dys*topian scenario:

The New Luddite Challenge

First let us postulate that the computer scientists succeed in developing intelligent machines that can do all things better than human beings can do them. In that case presumably all work will be done by vast, highly organized systems of machines and no human effort will be necessary. Either of two cases might occur. The machines might be permitted to make all of their own decisions without human oversight, or else human control over the machines might be retained.

If the machines are permitted to make all their own decisions, we can't make any conjectures as to the results, because it is impossible to guess how such machines might behave. We only point out that the fate of the human race would be at the mercy of the machines. It might be argued that the human race would never be foolish enough to hand over all the power to the machines. But we are suggesting neither that the human race would voluntarily turn power over to the machines nor that the machines would willfully seize power. What we do suggest is that the human race might easily permit itself to drift into a position of such dependence on the machines that it would have no practical choice but to accept all of the machines' decisions. As society and the problems that face it become more and more complex and machines become more and more intelligent, people will let machines make more of their decisions for them, simply because machine-made decisions will bring better results than man-made ones. Eventually a stage may be reached at which the decisions necessary to keep the system running will be so complex that human beings will be incapable of making them intelligently. At that stage the machines will be in effective control. People won't be able to just turn the machines off, because they will be so dependent on them that turning them off would amount to suicide.

On the other hand it is possible that human control over the machines may be retained. In that case the average man may have control over certain private machines of his own, such as his car or his personal computer, but control over large systems of machines will be in the hands of a tiny elite—just as it is today, but with two differences. Due to improved techniques the elite will have greater control over the masses; and because human work will no longer be necessary the masses will be superfluous, a useless burden on the system. If the elite is ruthless they may simply decide to exterminate the mass of humanity. If they are humane they may use propaganda or other psychological or biological techniques to reduce the birth rate until the mass of humanity becomes extinct, leaving the world to the elite. Or, if the elite consists of soft-hearted liberals, they may decide to play the role of good shepherds to the rest of the human race. They will see to it that everyone's physical needs are satisfied, that all children are raised under psychologically hygienic conditions, that everyone has a wholesome hobby to keep him busy, and that anyone who may become dissatisfied undergoes "treatment" to cure his "problem." Of course, life will be so purposeless that people will have to be biologically or psychologically engineered either to remove their need for the power process or make them "sublimate" their drive for power into some harmless hobby. These engineered human beings may be happy in such a society, but they will most certainly not be free. They will have been reduced to the status of domestic animals.

In the book, you don't discover until you turn the page that the author of this passage is Theodore Kaczysnki—the Unabomber. I am no apologist for Kaczynski. His bombs killed three people during a 17-year terror campaign and wounded many others. One of his bombs gravely injured my friend David Gelernter, one of the most brilliant and visionary computer scientists of our time. Like many of my colleagues, I felt that I could easily have been the Unabomber's next target.

Kaczynski's actions were murderous and, in my view, criminally insane. He is clearly a Luddite, but simply saying this does not dismiss his argument; as difficult as it is for me to acknowledge, I saw some merit in the reasoning in this single passage. I felt compelled to confront it.

Kaczynski's dystopian vision describes unintended consequences, a well-known problem with the design and use of technology, and one that is clearly related to Murphy's law—"Anything that can go wrong, will." (Actually, this is Finagle's law, which in itself shows that Finagle was right.) Our overuse of antibiotics has led to what may be the biggest such problem so far: the emergence of antibiotic-resistant and much more dangerous bacteria. Similar things happened when attempts to eliminate malarial mosquitoes using DDT caused them to acquire DDT resistance; malarial parasites likewise acquired multi-drug-resistant genes.

The cause of many such surprises seems clear: The systems involved are complex, involving interaction among and feedback between many parts. Any changes to such a system will cascade in ways that are difficult to predict; this is especially true when human actions are involved.

I started showing friends the Kaczynski quote from *The Age of Spiritual Machines;* I would hand them Kurzweil's book, let them read the quote, and then watch their reaction as they discovered who had written it. At around the same time, I found Hans Moravec's book *Robot: Mere Machine to Transcendent Mind.* Moravec is one of the leaders in robotics research, and was a founder of the world's largest robotics research program, at Carnegie Mellon University. *Robot* gave me more material to try out on my friends—material surprisingly supportive of Kaczynski's argument. For example:

The Short Run (Early 2000s)

Biological species almost never survive encounters with superior competitors. Ten million years ago, South and North America were separated by a sunken Panama isthmus. South America, like Australia today, was populated by marsupial mammals, including pouched equivalents of rats, deers, and tigers. When the isthmus connecting North and South America rose, it took only a few thousand years for the northern placental species, with slightly more effective metabolisms and reproductive and nervous systems, to displace and eliminate almost all the southern marsupials.

In a completely free marketplace, superior robots would surely affect humans as North American placentals affected South American marsupials (and as humans have affected countless species). Robotic industries would compete vigorously among themselves for matter, energy, and space, incidentally driving their price beyond human reach. Unable to afford the necessities of life, biological humans would be squeezed out of existence.

There is probably some breathing room, because we do not live in a completely free marketplace. Government coerces nonmarket behavior, especially by collecting taxes. Judiciously applied, governmental coercion could support human populations in high style on the fruits of robot labor, perhaps for a long while.

A textbook dystopia—and Moravec is just getting wound up. He goes on to discuss how our main job in the 21st century will be "ensuring continued cooperation from the robot industries" by passing laws decreeing that they be "nice," and to describe how seriously dangerous a human can be "once transformed into an unbounded superintelligent robot." Moravec's view is that the robots will eventually succeed us—that humans clearly face extinction.

I decided it was time to talk to my friend Danny Hillis. Danny became famous as the cofounder of Thinking Machines Corporation, which built a very powerful parallel supercomputer. Despite my current job title of Chief Scientist at Sun Microsystems, I am more a computer architect than a scientist, and I respect Danny's knowledge of the information and physical sciences more than that of any other single person I know. Danny is also a highly regarded futurist who thinks long-term—four years ago he started the Long Now Foundation, which is building a clock designed to last 10,000 years, in an attempt to draw attention to the pitifully short attention span of our society. (See "Test of Time," *Wired* 8.03, page 78.)

So I flew to Los Angeles for the express purpose of having dinner with Danny and his wife, Pati. I went through my now-familiar routine, trotting out the ideas and passages that I found so disturbing. Danny's answer—directed specifically at Kurzweil's scenario of humans merging with robots—came swiftly, and quite surprised me. He said, simply, that the changes would come gradually, and that we would get used to them.

But I guess I wasn't totally surprised. I had seen a quote from Danny in Kurzweil's book in which he said, "I'm as fond of my body as anyone, but if I can be 200 with a body of silicon, I'll take it." It seemed that he was at peace with this process and its attendant risks, while I was not.

While talking and thinking about Kurzweil, Kaczynski, and Moravec, I suddenly remembered a novel I had read almost 20 years ago—*The White Plague,* by Frank Herbert—in which a molecular biologist is driven insane by the senseless murder of his family. To seek revenge he constructs and disseminates a new and highly contagious plague that kills widely but selectively. (We're lucky Kaczynski was a mathematician, not a molecular biologist.) I was also reminded of the Borg of *Star Trek,* a hive of partly biological, partly robotic creatures with a strong destructive streak. Borg-like disasters are a staple of science fiction, so why hadn't I been more concerned about such robotic dystopias earlier? Why weren't other people more concerned about these nightmarish scenarios?

Part of the answer certainly lies in our attitude toward the new—in our bias toward instant familiarity and unquestioning acceptance. Accustomed to living with almost routine scientific breakthroughs, we have yet to come to terms with the fact that the most compelling 21st-century technologies—robotics, genetic engineering, and nanotechnology—pose a different threat than the technologies that have come before. Specifically, robots, engineered organisms, and nanobots share a dangerous amplifying factor: They can self-replicate. A bomb is blown up only once—but one bot can become many, and quickly get out of control.

Much of my work over the past 25 years has been on computer networking, where the sending and receiving of messages creates the opportunity for out-of-control replication. But while replication in a computer or a computer network can be a nuisance, at worst it disables a machine or takes down a network or network service. Uncontrolled self-replication in these newer technologies runs a much greater risk: a risk of substantial damage in the physical world.

Each of these technologies also offers untold promise: The vision of near immortality that Kurzweil sees in his robot dreams drives us forward; genetic engineering may soon provide treatments, if not outright cures, for most diseases; and nanotechnology and nanomedicine can address yet more ills. Together they could significantly extend our average life span and improve the quality of our lives. Yet, with each of these technologies, a sequence of small, individually sensible advances leads to an accumulation of great power and, concomitantly, great danger.

What was different in the 20th century? Certainly, the technologies underlying the weapons of mass destruction (WMD)—nuclear, biological, and chemical (NBC)—were powerful, and the weapons an enormous threat. But building nuclear weapons required, at least for a time, access to both rare—indeed, effectively unavailable—raw materials and highly protected information; biological and chemical weapons programs also tended to require large-scale activities.

The 21st-century technologies—genetics, nanotechnology, and robotics (GNR)—are so powerful that they can spawn whole new classes of accidents and abuses. Most dangerously, for the first time, these accidents and abuses are widely within the reach of individuals or small groups. They will not require large facilities or rare raw materials. Knowledge alone will enable the use of them.

Thus we have the possibility not just of weapons of mass destruction but of knowledge-enabled mass destruction (KMD), this destructiveness hugely amplified by the power of self-replication.

I think it is no exaggeration to say we are on the cusp of the further perfection of extreme evil, an evil whose possibility spreads well beyond that which weapons of mass destruction bequeathed to the nation-states, on to a surprising and terrible empowerment of extreme individuals. . . .

Perhaps it is always hard to see the bigger impact while you are in the vortex of a change. Failing to understand the consequences of our inventions while we are in the rapture of discovery and innovation seems to be a common fault of scientists and technologists; we have long been driven by the overarching desire to know that is the nature of science's quest, not stopping to notice that the progress to newer and more powerful technologies can take on a life of its own.

I have long realized that the big advances in information technology come not from the work of computer scientists, computer architects, or electrical engineers, but from that of physical scientists. The physicists Stephen Wolfram and Brosl Hasslacher introduced me, in the early 1980s, to chaos theory and nonlinear systems. In the 1990s, I learned about complex systems from conversations with Danny Hillis, the biologist Stuart Kauffman, the Nobel-laureate physicist Murray Gell-Mann, and others. Most recently, Hasslacher and the electrical engineer and device physicist Mark Reed have been giving me insight into the incredible possibilities of molecular electronics.

In my own work, as codesigner of three microprocessor architectures—SPARC, picoJava, and MAJC—and as the designer of several implementations thereof, I've been afforded a deep and firsthand acquaintance with Moore's law. For decades, Moore's law has correctly predicted the exponential rate of improvement of semiconductor technology. Until last year I believed that the rate of advances predicted by Moore's law might continue only until roughly 2010, when some physical limits would begin to be reached. It was not obvious to me that a new technology would arrive in time to keep performance advancing smoothly.

But because of the recent rapid and radical progress in molecular electronics—where individual atoms and molecules replace lithographically drawn transistors—and related nanoscale technologies, we should be able to meet or exceed the Moore's law rate of progress for another 30 years. By 2030, we are likely to be able to build machines, in quantity, a million times as powerful as the personal computers of today—sufficient to implement the dreams of Kurzweil and Moravec.

As this enormous computing power is combined with the manipulative advances of the physical sciences and the new, deep understandings in genetics, enormous transformative power is being unleashed. These combinations open up the opportunity to completely redesign the world, for better or worse: The replicating and evolving processes that have been confined to the natural world are about to become realms of human endeavor.

In designing software and microprocessors, I have never had the feeling that I was designing an intelligent machine. The software and hardware is so fragile and the capabilities of the machine to "think" so clearly absent that, even as a possibility, this has always seemed very far in the future.

But now, with the prospect of human-level computing power in about 50 years, a new idea suggests itself: that I may be working to create tools which will enable the construction of the technology that may replace our species. How do I feel about this? Very uncomfortable. Having struggled my entire career to build reliable software systems, it seems to me more than likely that this future will not work out as well as some people may imagine. My personal experience suggests we tend to overestimate our design abilities.

Given the incredible power of these new technologies, shouldn't we be asking how we can best coexist with them? And if our own extinction is a likely, or even possible, outcome of our technological development, shouldn't we proceed with great caution?

The dream of robotics is, first, that intelligent machines can do our work for us, allowing us lives of leisure, restoring us to Eden. Yet in his history of such ideas, *Darwin Among the Machines,* George Dyson warns: "In the game of life and evolution there are three players at the table: human beings, nature, and machines. I am firmly on the side of nature. But nature, I suspect, is on the side of the machines." As we have seen, Moravec agrees, believing we may well not survive the encounter with the superior robot species.

How soon could such an intelligent robot be built? The coming advances in computing power seem to make it possible by 2030. And once an intelligent robot exists, it is only a small step to a robot species—to an intelligent robot that can make evolved copies of itself.

A second dream of robotics is that we will gradually replace ourselves with our robotic technology, achieving near immortality by downloading our consciousness; it is this process that Danny Hillis thinks we will gradually get used to and that Ray Kurzweil elegantly details in *The Age of Spiritual Machines*. . . .

But if we are downloaded into our technology, what are the chances that we will thereafter be ourselves or even human? It seems to me far more likely that a robotic existence would not be like a human one in any sense that we understand, that the robots would in no sense be our children, that on this path our humanity may well be lost.

Genetic engineering promises to revolutionize agriculture by increasing crop yields while reducing the use of pesticides; to create tens of thousands of novel species of bacteria, plants, viruses, and animals; to replace reproduction, or supplement it, with cloning; to create cures for many diseases, increasing our life span and our quality of life; and much, much more. We now know with certainty that these profound changes in the biological sciences are imminent and will challenge all our notions of what life is.

Technologies such as human cloning have in particular raised our awareness of the profound ethical and moral issues we face. If, for example, we were to reengineer ourselves into several separate and unequal species using the power of genetic engineering, then we would threaten the notion of equality that is the very cornerstone of our democracy.

Given the incredible power of genetic engineering, it's no surprise that there are significant safety issues in its use. My friend Amory Lovins recently cowrote, along with Hunter Lovins, an editorial that provides an ecological view of some of these dangers. Among their concerns: that "the new botany aligns the development of plants with their economic, not evolutionary, success." [Amory B. Lovins and L. Hunter Lovins, "A Tale of Two Botanies." *Wired*, Vol. 8, April 2000, p. 247] Amory's long career has been focused on energy and resource efficiency by taking a whole-system view of human-made systems; such a whole-system view often finds simple, smart solutions to otherwise seemingly difficult problems, and is usefully applied here as well.

After reading the Lovins' editorial , I saw an op-ed by Gregg Esterbrook in *The New York Times* (November 19, 1999) about genetically engineered crops, under the headline: "Food for the Future: Someday, rice will have built-in vitamin A. Unless the Luddites win."

Are Amory and Hunter Lovins Luddites? Certainly not. I believe we all would agree that golden rice, with its built-in vitamin A, is probably a good thing, if developed with proper care and respect for the likely dangers in moving genes across species boundaries.

Awareness of the dangers inherent in genetic engineering is beginning to grow, as reflected in the Lovins' editorial. The general public is aware of, and uneasy about, genetically modified foods, and seems to be rejecting the notion that such foods should be permitted to be unlabeled.

But genetic engineering technology is already very far along. As the Lovins note, the USDA has already approved about 50 genetically engineered crops for unlimited release; more than half of the world's soybeans and a third of its corn now contain genes spliced in from other forms of life.

While there are many important issues here, my own major concern with genetic engineering is narrower: that it gives the power—whether militarily, accidentally, or in a deliberate terrorist act—to create a White Plague.

The many wonders of nanotechnology were first imagined by the Nobel-laureate physicist Richard Feynman in a speech he gave in 1959, subsequently published under the title "Theres Plenty of Room at the Bottom." The book that made a big impression on me, in the mid-'80s, was Eric Drexler's *Engines of Creation,* in which he described beautifully how manipulation of matter at the atomic level could create a utopian future of abundance, where just about everything could be made cheaply, and almost any imaginable disease or physical problem could be solved using nanotechnology and artificial intelligences.

A subsequent book, *Unbounding the Future: The Nanotechnology Revolution,* which Drexler cowrote, imagines some of the changes that might take place in a world where we had molecular-level "assemblers." Assemblers could make possible incredibly low-cost solar power, cures for cancer and the common cold by augmentation of the human immune system, essentially complete cleanup of the environment, incredibly inexpensive pocket supercomputers—in fact, any product would be manufacturable by assemblers at a cost no greater than that of wood—spaceflight more accessible than transoceanic travel today, and restoration of extinct species.

I remember feeling good about nanotechnology after reading *Engines of Creation.* As a technologist, it gave me a sense of calm—that is, nanotechnology showed us that incredible progress was possible, and indeed perhaps inevitable. If nanotechnology was our future, then I didn't feel pressed to solve so many problems in the present. I would get to Drexler's utopian future in due time; I might as well enjoy life more in the here and now. It didn't make sense, given his vision, to stay up all night, all the time.

Drexler's vision also led to a lot of good fun. I would occasionally get to describe the wonders of nanotechnology to others who had not heard of it. After teasing them with all the things Drexler described I would give a homework assignment of my own: "Use nanotechnology to create a vampire; for extra credit create an antidote."

With these wonders came clear dangers, of which I was acutely aware. As I said at a nanotechnology conference in 1989, "We can't simply do our science and not worry about these ethical issues." But my subsequent conversations with physicists convinced me that nanotechnology might not even work—or, at least, it wouldn't work anytime soon. Shortly thereafter I moved to Colorado, to a skunk works I had set up, and the focus of my work shifted to software for the Internet, specifically on ideas that became Java and Jini.

Then, last summer, Brosl Hasslacher told me that nanoscale molecular electronics was now practical. This was *new* news, at least to me, and I think to many people—and it radically changed my opinion about nanotechnology. It sent me back to *Engines of Creation.* Rereading Drexler's work after more than 10 years, I was dismayed to realize how little I had remembered of its lengthy section called "Dangers and Hopes," including a discussion of how nanotechnologies can become "engines of destruction." Indeed, in my rereading of this cautionary material today, I am struck by how naive some of Drexler's safeguard proposals seem, and how much greater I judge the dangers to be now than even he seemed to then. (Having anticipated and described many technical and political problems with nanotechnology, Drexler started the Foresight Institute in the late 1980s "to help prepare society for anticipated advanced technologies"—most important, nanotechnology.)

The enabling breakthrough to assemblers seems quite likely within the next 20 years. Molecular electronics—the new subfield of nanotechnology where individual molecules are circuit elements—should mature quickly and become enormously lucrative within this decade, causing a large incremental investment in all nanotechnologies.

Unfortunately, as with nuclear technology, it is far easier to create destructive uses for nanotechnology than constructive ones. Nanotechnology has clear military and terrorist uses, and you need not be suicidal to release a massively destructive nanotechnological device—such devices can be built to be selectively destructive, affecting, for example, only a certain geographical area or a group of people who are genetically distinct.

An immediate consequence of the Faustian bargain in obtaining the great power of nanotechnology is that we run a grave risk—the risk that we might destroy the biosphere on which all life depends.

As Drexler explained:

"Plants" with "leaves" no more efficient than today's solar cells could outcompete real plants, crowding the biosphere with an inedible foliage. Tough omnivorous "bacteria" could out-compete real bacteria: They could spread like blowing pollen, replicate swiftly, and reduce the biosphere to dust in a matter of days. Dangerous replicators could easily be too tough, small, and rapidly spreading to stop—at least if we make no preparation. We have trouble enough controlling viruses and fruit flies.

Among the cognoscenti of nanotechnology, this threat has become known as the "gray goo problem." Though masses of uncontrolled replicators need not be gray or gooey, the term "gray goo" emphasizes that replicators able to obliterate life might be less inspiring than a single species of crabgrass. They might be superior in an evolutionary sense, but this need not make them valuable.

The gray goo threat makes one thing perfectly clear: We cannot afford certain kinds of accidents with replicating assemblers.

Gray goo would surely be a depressing ending to our human adventure on Earth, far worse than mere fire or ice, and one that could stem from a simple laboratory accident. Oops.

It is most of all the power of destructive self-replication in genetics, nanotechnology, and robotics (GNR) that should give us pause. Self-replication is the modus operandi of genetic engineering, which uses the machinery of the cell to replicate its designs, and the prime danger underlying gray goo in nanotechnology. Stories of run-amok robots like the Borg, replicating or mutating to escape from the ethical constraints imposed on them by their creators, are well established in our science fiction books and movies. It is even possible that self-replication may be more fundamental than we thought, and hence harder—or even impossible—to control. A recent article by Stuart Kauffman in *Nature* titled "Self-Replication: Even Peptides Do It" discusses the discovery that a 52-amino-acid peptide can "autocatalyse its own synthesis." We don't know how widespread this ability is, but Kauffman notes that it may hint at "a route to self-reproducing molecular systems on a basis far wider than Watson-Crick base-pairing."

In truth, we have had in hand for years clear warnings of the dangers inherent in widespread knowledge of GNR technologies—of the possibility of knowledge alone enabling mass destruction. But these warnings haven't been widely publicized ; the public discussions have been clearly inadequate. There is no profit in publicizing the dangers.

The nuclear, biological, and chemical (NBC) technologies used in 20th-century weapons of mass destruction were and are largely military, developed in government laboratories. In sharp contrast, the 21st-century GNR technologies have clear commercial uses and are being developed almost exclusively by corporate enterprises. In this age of triumphant commercialism, technology—with science as its handmaiden—is delivering a series of almost magical inventions that are the most phenomenally lucrative ever seen. We are aggressively pursuing the promises of these new technologies within the now-unchallenged system of global capitalism and its manifold financial incentives and competitive pressures. . . .

As Thoreau said, "We do not ride on the railroad; it rides upon us"; and this is what we must fight, in our time. The question is, indeed, Which is to be master? Will we survive our technologies?

We are being propelled into this new century with no plan, no control, no brakes. Have we already gone too far down the path to alter course? I don't believe so, but we aren't trying yet, and the last chance to assert control—the fail-safe point—is rapidly approaching. We have our first pet robots, as well as commercially available genetic engineering techniques, and our nanoscale techniques are advancing rapidly. While the development of these technologies proceeds through a number of steps, it isn't necessarily the case—as happened in the Manhattan Project and the Trinity test—that the last step in proving a technology is large and hard. The breakthrough to wild self-replication in robotics, genetic engineering, or nanotechnology could come suddenly, reprising the surprise we felt when we learned of the cloning of a mammal.

And yet I believe we do have a strong and solid basis for hope. Our attempts to deal with weapons of mass destruction in the last century provide a shining example of relinquishment for us to consider: the unilateral US abandonment, without preconditions, of the development of biological weapons. This relinquishment stemmed from the realization that while it would take an enormous effort to create these terrible weapons, they could from then on easily be duplicated and fall into the hands of rogue nations or terrorist groups. The clear conclusion was that we would create additional threats to ourselves by pursuing these weapons, and that we would be more secure if we did not pursue them. We have embodied our relinquishment of biological and chemical weapons in the 1972 Biological Weapons Convention (BWC) and the 1993 Chemical Weapons Convention (CWC).

As for the continuing sizable threat from nuclear weapons, which we have lived with now for more than 50 years, the US Senate's recent rejection of the Comprehensive Test Ban Treaty makes it clear relinquishing nuclear weapons will not be politically easy. But we have a unique opportunity, with the end of the Cold War, to avert a multipolar arms race. Building on the BWC and CWC relinquishments, successful abolition of nuclear weapons could help us build toward a habit of relinquishing dangerous technologies. (Actually, by getting rid of all but 100 nuclear weapons worldwide—roughly the total destructive power of World War II and a considerably easier task—we could eliminate this extinction threat.)

Verifying relinquishment will be a difficult problem, but not an unsolvable one. We are fortunate to have already done a lot of relevant work in the context of the BWC and other treaties. Our major task will be to apply this to technologies that are naturally much more commercial than military. The substantial need here is for transparency, as difficulty of verification is directly proportional to the difficulty of distinguishing relinquished from legitimate activities. . . .

It is now more than a year since my first encounter with Ray Kurzweil and John Searle. I see around me cause for hope in the voices for caution and relinquishment and in those people I have discovered who are as concerned as I am about our current predicament. I feel, too, a deepened sense of personal responsibility—not for the work I have already done, but for the work that I might yet do, at the confluence of the sciences.

But many other people who know about the dangers still seem strangely silent. When pressed, they trot out the "this is nothing new" riposte—as if awareness of what could happen is response enough. They tell me, There are universities filled with bioethicists who study this stuff all day long. They say, All this has been written about before, and by experts. They complain, Your worries and your arguments are already old hat.

I don't know where these people hide their fear. As an architect of complex systems I enter this arena as a generalist. But should this diminish my concerns? I am aware of how much has been written about, talked about, and lectured about so authoritatively. But does this mean it has reached people? Does this mean we can discount the dangers before us?

Knowing is not a rationale for not acting. Can we doubt that knowledge has become a weapon we wield against ourselves?

The experiences of the atomic scientists clearly show the need to take personal responsibility, the danger that things will move too fast, and the way in which a process can take on a life of its own. We can, as they did, create insurmountable problems in almost no time flat. We must do more thinking up front if we are not to be similarly surprised and shocked by the consequences of our inventions.

My continuing professional work is on improving the reliability of software. Software is a tool, and as a toolbuilder I must struggle with the uses to which the tools I make are put. I have always believed that making software more reliable, given its many uses, will make the world a safer and better place; if I were to come to believe the opposite, then I would be morally obligated to stop this work. I can now imagine such a day may come.

This all leaves me not angry but at least a bit melancholic. Henceforth, for me, progress will be somewhat bittersweet.

Boolean Logic

Michael Heim examines the cognitive implications of Boolean logic and argues that it emphasizes reason and control over intuition and surprise. The problem, he suggests, is that when we use computers, the logic of the machine unconsciously affects the way we apprehend the world. Heim therefore concludes that we must consciously recognize the power that technologies have to shape thinking.

Michael Heim

How does thinking at the computer differ from thinking with paper and pencil or thinking at the typewriter? The computer doesn't merely place another tool at your fingertips. It builds a whole new environment, an information environment in which the mind breathes a different atmosphere. The computing atmosphere belongs to an information-rich world—which soon becomes an information-polluted world.

First, the files you create grow rapidly, forming an electronic library of letters, papers, and other documents. Through on-line connections, you save pieces from the work of colleagues and friends, notes about future projects, and leftovers from database searches. Add some serendipitous items to disk storage—maybe the Gettysburg Address, the Constitution, or the King James Bible—and you find yourself soon outgrowing your disk-storage capacity. CD-ROMS then spin out encyclopedias, the *Oxford English Dictionary,* or the entire corpus of ancient Greek literature. As the load of information stresses your mental capacity, you sense that you've come down with infomania.

Because the computer helped generate all this information, you naturally hope that the computer will in turn help mop up the mess. The computer can indeed hack a neat pathway through the dense information jungle. Computer data searches find references, phrases, or ideas in an instant, in the nanoseconds it takes the microprocessor to go through huge amounts of data. A word processor or database takes a key phrase and in a flash snaps a piece of information into view. So there you are, lifted by the computer out of the morass generated by computers. You can search through thousands of periodicals in minutes, without ever having to know anything about silicon microchips, high-level code, or sorting algorithms. All you need is some elementary search logic that you can learn in about an hour. Today most computer searches use elementary Boolean logic.

What is Boolean logic? Alfred Glossbrenner in *How to Look It Up On-line* describes Boolean logic in terms simple enough for most computer users: "AND means a record must have both terms in it. OR means it can have either term. NOT means it cannot have the specified term." Glossbrenner chides those who belabor the complexities of Boolean logic and bewilder the user: "You sometimes get the impression that the authors would be drummed out of the manual-writers union if they didn't include complicated discussion of search logic laced with plenty of Venn diagrams—those intersecting, variously shaded circles you learned about in sophomore geometry. Forget it!"[1]

But alas, what Glossbrenner wants us to forget will soon enough slip into oblivion as technology enfolds us in its web of assumptions. Frequent reading and writing on computers will soon allow us little distance from the tools that trap our language. They will fit like skin. The conditions under which we work will grow indiscernible, invisible to all but the keenest eye. Present everywhere like eyeglasses on the end of our noses, computers will hide the distortion they introduce, the vivid colors they overshadow, the hidden vistas they occlude. Like microscopes, computers extend our vision vastly, but unlike microscopes, computers process our entire symbolic life, reflecting the contents of the human psyche. Boolean search logic and other computer strategies will soon enough become second nature for literate people, something they take for granted.

What people take for granted was once something startling and unprecedented. A felt transition like the present alerts us to the change, and so we have an opportunity to ponder the initial shifts in the life of the psyche. We can ask, How does Boolean search logic affect our thought processes and mental life? What dark side of infomania is hiding behind those "intersecting, variously shaded circles you learned about in sophomore geometry"?

The significance of Boolean search logic deserves far more than a side-bar in how-to manuals. Boolean logic, displayed graphically by the circles of the Venn diagrams, constitutes a central achievement of modern logic. Modern logic, which makes the computer possible, got its footing in the work of Gottfried Leibniz (1646–1716), whose discoveries laid the foundations of computer systems and the information age. So when we inspect Boolean logic for its side effects, we are looking at the implicit heart of the world we inhabit. Boolean logic functions as a metaphor for the computer age, since it shows how we typically interrogate the world of information.

Humans have always interrogated the world in a variety of ways, and each way reveals a distinct approach to life: Socrates pushed for personal definitions; Descartes and Galileo taught scientists to pose questions with empirical hypotheses; McLuhan teased our awareness with his enigmatic slogans; Heidegger drew on a scholarly history of reality; and Wittgenstein worried over odd locutions. The type of question we ask, philosophers agree, shapes the possible answers we get. The way in which we search limits what we find in our searching.

Today we interrogate the world through the computer interface, where many of our questions begin with Boolean terms. The Boolean search then guides the subconscious processes by which we characteristically model the world. Once we notice how computers structure our mental environment, we can reflect on the subconscious agencies that affect our mental life, and we are then in a position to grasp both the potential and the peril. So let's return again to those simple Venn diagrams from sophomore geometry and to the Boolean logic on which they are based.

George Boole (1815–1864) discovered the branch of mathematics known as *symbolic logic*. Boole's "algebra of logic" uses formulas to symbolize logical relations. The formulas in algebraic symbols can describe the general relationships among groups of things that have certain properties. Given a question about how one group relates to another, Boole could manipulate the equations and quickly produce an answer. First, his algebra classifies things, and then the algebraic symbols express any relationship among the things that have been classified—as if we were shuffling things in the nested drawers of a Chinese puzzle box.

Take two referential terms, such as *brown* and *cows*: all objects that are brown = B; all objects that are cows = C. An algebraic formula can represent the relationship between these two terms as a product of mutual inclusion: "All brown cows" = BC. For more complex formulas, add a logical NOT ($—C$) as well as an AND *(BC and C — B)*. Once you know that *(BC and C — B) = F* (where F means any animal that "lives on the farm"), you can conclude that $BC = F$ or also that any cow, no matter what color, lives on the farm. You can build up terms that represent a whole series of increasingly complex relationships, and then you can pose and calculate any implication from that series. You can even make symbolic formulas represent a very long chain of deductive reasoning so that the logical form of each part of the argument rises to the surface for review and criticism, making it possible to scan an argument as if it were a mathematical problem.

Historically, Boole's logic was the first system for calculating class membership, for rapidly determining whether or not something falls into one or another category or class of things. Before Boole, logic was a study of statements about things referred to directly and intuitively at hand. After Boole, logic became a system of pure symbols. Pre-Boolean logic focused on the way that direct statements or assertions connect and hold together. A set of statements that hangs together can be a valid deductive pattern. Validity is the way that conclusions connect with their supporting reasons or premises. The traditional study of logic harked back to Aristotle, who first noticed patterns in the way we assemble statements into arguments. Aristotle called the assemblage of statements *syllogisms,* from the Greek for a pattern of reasoning. Aristotle himself used symbols sparingly in his logic, and when he did use symbols, they served merely to point out language patterns. Aristotle's symbols organized what was already given in direct statements. With Boolean logic, on the contrary, direct statements have value only as instances of the relationships among abstract symbols. Direct language becomes only one possible instance of algebraic mathematics, one possible application of mathematical logic.

Boole inverted the traditional relationship between direct and symbolic languages. He conceived of language as a system of symbols and believed that his symbols could absorb all logically correct language. By inverting statement and symbol, Boole's mathematical logic could swallow traditional logic and capture direct statements in a web of symbolic patterns. Logical argument became a branch of calculation.

The term *symbolic logic* first appeared in 1881 in a book by that title. The book's author, John Venn, introduced the first graphic display of Boole's formulas. Venn continued Boole's plan to absorb the direct statements of language into a general system of abstract algebra. With mathematics as a basis, Venn could solve certain logical difficulties that had perplexed traditional Aristotelian logicians. With mathematical precision, modern logic could present linguistic arguments and logical relationships within a total system, a formal organization having its own axioms and theorems. Systemic consistency became more important than the direct reference to things addressed in our experience.

Note already one telltale sign of infomania: the priority of system. When system precedes relevance, the way becomes clear for the primacy of information. For it to become manipulable and transmissible as information, knowledge must first be reduced to homogenized units. With the influx of homogenized bits of information, the sense of overall significance dwindles. This subtle emptying of meaning appears in the Venn diagrams that graphically display Boolean logic.

The visual display that John Venn created begins with empty circles. Venn noted how Boolean logic treats terms, like *brown* and *cows,* strictly as algebraic variables and not as universal terms referring to actually existing things. In Boole's logic, terms function like compartments or drawers that may or may not contain any actual members. Boole's logic can use terms that are empty, the class of unicorns, for example. A term with no actually existing members is a null set, an empty compartment. As modern logicians say, the terms of logic do not in themselves carry existential import. The terms reveal relationships among themselves, but they remain unconnected to existence or to the direct references of firsthand experience. (Mathematics also shares this existential vacuum: $2 + 2 = 4$ remains mathematically true whether or not four things actually exist anywhere.) Boolean logic uses terms only to show relationships—of inclusion or exclusion—among the terms. It shows whether or not one drawer fits into another and ignores the question of whether there is anything in the drawers. The Boolean vocabulary uses abstract counters, tokens devoid of all but systemic meaning.

On Venn diagrams, then, we begin with empty circles to map statements that contain universal terms. We can map the statement "All the cows are brown" by drawing two overlapping circles: one representing cows and the other, brown things. Shade in (exclude) the area that represents cows and that does not overlap the area representing "brown things," and you have a graphic map of the statement "All the cows are brown." The map remains accurate regardless of whether or not any cows actually exist; you could equally well have drawn a map of the unicorns that are white. Add a third circle to represent spotted things, and you can map "No brown cows are spotted" or "All brown cows are spotted," and so on.

What does this procedure really map? According to Boolean logic, no cows or brown things or spotted things need actually exist. All we have mapped is the relationship between sets or classes. The sets could refer to custards or quarks or square circles.

In its intrinsic remoteness from direct human experience, Boolean search logic shows another part of the infomania syndrome: a gain in power at the price of our direct involvement with things. The Boolean search affects our relationship to language and thought by placing us at a new remove from subject matter, by directing us away from the texture of what we are exploring.

To add particular statements to our map, like "Some spotted cows are brown," we need to introduce more symbols. We can map statements about particular things on the diagrams by stipulating another conventional symbol, often a star, an asterisk, or some other mark. Statements that imply that a particular member of a class actually exists must be specifically marked as such; otherwise, the general term labels a potentially empty compartment. From the outset, then, Boolean logic assumes that as a rule, we stand at a remove from direct statements about particular things in which we existing beings are actually, personally involved.

This shift in the meaning of logical terms has drastic consequences for logic itself and for logic as a formal study. Traditional Aristotelian logic presupposed an actual subject, ideal or real, to which logical terms or words refer. Traditional logic also presupposed that logical thinking is, like spontaneous thought and speech, intimately involved with a real subject matter. Mathematical logic gained the upper hand by severing its significance from the conditions under which we make direct statements. Today, logicians like Willard Van Orman Quine can argue that a concrete and unique individual thing (to which we refer as such) has no more reality than "to be the value of a variable," at least when we consider things "from a logical point of view." The modern logical point of view begins with the system, not with concrete content. It operates in a domain of pure formality and abstract detachment. The modern logical point of view proceeds from an intricate net of abstract relations having no inherent connection to the things we directly perceive and experience.

We can contrast this aloof abstraction with the traditional logic that still swam in the element of direct experience. Traditional logic began with direct statements, insofar as its logical language presupposed as necessary the existential interpretation of statements. When we state something in everyday language, we attribute something to something; we attribute the color mauve to the wall, the quality of mercy to a creditor. We speak of what is before us, and we speak in the context of other people who may also have access to what we are talking about. We commonly assume the existence or at least the existential relevance of what we are talking about. Modern symbolic logic, on the contrary, mimics modern mathematics, which has no interest in the actually existing world, not even the world of direct statements. In this sense, modern logic operates at a remove from our everyday involvement with things.

But why pick on modern Boolean logic? Don't all logics bring abstraction and alienation? Even the words we use to pose any question testify to a gap between us and the wordless subject we are thinking or talking about. Any logic can distance us. We sometimes run across a person arguing with impeccable logic for a conclusion contrary to our own gut feelings, and we often feel overwhelmed, and forcibly so, by the sheer power of the argument itself. Logic can move like a juggernaut adrift from any personal engagement with its subject matter. Someone with a great deal less experience, for example, can make us feel compelled to accept a conclusion we know instinctively to be wrong. We feel the logical coercion even though we may have much more familiarity with the matter under discussion. Arguing with someone like Socrates or William F. Buckley can be disconcerting. We sense a line of thought pushing inexorably through the topic, perhaps even in spite of the topic. Logic, like mathematics, operates outside the intuitive wisdom of experience and common sense. Hence the mathematical idiot savant. Like math, logic can hover above particular facts and circumstances, linking chains of statements trailing from some phantom first premise. We can be perfectly logical yet float completely adrift from reality. By its very nature, logic operates with abstractions. But modern logic operates with a greater degree of abstraction than does Aristotelian logic, placing us at a further remove from experience and from felt insight.

When college students study those Venn diagrams from "sophomore geometry," they feel the pain of that disengaged logic. When they first learn to symbolize statements and arguments in symbolic logic, they must pass through a lengthy and painful process of converting their English language into abstract symbols. So far removed does this logic stand from the direct everyday use of language that the textbook refers to the process of converting arguments into symbols as "translation." Before analyzing their thoughts logically, students must translate them to fit the system of modern logic. Statements in direct English must first undergo a sea change.

The painful translation into symbols signals acute infomania. But when logic works on the computer, this pain turns into convenience. When the computer automatically and invisibly converts input into algebraic bytes, the user is shielded from the translation into modern logic. Instead of the human mind puzzling over how language fits the system, the computer does the fitting; it transforms our alphabet into manipulable digits.

As a medium, the computer relieves us of the exertion needed to pour our thoughts into an algebraic mold. The shift from intuitive content to bit-size information proceeds invisibly and smoothly. On the machine level, the computer's microswitches in the central processing unit organize everything through a circuit based on symbolic logic, and Boolean searches simply apply that same logic to text processing. Hardly noticing this spiderlike, nondirect logic, we stand at a new remove from concretely embedded language. The computer absorbs our language so we can squirt symbols at lightning speeds or scan the whole range of human thought with Boolean searches. Because the computer, not the student, does the translating, the shift takes place subtly. The computer system slides us from a direct awareness of things to the detached world of logical distance. By encoding language as data, the computer already modifies the language we use into mathematized ASCII (American Standard Code for Information Interchange). We can then operate with the certitude of Boolean formulas. The logical distance we gain offers all the allure of control and power without the pain of having to translate back and forth from our everyday approach to the things we experience.

But so what if computer power removes us from direct intuitive language? So what if Boolean logic injects greater existential distance from practical contexts than any previous logic? Don't our other text tools also operate at a remove from direct context-embedded language? Isn't any medium, by definition, a mediation? If the Boolean search operates at a great remove from direct oral discourse, don't also pen and paper, not to mention rubber erasers and Linotype typesetting machines?

Nonlinguistic tools, like erasers, do indeed insert a distance between ourselves and our context-embedded mother tongue. And, yes, using a rubber eraser does affect us in subtle, psychological ways. Teachers understand that getting a student to use an eraser marks a significant step on the road to good writing. A self-critical attitude distinguishes good from bad writing, and picking up an eraser means that we are beginning to evaluate our own words and thoughts.

But using Boolean search logic on a computer marks a giant step in the human species's relationship to thought and language. Just as the invention of the wax tablet made a giant stride in writing habits, forever marginalizing chiseled stones, so too Boolean search logic marks the new psychic framework of electronic text woven around us by computers. With electronic text we speed along a superhighway in the world of information, and Boolean search logic shifts our mental life into a high gear.

The Boolean search shows the characteristic way that we put questions to the world of information. When we pose a question to the Boolean world, we use keyboards, buzzwords, and thought bits to scan the vast store of knowledge. Keeping an abstract, cybernetic distance from the sources of knowledge, we set up tiny funnels to capture the onrush of data. The funnels sift out the "hits" triggered by our keywords. Through minute logical apertures, we observe the world much like a robot rapidly surveying the surface of things. We cover an enormous amount of material in an incredibly short time, but what we see comes through narrow thought channels.

Because they operate with potentially empty circles, the Boolean search terms propel us at breakneck pace through the knowledge tunnel. The computer supports our rapid survey of knowledge in the mode of scanning, and through the computer's tools we adapt to this mode of knowing. The scanning mode infiltrates all our other modes of knowing. The byte, the breezy bit, and the verbal/visual hit take the place of heavier substance.

Of course, the computerized reader doesn't pluck search terms out of pure air. The funnels we fashion often result from a carefully honed search strategy. In *How to Look It Up Online,* Glossbrenner advises the reader:

> Meditate. Seriously. You may not be a Ninja warrior preparing for battle, but it's not a bad analogy. If you ride in like a cowboy with six-guns blazing, firing off search terms as they come into your head, you'll stir up a lot of dust, expend a lot of ammunition, and be presented with a hefty bill but very little relevant information when you're done. . . . *Think* about the topic beforehand. Let your mind run free and flow into the subject. What do you know and what can you extrapolate about the subject?[2]

What Glossbrenner calls meditation actually works to serve calculation. What he describes is no more than a deep breath before taking the plunge. Meditation of this kind only sharpens an already determined will to find something definite. The user meditates in order to construct a narrower and more efficient thought tunnel. But even if we build our tunnels carefully, we still remain essentially tunnel dwellers.

The word *meditate* came originally from the Latin *meditari,* meaning "to be in the midst of, to hover in between." The meditation that Glossbrenner prescribes—prudent advice as far as it goes—helps the user zero in more closely on a target. It is the fill-up before a drive on the freeway, not the notion to hike in the countryside.

If we in fact take inspiration from the ninja warrior, we should recall Kitaro Nishida's teachings about "the logic of nothingness" *(mu no ronri).* The ninja warrior empties his mind before battle precisely by abandoning all specifics, by relaxing his attention so that the windows of awareness open to fresh perceptions. Genuine meditation refreshes our original potential to move in any direction. Our highest mind remains alert but flexible, firm but formless—in short, omnidirectional. Meditation truly expands the psyche and opens it to the delicate whisperings of intuition.

A Taoist sage once wrote that "thinking is merely one way of musing." Tightly controlled thought remains but a trickle in the daily stream of thoughts flowing through the psyche. Most of the time, the background mind muses with a soft undercurrent that quietly sorts things out, gently putting things together and taking them apart. We do our best thinking when sitting before the fireplace on a crisp winter night or lying on the grass on a balmy spring day. That's when our minds are most fully engaged, when we are musing.

Computer-guided questions sharpen thinking at the interface, but sharpness is not all. A more relaxed and natural state of mind, according to Siu, a Taoist, increases mental openness and allows things to emerge unplanned and unexpected. Rather than sharpen the determined will, we must preserve a state of no-mind in which our attention moves free of the constricted aims of consciousness. The musing mind operates on a plane more sensitive and more complex than that of consciously controlled thought. Musing is not wild in the sense of wanton but wild in the sense of flowing, unforced, and unboundedly fruitful. Thinking itself happens only when we suspend the inner musings of the mind long enough to favor a momentary precision, and even then thinking belongs to musing as a subset of our creative mind.

Now contrast the Boolean scan with a meditative perusal through traditional books. The book browser moves through symbols in the mode of musing. Books do in fact have a linear structure that unfolds sequentially, page by page, chapter by chapter, but seldom do readers tick to reading in this way. When we look something up in books, we often find ourselves browsing in ways that stir fresh discoveries, often turning up something more important than the discovery we had originally hoped to make. Some of our best reading is browsing. The book browser welcomes surprise, serendipity, new terrain, fresh connections where the angle of thought suddenly shifts. The browser meditates every moment while under way, musing along a gentle, wandering path through haphazard stacks of material. The browser forgoes immediate aims in order to ride gently above conscious purposes, in order to merge with an unexpected content in the pages. The browser feels wilderness beckon from afar.

The Boolean reader, on the contrary, knows in advance where the exits are, the on-ramps, and the well-marked rest stops. Processing texts through the Boolean search enhances the power of conscious, rational control. Such rationality is not the contemplative, meditative meander along a line of thinking, that the search through books can be. The pathway of thought, not to mention the logic of thought, disappears under a Boolean arrangement of freeways.

The Boolean search treats texts as data. When you search a database, you browse through recent material, often covering no more than the last ten years. Cutting off the past in this way streamlines the search. But a musing cut off from historical roots loses the fertile exposure to false starts, abandoned pathways, and unheard-of avenues. An exclusive focus on the recent past curtails our mental musings, and a narrow awareness sacrifices the intuitive mind.

Boolean search logic affects our mental vision just as long hours at the computer screen affect our eyesight. In a relaxed state, our eyes accept the world passively as a spectacle of discovery. Only when we strain to see do our eyes lose the surprise of perceptions. Constant straining induces a sensory myopia in which we need to strain in order to see better what we wish to see. We lose much of our peripheral vision when we use our eyes willfully. Likewise with the mind's eye. A relaxed and easy thought enjoys intuitive turns, and thinking at its best muses over human symbols. Boolean search logic cuts off the peripheral vision of the mind's eye. The computer interface can act like the artificial lens that helps us persist in our preconceptions. Boolean logic can unconsciously entrench us in our straining ways, hurting us as much mentally as the carpal tunnel syndrome hurts us physically. We may see more and see it more sharply, but the clarity will not hold the rich depth of natural vision. The world of thought we see will be flattened by an abstract remoteness, and the mind's eye, through its straining, will see a thin, flattened world with less light and brightness.

But notice how we do in fact always use some holistic guesswork, even when we are trying our best to shut off the mind's peripheral vision. Our Boolean searches could never begin without vague hunches and half-seen surmises. We need hunches and inklings to start with. Unfortunately, the Boolean search places our hunches in the service of a skeletal logic far removed from the direct operations of language.

If computers aid our searching minds, we must not abandon the books during our leisure time. The serendipitous search through books is necessary for knowledge and learning. Browsing often evokes daydreams and unsuspected connections; analogies and pertinent finds happen among the stacks of physically accessible pages. Although not as efficient as the

Boolean search, library browsing enriches us in unpredictable ways. Looking for something in a book library frequently leads to discoveries that overturn the questions we originally came to ask.

Book libraries hold unsystematic, unfiltered collections of human voices and thoughts. Libraries are repositories not so much of information as of the intuitions of countless authors. The books in libraries remain physical reminders of the individual voices of the authors, who often speak to us in ways that shock and disturb, in ways that break through our assumptions and preconceptions, in ways that calm and deepen. The word museum derives from the Greek word for the Muses, goddesses of dream, spontaneous creativity, and genial leisure. Libraries may be, in this strict sense, the last museums of the stored language, the last outposts of predigital intuition.

Today libraries are becoming information centers rather than places for musing. The Los Angeles County Public Library, the world's largest circulating library, receives more requests for information than requests for books. In 1989, one university in California opened the first library without books, a building for searching electronic texts. Books still remain a primary source, but they are rapidly becoming mere sources of information. A large volume of book sales doesn't necessarily prove that the book, with its special psychic framework, endures as such. Many books today gain attention as nonbooks linked to cinema, television, or audio recordings.

Searching through books was always more romance than busyness, more rumination than information. Information is by nature timebound. Supported by technological systems, information depends on revision and updating. When books become mere sources of information, they lose the atmosphere of contemplative leisure and timeless enjoyment. Old books then seem irrelevant, as they no longer pertain to current needs. One of the new breed of information publishers epitomizes this attitude in a pithy warning: "Any book more than two years old is of questionable value. Books more than four or five years old are a menace. OUT OF DATE = DANGEROUS."[3]

As book libraries turn into museums of alphabetic life, we should reclaim their original meaning. Museums are places for play, for playing with the muses that attract us, for dreams, intuitions, and enthusiasms. Information plugs us into the world of computerized productivity, but the open space of books balances our computer logic with the graces of intuition.

Notes

1. Alfred Glossbrenner, *How to Look It Up Online* (New York: St. Martin's Press, 1987), p. 109.
2. Ibid., p. 116.
3. Daniel Remer and Stephen Elias, *Legal Care for Your Software* (Berkeley, Calif.: Nolo Press, 1987), p. ii.

III

Social Contexts

What social impact do computers have? Are they transforming the workplace? Politics? Law? Are they changing our ideas on such matters as privacy and ownership? This section examines the social contexts of computing and the ways in which technologies affect the institutions and ideas that organize contemporary society. As you study these readings, you may also consult the website of the Electronic Frontier Foundation, which discusses many of these same issues, at eff.org.

16

Privacy in a Database Nation

Simson Garfinkel looks at the many threats to privacy that computer technology facilitates. Because they are repositories of vast amounts of data, databases, in particular, make it easy to "repurpose" information for uses other than that for which it was initially gathered. As you read this selection, you may also consult the following on-line sources on computers and privacy: the Electronic Privacy Information Center at epic.org and privacyfoundation.org.

Simson Garfinkel

WASHINGTON, DC, 1965. The Bureau of the Budget's proposal was simple yet revolutionary. Instead of each federal agency's investing in computers, storage technology, and operations personnel, the United States government would build a single National Data Center. The project would start by storing records from four federal agencies: population and housing data from the Bureau of the Census; employment information from the Bureau of Labor Statistics; tax information from the Internal Revenue Service; and benefit information from the Social Security Administration. Eventually, it would store far more.

While the original motivation was simply to cut costs, it soon became clear that there would be additional benefits. Accurate statistics could be created quickly and precisely from the nation's data. By building a single national database, the government could track down and stamp out the misspelled names and other inconsistent information that haunts large-scale databank projects. A single database would also let government officials and even outsiders use the data in the most efficient manner possible.

From "Database Nation" by Simson Garfinkel, 2000. Reprinted by permission of O'Reilly and Associates, Inc., www.oreilly.com.

The Princeton Institute for Advanced Study issued a report enthusiasti-cally supporting the databank project, saying that centralized storage of the records could actually improve the security of the information, and there-fore the privacy of the nation. Carl Kaysen, the Institute's director and the chairman of the study group, further urged that Congress pass legislation that would give the records additional protections, provide for privacy, and promote accountability of the databank workers. Others latched on to the idea, and the concept of the National Data Center slowly evolved into that of a massive databank containing cradle-to-grave electronic records for every U.S. citizen. The database would contain every person's electronic birth certificate, proof of citizenship, school records, draft registration and military service, tax records, Social Security benefits, and ultimately, their death records and estate information. The FBI might even use the system to store criminal records.

An article promoting the project appeared in the July 23, 1966 issue of the *Saturday Review*. Its title said everything: "Automated Government—How Computers Are Being Used in Washington to Streamline Personnel Administration to the Individual's Benefit."[1] But the article didn't have the intended result. Instead of applauding the technocratic vision, the U.S. Congress commenced a series of hearings on the threats of computerized databanks. Six months later, the *New York Times Magazine* ran an article titled "Don't Tell It to the Computer," which viciously attacked the idea of a centralized government data warehouse. Written by Vance Packard, au-thor of *The Naked Society* (a best-selling book that describes the invasion of privacy by government, business, and schools), the *Times* piece articu-lated what was to become a key argument against the project:

> The most disquieting hazard in a central data bank would be the placing of so much power in the hands of the people in a position to push computer buttons. When the details of our lives are fed into a central computer or other vast file-keeping systems, we all fall under the control of the machine's managers to some extent.[2]

The tide was turning. By 1968, the Bureau of the Budget said that it was doubtful that a practical plan for the center would be presented to the Ninetieth Congress. Meanwhile, the House Special Subcommittee on Inva-sion of Privacy issued a report holding that privacy must be the primary consideration in establishing computerized databanks, that no work should be done on a National Data Center until privacy could be guaranteed, and that the Bureau was at fault for not developing procedures to ensure privacy.

A poll by the Harvard University Program on Technology and Society the following year found that 56% of Americans opposed development of the National Data Center, on the grounds that it would invade their privacy.

That same year, in his book, *The Death of Privacy,* Jerry M. Rosenberg opened with this grave warning:

> When Adolf Hitler was aspiring to the Chancellorship of Germany, he acquired the confidential European Census and used it to weed out some of his potential antagonists.
>
> With the advance of technology, centralized data accumulation becomes easier, the reward for intrusion is increased, and control shifts to still fewer people.[3]

The National Data Center was never built. Instead, each federal agency was told to continue building its own computer systems. In lieu of creating a single databank, which could be used by unscrupulous bureaucrats to exercise inappropriate control over some people's lives, the government created dozens of databanks.

American businesses followed the government's example, often purchasing the same computers that had first been developed to fill government needs. The political decision not to build a central data repository set the direction that computers would follow for the next 30 years. Whereas a central databank would have pushed the development of massive mainframes and high-speed communications networks , developers created smaller, regional mainframes with basically no interconnecting networks until the late 1980s. But the decision to kill the project also had a profound impact on personal privacy—and not necessarily the impact that was expected. . . .

Almost Forty Years Later

I order a pair of white chocolate lattés, and hand my Mileage Plus First Card to the barista for payment. Although the drinks cost only $3 each, I'd rather charge the transaction than pay cash. But putting every single purchase on my credit card, I've managed to accumulate a balance of more than 50,000 frequent-flyer miles in less than a year—enough to buy my wife and myself a pair of roundtrip tickets anywhere in the United States.

Thirty years ago, the idea of a centralized computer tracking one's every purchase seemed like part of an Orwellian nightmare. Fifteen years ago, the mathematical genius Dr. David Chaum invented "E-Cash," an anonymous payment system designed to let consumers buy things electronically without revealing their identities. Who could have imagined that the day would come when millions of people would not only wish to have their purchases tracked—but would complain when transactions were missed? Yet that is one of the most intriguing results of socalled loyalty programs such as United's credit card: they have created massive databanks that paint a detailed electronic mosaic of consumer behavior, and they have done so with the willing participation of the monitored.

I call my mother when I get home. In the back of my mind, I know that a record of my call is being kept in the phone company's computer system. My records will probably never be reviewed by a human being, but at least once a month I hear of some big crime in which the suspect's guilt was "proven," in part, with these kinds of telephone records. In trials after the bombing of the Murrah Federal Building in Oklahoma City in 1995, for instance, one critical piece of evidence presented by the prosecution was the telephone call records from prepaid calling cards used by Timothy McVeigh and Terry Nichols. Rightwing extremists in the militia movement thought that calls made with these calling cards, purchased with cash, would be anonymous and untraceable. In fact, records of every call made with each card had been carefully kept. Prosecutors presented hundreds of pages of phone card records, with calls to auto racing tracks, chemical companies, motels, storage facilities, and rental truck outlets.[4] Those records allowed the prosecution to show that Timothy McVeigh and Terry Nichols had been in frequent contact by telephone during the months and weeks leading up to the most murderous act of terrorism in U.S. history.[5]

In the 1960s, the federal government operated most of the computers in the country. Commentators warned that the centralization of personal information might be planting the seeds of some future totalitarian regime. "My own hunch is that Big Brother, if he comes to the United States, will turn out to be not a greedy power-seeker but a relentless bureaucrat obsessed with efficiency," wrote Vance Packard in his *New York Times Magazine* article.

Articles written by journalists like Packard helped kill the National Data Center. But they did not stop data progress. Today, a mesh of computers operated by banks, utilities, and private businesses records an astonishing amount of information about us on a daily basis. In many cases, personal information is there for the taking. Instead of building a national databank, we have built a nation of databanks.

Identity Theft: A Stolen Self

. . . . In recent years, there has been a sudden and dramatic growth of a new kind of crime, made possible by the ready availability of both credit and once-private information on Americans. In these cases, one person finds another's name and Social Security number, applies for a dozen credit cards, and proceeds to run up huge bills. (Many banks made this kind of theft far easier than it should be by printing their customers' Social Security numbers on their bank statements.) Sometimes the thieves enjoy the merchandise for themselves, go on lavish trips, and eat in fine restaurants. Other times, the thieves fence the ill-gotten merchandise, turning it into cash. This crime has become so common that it has earned its own special name: *identity theft.*

Sometimes the crook gets the personal information from inside sources:

in April 1996, federal prosecutors charged a group of Social Security Administration employees with stealing personal information on more than 11,000 people and selling the data to credit fraud rings, who used the information to activate stolen credit cards and ring up huge bills.[6] Other times, crooks pose as homeless people and rummage through urban trash cans, looking for bank and credit card statements.

A typical case is what happened to Stephen Shaw, a Washington-based journalist.[7] Sometime during the summer of 1991, a car salesman from Orlando, Florida with a similar name—Steven Shaw—obtained Stephen Shaw's credit report. This is actually easier than it sounds. For years, Equifax had aggressively marketed its credit reporting service to car dealers. The service lets salespeople weed out the Sundy window-shoppers from the serious prospects by asking a customer's name and then surreptitiously disappearing into the back room and running a quick credit check. In all likelihood, says the Washington-based Shaw, the Shaw in Florida had simply gone fishing for someone with a similar-sounding name and a good credit history.

Once Steven Shaw in Florida had Stephen Shaw's Social Security number and credit report, he had everything he needed to steal the journalist's identity. Besides stating that Stephen Shaw had excellent credit, the report listed his current and previous addresses, his mother's maiden name, and the account numbers of all of his major credit cards. Jackpot!

"He used my information to open 35 accounts and racked up $100,000 worth of charges," says Stephen Shaw. "He tagged me for everything under the sun—car loans, personal loans, bank accounts, stereos, furniture, appliances, clothes, airline tickets."

Because all the accounts were opened using Stephen Shaw's name and Social Security number, all of the businesses held the Washington-based Stephen Shaw liable for the money that the other Shaw spent. And when the bills weren't paid, the companies told Equifax and the other credit bureaus that Stephen Shaw, the man who once had stellar credit, was now a deadbeat.

Not all cases of identity theft start with a stolen credit report or a misappropriated bank statement. Some cases begin with a fraudulently filed change of address form, directing the victim's mail to an abandoned building. And no paper trail need be created at all. In May 1997, the *Seattle Times* reported that hundreds of people in the Seattle area had received suspicious crank phone calls. The caller claimed to be from a radio station that was giving away money; the check would be in the mail as soon as the people picking up the phone provided their Social Security numbers.

Some people found the calls suspicious and telephoned the station or the police. Others presumably handed over the information that the callers requested. Similar scams are epidemic on America Online, the world's largest online service, where they have been given the evocative name *phishing.*

Shaw says it took him more than four years to resolve his problems—a period that appears to be typical for most identity theft victims. That's four years of harassing calls from bill collectors, of getting more and more angry letters in the mail, of not knowing what else is being done in your name. Four years of having your creditors think of you as a deadbeat. During this period, it's virtually impossible for the victim to obtain a new credit card or a mortgage. One of the cruelest results of identity theft is that many victims find themselves unemployable; in addition to job references, many businesses routinely check the credit reports of their job applicants.

Identity theft is made possible because credit card companies, always on the lookout for new customers, don't have a good way to verify the identity of a person who mails in an application or orders a credit card over the telephone. So the credit card companies make a dangerous assumption: they take it for granted that if you know a person's name, address, telephone number, Social Security number, and mother's maiden name, *you must be that person.* And when the merchandise is bought and the bills aren't paid, that person is the one held responsible.

Of course, it's relatively easy to learn a person's name, address, telephone number, Social Security number, and mother's maiden name. Credit bureaus hand this data out to their customers. Lookup services make this information available, at minimal cost, over the Internet. And many consumers, unaware of the risk, will readily divulge this information to people who call on the phone and claim to be from a bank or credit card agency.

Identity theft isn't a fundamentally new kind of crime. There are many stories from fairy tales and from the American West of con men who scammed a place to stay, fancy meals, and even the affection of an unknowing lady, by claiming to be somebody else. What's different now is that corporate willingness to extend credit has made many more people vulnerable to having their identity and reputation exploited without their knowledge. And because the credit is offered by mail or by telephone— often by either a computer running a program or by a low-paid customer service representative reading a script—it has become nearly impossible for the hero to convince the lady that she has been duped by a rogue.

Nobody is really sure how prevalent identity theft is today—estimates vary between 100,000 and 400,000 cases a year—but it is definitely on the rise. Ideally, the perpetrators should be jailed, fined, and otherwise punished. But law enforcement agencies are overwhelmed, and the courts have not allowed the true victims—the people who have had their identities stolen—to press charges against the perpetrators. That's because the law sees the company that issued the credit as the aggrieved party, not the people who have had their identities stolen. And most banks won't prosecute; it is easier to simply write off the loss and move on.

There are lots of technical changes that could be made to lower the incidence of identity theft. One change, for example, would be to require a person applying for a credit card to show up in person and have a photograph taken, recorded, and put on the back of the credit card. This would act as a deterrent, since most identity thieves don't want to have records created that could be used to trace back to their actual identity. But few credit card issuers would ever mandate the use of photographs, since it would effectively end the industry's marketing strategy of sending credit cards to new customers through the mail, without the need to have local branch offices.

Ultimately, identity theft is flourishing because credit-issuing companies are not being forced to cover the costs of their lax security procedures. The eagerness with which credit companies send out preapproved credit card applications creates the risk of fraud. When the fraud takes place, the credit issuer simply notes that information in the consumer's credit file and moves on; the consumer is left to pick up the pieces and otherwise deal with the cost of a stolen identity. It stands to reason, then, that the easiest way to reduce fraud would be to force the companies that are creating the risk to suffer the consequences. One way to do that would by penalizing companies that add provably false information to a consumer credit report in the same way we penalize individuals who file false police reports. Such penalties would force credit grantors to do a better job of identifying the individuals to whom they grant credit, and this, in turn, would do a good job of limiting the crime of identity theft.

Our Databanked Future

And what if we look in the other direction? Looking forward, we can see a future in which technology will increasingly be used to limit ambiguity. Anything that can be known will be known, and it will be known to a greater degree of precision than was ever thought possible. Left to its own devices, it's quite likely that business will repeat the mistakes of the past, designing systems that are fundamentally unfair, undemocratic, and unaccountable.

Back in 1965, the United States government stood at a computational crossroads. On the table was a proposal to create a massive government database. But when details of the project reached the public, the project was terminated. Instead, the U.S. Congress held hearings on the threat of computers to privacy, a U.S. government commission formulated the idea of data protection, and a (relatively) small part of the U.S. government's executive branch was given the mission to enforce a new set of laws.

We blew it. A national database could have headed off the excesses of the credit reporting industry. If the system had allowed strong user controls, or had avenues for redress, it further could have prevented the sea of errors that exist in the plethora of private databanks today. Moreover, with a public system, uses of the data for purposes other than those originally intended would have been debated in public, rather than proposed and approved behind closed doors.

Today, we stand at another computational crossroads. We are moving past the 1960s vision of computers that hold important financial, educational, and credit information. We are moving into an integrated future in which computers will track the most mundane and the most intimate aspects of our lives. They will measure and record the happenings on our planet. They will let us distinguish one person from another with the most fine-grained precision. Once again, there may be a need for the government to step in and set the rules for what can and cannot be done with this advanced information technology. Otherwise, we risk recreating the information abyss that we handled so deftly before. Sadly, this level of analysis is missing from most public discourse on credit card fraud, unauthorized uses of database information, and identity theft.

Databank technology has a fundamental problem: there is no way to guarantee that the information in the databank is correct. We should focus on this problem, and try to build computer and societal systems that are resilient in the face of error. Instead, we are doing the reverse. Bankers, law enforcement and immigration officials, and policymakers are looking for a quick technological fix to the problem of identifying individuals. . . . We'll see why this approach ultimately can't work.

The Information Crisis

As an experiment, make a list of the data trails that you leave behind on a daily basis. Did you buy lunch with a credit card? Write that down. Did you buy lunch with cash, but visit the automatic teller machine (ATM) beforehand? If so, then that withdrawal makes up your data shadow as well. Every long distance phone call, any time you leave a message inside a voice mailbox, and every web page you access on the Internet—all of these are part of your comprehensive data profile.

You are more likely to leave records if you live in a city, if you pay for things with credit cards, and if your work requires that you use a telephone or a computer. You will leave fewer records if you live in the country or if you are not affluent. This is really no surprise: detailed records are what makes the modern economy possible.

What is surprising, though, is the amount of collateral information that these records reveal. Withdraw cash from an ATM, and a computer records not just how much money you took out, but the fact that you were physically located at a particular place and time. Make a telephone call to somebody who has Caller ID, and a little box records not just your phone number (and possibly your name), but also the exact time that you placed your call. Browse the Internet, and the web server on the other side of your computer's screen doesn't just record every page that you download—it also records the speed of your computer's modem, the kind of web browser you are using, and even your geographical location.

There's nothing terribly new here, either. In 1986, John Diebold wrote about a bank that seven years earlier

> had recently installed an automatic teller machine network and noticed "that an unusual number of withdrawals were being made every night between midnight and 2:00 a.m." . . . Suspecting foul play, the bank hired detectives to look into the matter. It turns out that many of the late-night customers were withdrawing cash on their way to a local red light district.[8]

An article about the incident that appeared in the Knight News Service observed: "there's a bank someplace in America that knows which of its customers paid a hooker last night."[9] (Diebold, one of America's computer pioneers in the 1960s and 1970s, had been an advocate of the proposed National Data Center. But by 1986, he had come to believe that building the Data Center would have been a tremendous mistake, because it would have concentrated too much information in one place.)

I call records such as banks' ATM archives *hot files*. They are juicy, they reveal unexpected information, and they exist largely outside the scope of most people's understanding.

Over the past 15 years, we've seen a growing use of hot files. One of the earliest cases that I remember occurred in the 1980s, when investigators for the U.S. Drug Enforcement Agency started scanning through the records of lawn-and-garden stores and correlating the information with data dumps from electric companies. The DEA project was called Operation Green Merchant; by 1993, the DEA, together with state and local authorities, had seized nearly 4,000 growing operations, arrested more than 1,5000 violators, and frozen millions of dollars in illicitly acquired profits and assets.[10] Critics charged that the program was a dragnet that caught both the innocent and the guilty. The investigators were searching out people who were clandestinely raising marijuana in their basements. While the agents did find some pot farmers, they also raided quite a few innocent gardeners—including one who lived next to an editor at the *New York Times*. The *Times* eventually wrote an editorial, but it didn't stop the DEA's practices.

Americans got another dose of hot file surprise in the fall of 1987, when President Ronald Reagan nominated Judge Robert Bork to the Supreme Court of the United States. Bork's nomination was fiercely opposed by women's groups, who said that the judge had a history of ruling against women's issues; they feared that Bork would be the deciding vote to help the Court overturn a woman's right to an abortion. Looking for dirt, a journalist from Washington, D.C.'s liberal *City Paper* visited a video rental store in Bork's neighborhood and obtained a printout from the store's computer of every movie that Bork had ever rented there. The journalist had hoped that Bork would be renting pornographic films. As it turned out, Bork's tastes in video veered towards mild fare: the 146 videos listed on the printout were mostly Disney movies and Hitchcock films.

Nevertheless, Bork's reputation was still somewhat damaged. Some accounts of the Bork story that have been published and many offhanded remarks at cocktail parties often omit the fact that the journalist came up empty in the search for pornography. Instead, these accounts erroneously give the impression that Bork was a fan of porn, or at least allow the reader to draw that conclusion.

The problem with hot files, then, is that they are too hot: on the one hand, they reveal information about us that many people think a dignified society keeps private; on the other hand, they are easily misinterpreted. And it turns out that these records are also easily faked: if the clerk at the video rental store had wanted to do so, that person could easily have added a few dozen porno flicks to the record, and nobody could have proved that the record had been faked.

As computerized record-keeping systems become more prevalent in our society, we are likely to see more and more cases in which the raw data collected by these systems for one purpose is used for another. Indeed, advancing technology makes such releases all the more likely. In the past, computer systems simply could not store all of the information that they could collect: it was necessary to design systems so that they would periodically discard data when it was no longer needed. But today, with the dramatic developments in data storage technology, it's easy to store information for months or years after it is no longer needed. As a result, computers are now retaining an increasingly more complete records of our lives— as they did with Judge Bork's video rental records. Ask yourself this: what business did the video rental store have keeping a list of the movies that Bork had rented, after the movies had been returned?

This sea of records is creating a new standard of accountability for our society. Instead of relying on trust or giving people the benefit of the doubt, we can now simply check the record and see who was right and who was wrong. The ready availability of personal information also makes things easier for crooks, stalkers, blackmail artists, con men, and others who are up to no good. One of the most dramatic cases was the murder of actress Rebecca Schaeffer in 1989. Schaeffer had gone to great lengths to protect her privacy. But a 19-year-old crazed fan, who allegedly wanted to meet her, hired a private investigator to find out her home address. The investigator went to California's Department of Motor Vehicles, which at the time made vehicle registration information available to anyone who wanted it, since the information was part of the public record. The fan then went to Schaeffer's house, waited for four hours, and shot her once in the chest when she opened her front door.[11]

False Data Syndrome

Another insidious problem with this data sea is something I call *false data syndrome*. Because much of the information in the data sea is correct, we are predisposed to believe that it is all correct—a dangerous assumption that is all too easy to make. The purveyors of the information themselves often encourage this kind of sloppy thinking by failing to acknowledge the shortcomings of their systems.

For example, in 1997, the telephone company NYNEX (now part of Bell Atlantic) launched an aggressive campaign to sell the new Caller ID service to its subscribers. With the headline "See Who's Calling Before You Pick Up the Phone," the advertisement read:

> Caller ID lets you see both the *name and number* of the incoming call so you can decide to take the call now or return it later. Even if the caller doesn't leave a message, your Caller ID box automatically stores the name, number, and time of the incoming call. Caller ID also works with Call Waiting, so you can see who's calling *even while you're talking to someone else.*[12]

Clearly, NYNEX was confusing human identities with telephone numbers. Caller ID doesn't show the telephone number that belongs to the person who is making the call—it shows the number of the telephone from which the call is being placed. So-called "enhanced" Caller ID services that display a name and number don't really display the caller's name—they display the name of the person who is listed in the telephone book. If I make an obscene call from your house during a party, or if I use your telephone to make a threat on the life of the president of the United States (a federal crime), Caller ID will say that you are the culprit—not me.

The Tracking Process: How Our Information Is Turned Against Us

Nobody set out to build a society in which the most minute details of everyday life are permanently recorded for posterity. But this is the future that we are marching towards, thanks to a variety of social, economic, and technological factors.

Humans are born collectors. Psychologically, it's much easier to hold on to something than to throw it away. This is all the more true for data. Nobody really feels comfortable erasing business correspondence or destroying old records—you never know when something might be useful. Advancing technology is making it possible to realize our collective dream of never throwing anything away—or at least never throwing away a piece of information.

The first computer that I bought in 1978 stored information on cassette tapes. I could fit 200 kilobytes on a 30-minute cassette, if I was lucky. The computer that I use today has an internal hard disk that can store 6 gigabytes of information—a 30,000-fold increase in just two decades. And this story is hardly unique: all over the world, businesses, governments, and individuals have seen similar improvements in their ability to store data. As a civilization, we've used this newfound ability to store more and more minute details of everyday existence. We are building the world's *datasphere:* a body of information that describes the Earth and our actions upon it.

Building the world's database is a three-step process—one that we've been blindly following without considering its ramifications for the future of privacy. First, industrialized society creates new opportunities for data collection. Next, we dramatically increase the ease of automatically capturing information into a computer. The final step is to arrange this information into a large-scale database so it can be easily retrieved at a moment's notice.

Once the day-to-day events of our lives are systematically captured in a machine-readable format, this information takes on a life of its own. It finds new uses. It becomes indispensable in business operations. And it often flows from computer to computer, from business to business, and between industry and government. If we don't step back and stop the collection and release of this data, we'll soon have a world in which every moment and every action is permanently "on the record."

The Extraction of Self

Before she resigned from the Federal Trade Commission, Commissioner Christine Varney painted the following agent-based marketing scenario for National Public Radio:

> Suppose that every year you send your wife flowers on your anniversary, and I notice that this year you don't, and I notice that she is not in San Francisco but in Los Angeles at the Four Seasons Hotel, and I ask you if I should send her flowers? Your reaction, whether you are ecstatic or horrified, depends on one thing: consent.[13]

Actually, whether you are ecstatic or horrified would probably depend on many other factors. If you were planning to meet your wife at the hotel, you might be pleased with the helpful suggestion. If you thought your wife was visiting her sick mother in upstate New York, the message might hasten your eventual separation and divorce. And if your wife had been reported missing, the message might help you locate her. Consent doesn't really enter into this story; you might have given consent for such a matching program when you signed up for the credit card, but nevertheless be tremendously disturbed by the outcome. On the other hand, if you did not give consent for the program, but it nevertheless told you an important piece of information you didn't know, you might be thankful just the same. Varney's statement was misleading for another reason: consent is not needed to execute this not-so-furistic agent-based marketing strategy. All of the information necessary to complete Varney's example is available today to banks and credit card companies. What's holding back these applications isn't the lack of consumer consent, but the lack of a strong business case that such software will make money for the companies.

The Electronic Privacy Information Center's Marc Rotenberg predicts that next-generation agents will scan the world for personal information about an individual, then construct a predictive model for use by marketers and others. Rotenberg calls this *the extraction of self.*

The extraction of self is one of the greatest threats posed by computers to personal privacy and human identity. The profile could know every document you've ever read, every person you've ever known, every place you've ever been, and every word you've ever said that has been recorded. Your identity would no longer exist just inside of you, but in the model. "It would know more about you than you know about yourself," Rotenberg says. "At such a point, we don't lose just individuality, we lose the individual."[14]

In fact, the first self has already been extracted. Back in 1980, Janet Kolodner, a graduate student of AI pioneer Roger Schank at Yale University, created a program called CYRUS. Kolodner's program was an attempt to model the memory of President Carter's Secretary of State, Cyrus Vance. Writes AI historian Daniel Crevier:

> The program actually thought of itself as Vance and obtained its "memories" from news stories about Vance intercepted by FRUMP (another AI program). Once asked whether his wife had ever met the wife of Israel's Prime Minister Begin, CYRUS remembered that Vance and Begin had participated in a social occasion to which it was likely they had taken their wives, and thus replied—accurately, as it turned out—"Yes, at a state dinner in Israel in January 1980."[15]

There is no technological means of preventing the extraction of self. But if privacy is to exist in the future, then this technology must be regulated. And there are many ways that such regulation could take place.

One legal tool to prevent the extraction of self might be copyright. U.S. law and international treaty recognize a special kind of copyright called a *compilation copyright.* This copyright protects newspapers, compact discs, and other sorts of information-rich media from illegal copying even when the individual items they contain are not subject to copyright protection. The doctrine of compilation copyright could be extended to cover individual components of a person's life. You might not have copyright protection on each sentence you say, each product you buy, or the names of each of the streets you've lived on since you were born. But when these facts are assembled into a whole, they might be held to be an unacceptable appropriation of your mortal essence. People or companies engaged in this practice could then be fined or jailed.

Another way to attack this problem could be the adoption and enforcement of rigorous privacy laws preventing the collection and compilation of personal information without the explicit permission of the data subject. In effect, lawmakers would be rigorously applying the third principle of the Code of Fair Information Practices: preventing information about a person that was obtained for one purpose from being used or made available for other purposes without the person's consent. Affirmative consent to data collection and intended uses should be a matter of law.

Technology Is Not Neutral

I met an undergraduate from the Massachusetts Institute of Technology at a conference once. He told me, in all sincerity, that technology is *privacy neutral*. "Technology can be used to invade privacy, or it can be used to protect privacy," he said.

The MIT undergraduate reminded me a lot of myself: I had said much the same thing when I was an undergraduate at the Institute. This "technology is neutral" argument is a very comforting idea for people who are being trained to work with the world's most advanced technology. "Technology isn't the problem," we like to think. "It's the way people use technology that's the problem!"

"Technology is neutral" is a comforting idea, but it's wrong. History is replete with the dehumanizing effects of technology.[16] Although it's possible to use technology to protect or enhance privacy, the tendency of technological advances is to do the reverse. It is harder, and frequently more expensive, to build devices and construct services that protect people's privacy than to destroy it.

For example, in my last year at MIT, the Institute purchased a very expensive electronic telephone switch called a 5ESS. Within a few years, digital ISDN telephones were widely deployed throughout the Institute. Each telephone instrument had a little computer screen, a dozen or more pushbuttons, twice as many lights, and a microphone for the phone's built-in speakerphone. As I learned more about the phones, I discovered that each button and light on the instrument was "soft"—that is, any button and any light could be programmed by the 5ESS to have any feature: it was all a question of software.

Unfortunately, the design of the ISDN telephones allows them to be used for a purpose that was never intended: bugging offices on campus. The bug is the built-in microphone that's used for the speakerphone. Normally, when you use the ISDN telephone to place a speakerphone call, a little red light next to the mike turns on to let you know that the mike is recording. But because the phone is completely driven by software, turning on the microphone and turning on the little red light are distinct operations. By reprogramming the 5ESS, it's possible to turn on the mike without turning on the light. The telephone could just as easily have been designed a different way—for example, the little red light could have been designed to turn on automatically whenever the microphone was activated without any intervention from the 5ESS. The phone wasn't built this way because the designers at AT&T didn't make privacy a primary design goal.

On the other hand, an example of pro-privacy engineering is the small video camera that computer maker Silicon Graphics included with many of its desktop workstations. The video camera is for teleconferencing: it sits on top of the computer monitor, its lens pointed at the computer's user. Normally, the camera's shutter is controlled by software: run a program and the camera starts recording. Kill the program, and the camera stops. But the camera has a physical shutter as well—there is a small plastic slider that can be slipped in front of the camera's eye, blocking its view. Surely, the camera with the plastic shutter is more expensive to make than other low-cost video cameras that lack a physical blocking device. But if you sit down in front of the machine and slide the shutter in front of the lens, you know with certainty that the camera can't be monitoring your actions. Alas, this shutter is an extra design step that many other vendors choose to forgo.

One of the inherent problems with privacy-protecting technology is that it is very difficult to know whether or not the technology is working properly. If your privacy is being violated, you might observe a tell-tale symptom: you might get junk mail or harassing phone calls. You might see your personal information posted on the Internet. You might even discover a video camera in your bedroom. But it's impossible to know for sure if your privacy is being protected. What's more, when privacy violations are discovered and corrected, it's usually very difficult to know if the fixes were made in the technically correct manner.

Technology is not privacy neutral. The overwhelming tendency of technology is to out privacy. By its very nature, technology is intrusive. Advancing technology permits greater cataloging and measuring of the world around us. It allows us to create a global memory that can be easily searched. And technology allows greater control of nondeterministic processes, whether they're a person's selection of breakfast cereal or the election of a political candidate. We ignore this tendency at our own peril.

Notes

1. "Automated Government—How Computers Are Being Used in Washington to Streamline Personnel Administration to the Individual's Benefit," *Saturday Review,* July 23, 1966.
2. Vance Packard, "Don't Tell It to the Computer," *New York Times Magazine,* January 8, 1967.
3. Jerry M. Rosenberg, *The Death of Privacy* (New York: Random House, 1969), p. 1.
4. "McVeigh Prosecutor Cries During Trial," Associated Press, May 8, 1997. Available online at http://herald-mail.com/news/1997/bombing_trial/stories/may8_97.html.
5. "Answers for the Evidence," *Detroit Free Press,* December 17, 1997. Available online at http://www.freepress.com/news/bombtrial/qcase17.htm.
6. Jim Mallory, "Social Security Workers Charged with Data Theft" Newsbytes News Network (http://www.newsbytes.com/), August 4, 1996.
7. Interview by author, April 1995. See also "Separating the Equifax from Fiction," *Wired Magazine,* September 1995, p. 96.
8. James Finn and Leonard R. Sussman, eds., *Today's American: How Free?* (New York: Freedom House, 1986), p. 111.
9. Ibid.
10. U.S. Department of Justice Drug Enforcement Administration," U.S. Drug Threat Assessment: 1993. Drug Intelligence Report, Availability, Price, Purity, Use, and Trafficking of Drugs in the United States," September 1993, DEA-93042. Available online at http://mir.drugtext.org/druglibrary/schaffer/GOV-PUB/usdta.htm.
11. "TV-Movie Actress Slain in Apartment," Associated Press, July 19, 1989. "Arizona Holds Man in Killing of Actress," Associated Press, July 20, 1989. "Suspect in Slaying Paid to find Actress," Associated Press, July 23, 1989.
12. NYNEX advertisement, mailed to customers in Spring 1997.
13. Christine Varney, FTC commissioner, speaking to John McChesney on National Public Radio's *All Things Considered,* June 10, 1997.
14. Personal communication (email), August 27, 1997.
15. Daniel Crevier, *AI: The Tumultuous History of the Search for Artificial Intelligence* (New York: Basic Books, 1993).
16. Jacques Ellul, *The Technological Society* (New York: Random House, 1967).

17

The GNU Manifesto

Richard Stallman, one of the original developers of UNIX, argues in his GNU Manifesto that the proprietary systems that now govern software development and distribution undermine the true promise of computer technology. Though Stallman's essay was written well over a decade ago, it is considered a classic insofar as it is still invoked by those who argue that "information should be free." (See also Spafford, "Are Hacker Break-ins Ethical?)

Richard M. Stallman

What's GNU? GNU's Not Unix!

GNU, which stands for GNU's Not Unix, is the name of the complete Unix-compatible software system which I am writing so that I can give it away free to everyone who can use it.[1] Several other volunteers are helping me. Contributions of time, money, programs, and equipment are greatly needed.

So far we have a portable C and Pascal compiler which compiles for Vax and 6800 (though needing much rewriting), an Emacs-like text editor with Lisp for writing editor commands, a yacc-compatible parser generator, a linker, and around 35 utilities. A shell (command interpreter) is nearly completed. When the kernel and a debugger are written . . . it will be possible to distribute a GNU system suitable for program development. After this we will add a text formatter, an Empire game, a spreadsheet, and hundreds of other things, plus on-line documentation. We hope to supply, eventually, everything useful that normally comes with a Unix system, and more.

GNU will be able to run Unix programs, but will not be identical to Unix. We will make all improvements that are convenient, based on our experience with other operating systems. In particular, we plan to have longer filenames, file version numbers, a crashproof file system, filename completion perhaps, terminal-independent display support, and eventually a Lisp-based window system through which several Lisp programs and ordinary Unix programs can share a screen. Both C and Lisp will be available as system programming languages. We will try to support UUCP, MIT Chaosnet, and Internet protocols for communication.

GNU is aimed initially at machines in the 6800/16000 class, with virtual memory, because they are the easiest machines to make it run on. The extra effort to make it run on smaller machines will be left to someone who wants to use it on them.

Why I Must Write GNU

I consider that the golden rule requires that if I like a program I must share it with other people who like it. Software sellers want to divide the users and conquer them, making each user agree not to share with others. I refuse to break solidarity with other users in this way. I cannot in good conscience sign a nondisclosure agreement or a software license agreement. For years I worked within the artificial intelligence lab [at the Massachusetts Institute of Technology] to resist such tendencies and other inhospitalities, but now they have gone too far: I cannot remain in an institution where such things are done for me against my will.

So that I can continue to use computers without dishonor, I have decided to put together a sufficient body of free software so that I will be able to get along without any software that is not free. I have resigned from the AI lab to deny MIT any legal excuse to prevent me from giving GNU away.

Why GNU Will Be Compatible with Unix

Unix is not my ideal system, but it is not too bad. The essential features of Unix seem to be good ones, and I think I can fill in what Unix lacks without spoiling them. And a system compatible with Unix would be convenient for many other people to adopt.

How GNU Will Be Available

GNU is not in the public domain. Everyone will be permitted to modify and redistribute GNU, but no distributor will be allowed to restrict its further redistribution. That is to say, proprietary modifications will not be allowed. I want to make sure that all versions of GNU remain free.

Why Many Other Programmers Want to Help

I have found many other programmers who are excited about GNU and want to help.

Many programmers are unhappy about the commercialization of system software. It may enable them to make more money, but it requires them to feel in conflict with other programmers in general rather than feel as comrades. The fundamental act of friendship among programmers is the sharing of programs: marketing arrangements now typically used essentially forbid programmers to treat others as friends. The purchaser or software must choose between friendship and obeying the law. Naturally, many decide that friendship is more important. But those who believe in law often do not feel at ease with either choice. They become cynical and think that programming is just a way of making money.

By working on and using GNU rather than proprietary programs, we can be hospitable to everyone and obey the law. In addition, GNU serves as an example to inspire and a banner to rally others to join us in sharing. This can give us a feeling of harmony which is impossible if we use software that is not free. For about half the programmers I talk to, this is an important happiness that money cannot replace.

How You Can Contribute

I am asking computer manufacturers for donations of machines and money. I'm asking individuals for donations of programs and work.

One consequence you can expect if you donate machines is that GNU will run on them at an early date. The machines should be complete, ready-to-use systems, approved for use in a residential area, and not in need of sophisticated cooling or power.

I have found very many programmers eager to contribute part-time work for GNU. For most projects, such part-time distributed work would be very hard to coordinate; the independently written parts would not work together. But for the particular task of replacing Unix, this problem is absent. A complete Unix system contains hundreds of utility programs, each of which is documented separately. Most interface specifications are fixed by Unix compatibility. If each contributor can write a compatible replacement for a single Unix utility, and make it work properly in place of the original on a Unix system, then these utilities will work right when you put together. Even allowing for Murphy to create a few unexpected problems, assembling these components will be a feasible task. (The kernel will require closer communication and will be worked on by a small, tight group.)

If I get donations of money, I may be able to hire a few people full- or part-time. The salary won't be high by programmers' standards, but I'm looking for people for whom building community spirit is as important as making money. I view this as a way of enabling dedicated people to devote their full energies to working on GNU by sparing them the need to make a living in another way.

Why All Computer Users Will Benefit

Once GNU is written, everyone will be able to obtain good system software free, just like air.[2]

This means much more than just saving everyone the price of a Unix license. It means that much wasteful duplication of system programming effort will be avoided. This effort can go instead into advancing the state of the art.

Complete system sources will be available to everyone. As a result, a user who needs changes in the system will always be free to make them himself, or hire any available programmer or company to make them for him. Users will no longer be at the mercy of one programmer or company which owns the sources and is in sole position to make changes.

Schools will be able to provide a much more educational environment by encouraging all students to study and improve the system code. Harvard's computer lab used to have the policy that no program could be installed on the system if its sources were not on public display, and upheld it by actually refusing to install certain programs. I was very much inspired by this.

Finally, the overhead of considering who owns the system software and what one is or is not entitled to do with it will be lifted.

Arrangements to make people pay for using a program, including licensing of copies, always incur a tremendous cost to society through the cumbersome mechanisms necessary to figure out how much (that is, which programs) a person must pay for. And only a police state can force everyone to obey them. Consider a space station where air must be manufactured at great cost: charging each breather per liter of air may be fair, but wearing the metered gas mask all day and all night is intolerable even if everyone can afford to pay the air bill. And the TV cameras everywhere to see if you ever take the mask off are outrageous. It's better to support the air plant with a head tax and chuck the masks.

Copying all or parts of a program is as natural to a programmer as breathing, and as productive. It ought to be as free.

Some Easily Rebutted Objections to GNU's Goals

"Nobody will use it if it is free, because that means they can't rely on any support."

"You have to charge for the program to pay for providing the support."

If people would rather pay for GNU plus service than get GNU free without service, a company to provide just service to people who have obtained GNU free ought to be profitable.[3]

We must distinguish between support if the form of real programming work and mere hand-holding. The former is something one cannot rely on from a software vendor. If your problem is not shared by enough people, the vendor will tell you to get lost.

If your business needs to be able to rely on support, the only way is to have all the necessary sources and tools. Then you can hire any available person to fix your problem; you are not at the mercy of any individual. With Unix, the price of sources puts this out of consideration for most businesses. With GNU this will be easy. It is still possible for there to be no available competent person, but this problem cannot be blamed on distribution arrangements. GNU does not eliminate all the world's problems, only some of them.

Meanwhile, the users who know nothing about computers need handholding: doing things for them which they could easily do themselves but don't know how.

Such services could be provided by companies that sell just handholding and repair service. If it is true that users would rather spend money and get a product with service, they will also be willing to buy the service having got the product free. The service companies will compete in quality and price; users will not be tied to any particular one. Meanwhile, those of us who don't need the service should be able to use the program without paying for the service.

"You cannot reach many people without advertising, and you must charge for the program to support that."

It's no use advertising a program people can get free."

There are various forms of free or very cheap publicity that can be used to inform numbers of computer users about something like GNU. But it may be true that one can reach more microcomputer users with advertising. If this is really so, a business which advertises the service of copying and mailing GNU for a fee ought to be successful enough to pay for its advertising and more. This way, only the users who benefit from the advertising pay for it.

On the other hand, if many people get GNU from their friends, and such companies don't succeed, this will show that advertising was not really necessary to spread GNU. Why is it that free market advocates don't want to let the free market decide this?[4]

"My company needs a proprietary operating system to get a competitive edge."

GNU will remove operating system software from the realm of competition. You will not be able to get an edge in this area, but neither will your competitors be able to get an edge over you. You and they will compete in other areas, while benefiting mutually in this one. If your business is selling an operating system, you will not like GNU, but that's tough on you. If your business is something else, GNU can save you from being pushed into the expensive business of selling operating systems.

I would like to see GNU development supported by gifts from many manufacturers and users, reducing the cost to each.[5]

"Don't programmers deserve a reward for their creativity?"

If anything deserves a reward, it is social contribution. Creativity can be a social contribution, but only in so far as society is free to use the results. If programmers deserve to be rewarded for creating innovative programs, by the same token they deserve to be punished if they restrict the use of these programs.

"Shouldn't a programmer be able to ask for a reward for his creativity?"

There is nothing wrong with wanting pay for work, or seeking to maximize one's income, as long as one does not use means that are destructive. But the means customary in the field of software today are based on destruction.

Extracting money from users of a program by restricting their use of it is destructive because the restrictions reduce the amount and the ways that the program can be used. This reduces the amount of wealth that humanity derives from the program. When there is a deliberate choice to restrict, the harmful consequences are deliberate destruction.

The reason a good citizen does not use such destructive means to become wealthier is that, if everyone did so, we would all become poorer from the mutual destructiveness. This is Kantian ethics; or, the Golden Rule. Since I do not like the consequences that result if everyone hoards information, I am required to consider it wrong for one to do so. Specifically, the desire to be rewarded for one's creativity does not justify depriving the world in general of all or part of that creativity.

"Won't programmers starve?"

I could answer that nobody is forced to be a programmer. Most of us cannot manage to get any money for standing on the street and making faces. But we are not, as a result, condemned to spend our lives standing on the street making faces, and starving. We do something else.

But that is the wrong answer because it accepts the questioner's implicit assumption: that without ownership of software, programmers cannot possibly be paid a cent. Supposedly it is all or nothing.

The real reason programmers will not starve is that it will still be possible for them to get paid for programming; just not paid as much as now.

Restricting copying is not the only basis for business in software. It is the most common basis because it brings in the most money. If it were prohibited, or rejected by the customer, software business would move to other bases of organization which are now used less often. There are always numerous ways to organize any kind of business.

Probably programming will not be as lucrative on the new basis as it is now. But that is not an argument against the change. It is not considered an injustice that salesclerks make the salaries that they now do. If programmers made the same, that would not be an injustice either. (In practice they would still make considerably more than that.)

"Don't people have a right to control how their creativity is used?"

"Control over the use of one's ideas" really constitutes control over other people's lives; and it is usually used to make their lives more difficult.

People who have studied the issue of intellectual property rights carefully (such as lawyers) say that there is no intrinsic right to intellectual property. The kinds of supposed intellectual property rights that the government recognizes were created by specific acts of legislation for specific purposes.

For example, the patent system was established to encourage inventors to disclose the details of their inventions. Its purpose was to help society rather than to help inventors. At the time, the life span of 17 years for a patent was short compared with the rate of advance of the state of the art. Since patients are an issue only among manufacturers, for whom the cost and effort of a license agreement are small compared with setting up production, the patents often do not do much harm. They do not obstruct most individuals who use patented products.

The idea of copyright did not exist in ancient times, when authors frequently copied other authors at length in works of nonfiction. This practice was useful, and is the only way many authors' works have survived even in part. The copyright system was created expressly for the purpose of encouraging authorship. In the domain for which it was invented—books, which could be copied economically only on a printing press—it did little harm, and did not obstruct most of the individuals who read the books.

All intellectual property rights are just licenses granted by society because it was thought, rightly or wrongly, that society as a whole would benefit by granting them. But in any particular situation, we have to ask: are we really better of granting such license? What kind of act are we licensing a person to do?

The case of programs today is very different from that of books a hundred years ago. The fact that the easiest way to copy a program is from one neighbor to another, the fact that a program has both source code and object code which are distinct, and the fact that a program is used rather than read and enjoyed, combine to create a situation in which a person who enforces a copyright is harming society as a whole both materially and spiritually; in which a person should not do so regardless of whether the law enables him to.

"Competition makes things get done better."

The paradigm of competition is a race: by rewarding the winner, we encourage everyone to run faster. When capitalism really works this way, it does a good job; but its defenders are wrong in assuming it always works this way. If the runners forget why the reward is offered and become intent on winning, no matter how, they may find other strategies—such as attacking other runners. If the runners get into a fist fight, they will all finish late.

Proprietary and secret software is the moral equivalent of runners in a fist fight. Sad to say, the only referee we've got does not seem to object to fights; he just regulates them ("For every ten years you run, you can fire one shot"). He really ought to break them up, and penalize runners for even trying to fight.

"Won't everyone stop programming without a monetary incentive?"

Actually, many people will program with absolutely no monetary incentive. Programming has an irresistible fascination for some people, usually the people who are best at it. There is no shortage of professional musicians who keep at it even though they have no hope of making a living that way.

But really this question, though commonly asked, is not appropriate to the situation. Pay for programmers will not disappear, only become less. So the right question is, will anyone program with a reduced monetary incentive? My experience shows that they will.

For more than ten years, many of the world's best programmers worked at the artificial intelligence lab for far less money than they could have had anywhere else. They got many kinds of nonmonetary rewards: fame and appreciation, for example. And creativity is also fun, a reward in itself.

Then most of them left when offered a chance to do the same interesting work for a lot of money.

What the facts show is that people will program for reasons other than riches; but if given a chance to make a lot of money as well, they will come to expect and demand it. Low-paying organizations do poorly in competition with high-paying ones, but they do not have to do badly if the high-paying ones are banned.

"We need the programmers desperately. If they demand that we stop helping our neighbors, we have to obey."

You're never so desperate that you have to obey this sort of demand. Remember: millions for defense, but not a cent for tribute!

"Programmers need to make a living somehow."

In the short run, this is true. However, there are plenty of ways that programmers could make a living without selling the right to use a program.

This way is customary now because it brings programmers and businessmen the most money, not because it is the only way to make a living. It is easy to find other ways if you want to find them. Here are a number of examples.

A manufacturer introducing a new computer will pay for the porting of operating systems onto the new hardware.

The sale of teaching, hand-holding, and maintenance services could also employ programmers.

People with new ideas could distribute programs as freeway, asking for donations from satisfied users, or selling hand-holding services. I have met people who are already working this way successfully.

Users with related needs can form users' groups and pay dues. A group would contract with programming companies to write programs that the group's members would like to use.

All sorts of development can be funded with a Software Tax: Suppose everyone who buys a computer had to pay x percent of the price as a software tax. The government gives this to an agency like the NSF [National Science Foundation] to spend on software development. But if the computer buyer makes a donation to software development himself, he can take a credit against the tax. He can donate to the project of his own choosing— often chosen because he hopes to use the results when it is done. He can take credit for any amount of donation up to the total tax he had to pay. The total tax rate could be decided by a vote of the payers of the tax, weighted according to the amount they will be taxed on.

The consequences:

- The computer-using community supports software development.

- This community decides what level of support is needed.

- Users who care which projects their share is spent on can choose this for themselves.

In the long run, making programs free is a step toward the post-scarcity world, where nobody will have to work very hard just to make a living. People will be free to devote themselves to activities that are fun, such as programming, after spending the necessary ten hours a week on required tasks such as legislation, family, counseling, robot repair, and asteroid prospecting. There will be no need to be able to make a living from programming.,

We have already greatly reduced the amount of work that the whole society must do for its actual productivity, but only a little of this has translated itself into leisure for workers because much nonproductive activity is required to accompany productive activity. The main causes of this are bureaucracy and isometric struggles against competition. Free software will greatly reduce these drains in the area of software production. We must do this, in order for technical gains in productivity to translate into less work for us.

Notes

1. The wording here was careless. The intention was that nobody would have to pay for *permission* to use the GNU system. But the words don't make this clear, and people often interpret them as saying that copies of GNU should always be distributed at little or no charge. That was never the intent; later on, the manifesto mentions the possibility of companies providing the service of distribution for a profit. Subsequently I have learned to distinguish carefully between "free" in the sense of freedom and "free" in the sense of price. Free software is software that users have the freedom to distribute and change. Some users may obtain copies at no charge, while others pay to obtain copies—and if the funds help support improving the software, so much the better. The important thing is that everyone who has a copy has the freedom to cooperate with others in using it.

2. This is another place I failed to distinguish carefully between the two different meanings of "free." The statement as it stands is not false—you can get copies of GNU software at no charge, from your friends or over the net. But it does suggest the wrong idea.

3. Several such companies now exist.

4. The Free Software Foundation raises most of its funds from a distribution service, although it is a charity rather than a company. If *no one* chooses to obtain copies by ordering them from the FSF, it will be unable to do its work. But this does not mean that proprietary restrictions are justified to force every user to pay. If a small fraction of all the users order copies from the FSF, that is sufficient to keep the FSF afloat. So we ask users to choose to support us in this way. Have you done your part?

5. A group of computer companies recently pooled funds to support maintenance of the FNU C Compiler.

— 18 —

Crossing the Digital Divide

In the following selection, Jessica Brown considers the "digital divide" and the disparities in computer use and Internet access between middle-class and lower-income

Reprinted from the *Civil Rights Journal*, U.S. Commission of Civil Rights, 624 Ninth Street, NW, Washington, DC 20425.

households. Calling technology access a "civil rights issue," Brown argues that only a committed coalition of government, business, charities, and communities can bring everyone into the information age.

Jessica Brown

If you work for a corporation, and you're looking for a little face-time, a little positive publicity, the sort of thing P.R. people call "corporate goodwill," which is an industry term that refers to engendering a warm fuzzy feeling in people whenever they think about your product, a good thing to do is to hold a press conference and announce that you are donating a handful of computers to a local school. You'll pick an impoverished one, of course. The schools in wealthy neighborhoods already have computers; many have a few in every classroom. And it has to be computers. True, lots of impoverished schools don't have enough textbooks, or enough teachers, or even enough money for pencils, chalk, and toilet paper, but you can't really hold a press conference announcing that you are donating pencils or toilet paper to a low-income school because that makes people uncomfortable. Just thinking about schools that have to rely on corporate largesse to buy toilet paper is enough to make a lot of people change the channel. No, computers are better, mostly because they're still thought of as a luxury item. Unlike textbooks, it's okay that only wealthy schools are guaranteed to have them; and unlike textbooks, when poor children are given access to computers, this is still viewed as an act of generosity, and not the fulfillment of a basic right.

The Digital Divide

In August 1999, the U.S. Department of Commerce released a report that, for a couple of days at least, grabbed headlines. The report, Falling through the Net: Defining the Digital Divide, was conducted by the National Telecommunications and Information Administration (NTIA) and examined trends in Americans' access to, and usage of, the Internet, computers, and telephones. It found that, while the overall number of American homes, schools and businesses connected to the Internet is rapidly increasing, a large segment of society, namely people of color, the poor, and residents of rural and inner city communities, are seriously lagging behind in access to this and other types of information technology. "The good news," note the study's authors, "is that Americans are more connected than ever before. Access to computers and the Internet has soared for people in all demographic groups and geographic locations." . . . Accompanying this good news, however, was the persistence of what researchers and activists call the "digital divide," or the gap between the ability of privileged members of our society, and that of historically disadvantaged members, to access and use technology.

Not surprisingly, income remains a very strong factor in determining who will have access to electronic resources, and who will not. For instance, while about 80 percent of homes with annual incomes of $75,000 or more had computers by 1998, and about 60 percent were using the Internet, less than 40 percent of homes with annual incomes between $35,000 and $25,000 had home computers and less than 20 percent had Internet access. Of the poorest homes, those making less than $15,000 annually, computer ownership and Internet use fell to 15 percent and less than 10 percent, respectively. The data indicate, however, that income is not the only factor contributing to the digital divide. Whites of any income are still more likely to own computers and have Internet access than their black and Latino peers. For instance, while 33 percent of whites making between $15,000 and $35,000 had computers, only about 19 percent of blacks did. This overall discrepancy is so broad, reports NTIA, that a child in a low-income white family is still three times more likely to have Internet access than a black child in comparable family, and four times more likely than a Hispanic child.

Unfortunately, the data for schools and libraries isn't any more encouraging. "Traditionally," write Susan Goslee and Chris Conte in Losing Ground Bit by Bit: Low-Income Communities in the Information Age, . . . "we have looked to schools and libraries to help eliminate disparities in access to information resources." However, they note, "through no fault of their own, many of these institutions mirror the technology gap rather than mitigate it." According to a study released . . . by the Educational Testing Service (ETS), schools that serve historically disadvantaged communities are much less likely to offer computer and Internet services than schools serving other populations, and here, once again, race is a correlating factor. The ETS study found that while the average American school reported having about one computer for every ten students, schools where minority children made up 90 percent or more of the student body had average student to computer ratios of 17 to 1. The study also found that, while about 75 percent of schools in high-income areas had Internet access, only about 55 percent in low-income areas did. Libraries that serve low-income neighborhoods confront many of the same problems. Since most library funding occurs at the local level, institutions that serve poorer neighborhoods have fewer financial resources than those that serve wealthier areas. This often means that the communities that depend most heavily on public access points like schools and libraries to provide computer and Internet service are also the least likely to be able to afford them.

The most disturbing aspect of the technology gap, however, is that it is growing. For many groups the digital divide has widened in recent years as the information "haves" have outpaced the information "have nots" in gaining access to technology. . . .

Ramifications

Ironically, technology has always been viewed as a greater equalizer. The Internet especially has created high hopes for a future of free information, where totalitarian control of speech is impossible, borders are irrelevant, and each citizen participates equally in the global "conversation." The development of the Internet, in fact, is seen as having such a strong potential to revolutionize world culture that it has been likened to the invention of the printing press. This may be an apt analogy insofar as the Internet, like the printing press, has revolutionized the spread of information, making it faster, cheaper, and, theoretically at least, available to everyone. The Internet has also changed the stakes. As we all become more reliant on this marvelous new invention, as it transforms our society and our economy, what happens to those people who have no ability to access it? Do they become, as a result of their inability to operate a computer or go online, a disenfranchised underclass just as surely as if they could not read or write?

If the direction of the U.S. economy over the past few years is any indication, the answer to that question may be yes. With each passing year, computer skills become more and more of a prerequisite for basic participation in the workforce. According to the U.S. Department of Labor, almost 50 percent of all workers currently use a computer on the job, with these workers earning about 43 percent more than their less wired peers. Furthermore, . . . about 60 percent of all new jobs . . . require technology skills. Many of the jobs affected, moreover, will be in precisely those occupations that have traditionally been open to people without college degrees or specialized training. As offices become more computerized, for instance, it will become harder for workers to find secretarial and clerical positions that do not require word processing and database skills. Even the industrial sectors have been affected, notes Dorothee Benz, a New York journalist who covers labor issues. "Everyone, ranging from inventory workers in warehouses to cutters and graders in garment shops, may now be called upon to use a computer on the job."

The most lucrative jobs in the new U.S. economy, however, will require much more than the ability to simply operate a P.C. They will require the ability to engineer them: to write code, to design websites and software, to troubleshoot glitches, and to build networks. These jobs, in computer science, computer engineering, and systems analysis, are the three fastest growing occupational sectors in the new economy, and many labor analysts are holding out hope that they will soon move in to take the place of vanishing manufacturing jobs. If that happens, says Darin Kenley, the executive director of Kids Computer Workshop, an organization that provides computer access and mentoring for at-risk youth in Washington, DC, the digital divide will also have troubling ramifications for the general economy. "If, in the workplace, you have this large demographic of people who are being locked out of jobs," he says, "you risk a shortage in the labor pool."

However, the digital divide threatens to leave people sidelined from even more than the job market. The web has and will continue to change the way we interact with business, government, institutions of education, and even information itself. Sources of information that have traditionally been paper-based, such as government and municipal records, job listings, and even entire newspapers and magazines, have begun to shift resources from publishing hardcopy versions to publishing in electronic formats. Schools that have Internet access in each classroom have begun supplementing, and in some cases replacing, traditional materials like textbooks with the more current, in-depth, and dynamic information that can be found on the web. States have begun exploring the possibility of allowing citizens to cast votes online in elections, with the potential end goal of phasing out paper ballots altogether, and citizens can now lobby their elected representatives with the touch of a button, or download, in minutes, a particular legislator's voting record. For the privileged, the possibilities are endless, says David Geilhufe, director of the Eastmont Computing Center, a project that that provides low-income high school students with technology training in Oakland, California. However, he warns, people without access to technology risk falling farther and farther behind. "The electronic medium has become the preferred form of information," says Geilhufe. "When you have a segment of society that doesn't have the opportunity to access information in the preferred form you have a group of people that have been redefined from active participation in that society."

Technology as a Tool for Change

On the other hand, when historically disadvantaged communities do gain access to information technology, it really opens doors. That is the experience of activists working with two of the poorest demographic groups in the U.S. "The Internet is important because it allows Native Americans to live where they want, but have access to the rest of the world" notes Karen Buller, President of the National Indian Telecommunications Institute (NITI). "They can connect to the world while still keeping out of it, if they have Internet access." Another importance of the web is that it gives marginalized people the opportunity to have more of a voice. "On the Internet anyone can be an author," Buller says, "You don't need a Ph.D. or a big publishing house behind you. Native Americans have been misrepresented for hundreds of years by historians, anthropologists, and other outside observers. This allows us to correct those wrongs, and represent ourselves. I find it interesting that when most people get on the web, they do so to re-trieve information, but when Native Americans get on the web, they use it to put information out there about themselves."

Likewise, for people with disabilities, access to technology can be both a means to economic self-sufficiency, and a way to transcend physical limi-tations. "Traditionally," says Justin Dart, co-founder of Justice For All, a dis-ability rights advocacy group based in Washington DC, "people with dis-abilities have been employed in sheltered workshops, making sub-minimum wage and doing elementary labor work. Now the trend is moving toward technology and the potential is tremendous." Dale Brown of the President's Advisory Council on the Employment of People with Disabilities agrees. "Take a person with high level quadriplegia," she says by way of example. "There are computers that can be controlled with any muscle of the body. For instance, you can control a computer just through the movement of your eyes. Technology makes it easier to get information from the brain to the written page. In that regard, it's critical." Unfortunately, says Dart, most dis-abled people cannot use this type of technology, because it's just too expen-sive. "Statistically, people with disabilities are the poorest people in the U.S., so most, of course, do not have access to computers."

Barriers and Solutions

Although access to technology is beginning to gain recognition as a civil rights issue, our country has, for the most part, not yet found the political will to begin treating it like one. While most people agree that connecting all Americans to the Internet is a worthy goal, "nobody is quite sure who is actually responsible for bringing technology into communities," says Geil-hufe, "and nobody is sure who is going to pay for it." This is compounded by the fact that, for a lot of disadvantaged communities, the costs of a P.C. and a subscription to an Internet service provider are not the only barriers to getting online.

The problem is complex, explains Amy Borgstrom, the Executive Direc-tor of the Appalachian Center for Economic Networks (ACEnet), an or-ganization that works to connect citizens and small business operators in rural Appalachia to the World Wide Web. "I'm struck when I travel to any coast and people say `Oh, Internet access is universal and affordable, it only costs $15.95 a month.' In this community $15.95 a month can be the difference between having the ability to hire childcare so you can go to work, or having enough money to buy food." Nonetheless, she notes, the difficulties her low-income, rural clients face in getting access to the Inter-net don't end there. "We don't have the infrastructure, there's no affordable high bandwidth access. Some people out here still have party lines, and a surprising number of people don't even have phones."

Karen Buller, of NITI, agrees. "A major challenge is just getting the lines out here. A lot of phone companies won't even give us service, they don't see us as a profitable market." Although the NTIA reports that about 94 percent of American homes overall have phones, an examination of telephone penetration across racial and geographic lines illustrates a different facet of the digital divide. While about 95 percent of white families overall have phone service, only about 85 percent of black and Latino families do. For some populations, such as Native Americans, the combination of poverty and living in a remote area can be a particularly strong barrier to accessing basic telecommunications. The problem was compounded by the passage of the Telecommunications Act of 1996, which dismantled a framework of Federal subsidies that once helped to defray the cost of running telephone lines out to rural homes. Now, reports Buller, phone companies pass construction costs onto consumers. "To get the original line out can cost $10,000 to $50,000 in connection costs," she says. "That's just to get the line out to the first house! No one, no matter how much money they have, is going to pay that."

Even in communities that have phone lines, the telecommunications infrastructure does not always support Internet access, says David Geilhufe. "There is a spotty commitment on the part of corporate America to making advanced communications abilities available to low-income neighborhoods," he says, referring to practices documented in a report released by the Consumers Union and Consumer Federation of America . . . . The report, The Digital Divide Confronts the Telecommunications Act of 1996, notes that while phone companies are putting resources into building high-speed lines capable of providing fast Internet service to wealthier communities, many are lagging in building out these same services to low-income areas, unwilling to incur the cost for what they may believe is an inadequate return on investment. This creates a stark difference between each neighborhood's ability to access the web, Geilhufe explains. "Let's say I have a short health video on pre-natal care that I want to show people in the community, and I need to download it from the Net. In one neighborhood where you have high speed lines it takes 48 seconds, in another neighborhood where you're relying on old analog phone lines it takes 20 minutes."

One policy that partially addresses this issue is that of the education rate, or "e-rate." The e-rate, also A provision of the Telecommunications Act of 1996, provides discounts of up to 90 percent off of the cost of wiring qualifying schools, libraries, and health centers for Internet service. This is great, say advocates, but just getting the Internet into the schools and libraries will not meet the needs of an entire community. Many civil liberties groups, including the Civil Rights Forum on Communications Policy, and the National Urban League, have suggested that the e-rate be extended to provide discounted telecommunications services to community technology centers as well, insofar as these organizations also provide training and access and may reach a larger population. However, says Buller, what we really need is a renewed commitment to getting the information infrastructure into every home as well. "To make universal service really universal," she says, "the simplest thing would be to apply the same solution to getting people wired for telecommunications service that we did to getting them electricity. At first the cities had electricity and the rural areas didn't. Then legislators who represented rural people put in legislation causing the cities to pay a little extra; it was pennies really, to wire every home in the countryside for electricity. They felt rural people deserved it." A similar tax, she says, could be used to make sure everyone in the nation has access to telecommunications service. "This service is not an add-on, or an icing," she says, "it's a necessity."

Then there is the issue of acquiring the computer hardware itself, a problem that is often overlooked due to the fact that the overall cost of buying a P.C. has begun to go down. Although falling computer prices are good news for middle class buyers, a few hundred dollars per machine may still be too much for a lot of families, or for low-income schools and community access sites that have to struggle to cover basic expenses like books and staff salaries. A few companies have made headlines by offering computers to a handful of schools in exchange for the right to place a constant stream of advertisements, targeted toward children, at the sides and corners of the screen. Others have offered individual buyers a "free" P.C. in exchange for buying three years of Internet service at $20-$30 dollars a month. These programs have been somewhat limited, however, and are very controversial. This means that most institutions that do manage to get technology programs going are still relying on donated computers, the quality of which vary widely.

"In lower income areas, computers tend to be donated, and they may be older," says B. Keith Fulton, Director of Technology Programs and Policy for the National Urban League. "Most work fine, but there are limits in terms of running higher functions. They don't always have the capacity for some of the multimedia and Internet applications." It also means that having machines, or having enough of them, is by no means assured, and that library, community center, and school district staff may need to take on the additional burdens of writing grants, holding fundraisers, or soliciting donations to obtain the necessary P.C.s and software.

Beyond acquiring the machines, says Fulton, teachers and community organizers also need to be taught how to use them. "What people end up talking about, unfortunately, is who has computers and who doesn't. Then when computer prices go down they say 'Oh that solves the problem.' But you could give a laptop to everyone in the 'hood and does that solve the digital divide? No, you still need to provide training." Training is a vital, and often neglected, foundation for a successful community technology program. Without it computers may sit unused, or be used predominately for simple applications like computer games, because teachers or library staff don't necessarily know how to use them either. Often, staff are simply expected to acquaint themselves with the machines, sometimes on their own time. This means, says Fulton, that students in less wealthy districts aren't always getting the promised educational benefits even when their schools do get a computer program going.

Finally, says Elsa Macias, a senior researcher with the Tomas Rivera Policy Institute, a policy research center focusing on issues affecting Latinos in the U.S., you have to make people understand why this is something they need to learn how to do. Part of that is getting people over a general fear or mistrust of technology. Some people still approach computers with the fear that they might "break them" if they hit the wrong key; other people assume that they simply aren't smart enough to ever understand how to use a computer. The barrier for many though, says Macias, is apprehension over what computers, and particularly the Internet, might bring into the home. "People worry about what type of content their children will see," she says. "What if they start to access porn or hate sites? There is also the fear that using a computer is an anti-social activity that will take time away from the family."

In fact, many disadvantaged people approach the Internet with the assumption that the net is a white, upper class media that doesn't feature much content of possible interest to anybody else. Bob Johnson, the producer of the Black Entertainment Television (BET) cable network, and the CEO of BET Holdings, Inc., believes that this is one of the primary reasons people of color, in particular African Americans, do not use the Internet. "It's not so much a 'digital divide' as a mindset divide," Johnson told online news publication ZDnet. Blacks will use the web, he says, when web content producers make it clear they want their patronage. . . .

Mostly though, . . . coaxing people into sitting down at a computer and learning how to use it isn't so much of an issue anymore. Maybe it used to be that way, but now more people have come to understand that access to information technology is something that will eventually need to become competitive in the job market, and to fully participate in society. "People recognize that this is a train they need to get on," she says, "and if not them, they at least have to get their children on it, or they're going to be left behind." The big problem . . . is that the approach to bringing everybody into the information age is patchy, the commitment not yet solidified or even entirely earnest. Some neighborhoods get high-speed Internet access, while some do not have wiring for phones. Some schools have advanced computers in every classroom, while others make do with a handful of older models, or none at all. All in all, though donations of services and equipment, and the efforts of activists and local technology programs, are doing wonderful things in the communities they touch, it will take more to close the divide. It will take a commitment on the part of government, business, charitable organizations, and communities to an ideal of universal service, and an acknowledgment that equal access to technology is, for individuals, a basic right, and, for the country as a whole, an economic and democratic necessity.

— 19 —

Gender Bias in Instructional Technology

Katy Campbell shows the many ways in which prevailing teaching techniques and content place women at a distinct disadvantage for computer-based learning. She offers suggestions for a more inclusive learning design that would be amenable to a variety of learning styles.

Katy Campbell

Technology, and technology-based models of teaching and learning, are not value-neutral; and neither are the vocabulary and prevailing metaphors, which can exclude women or include them in undesirable ways [1].

Gender-related inequities in access and support for learning have been evident since microcomputers were first introduced into classrooms in the early 1980s. Research examining the experience of females in technology-based classrooms reveals a consistent pattern, established in the early years in school, in which girls are discouraged from computing both as a process and as a career choice. Psychological and sociocultural factors include attitudes toward math and science, math anxiety, motivation to learn, access to resources, learning context, learning design, nature of content, and learning and cognitive style differences. Much of this research involves students who attended school in the 1970s and 1980s, the undergraduate and adult learning population in post-secondary settings today. Thus there is a dearth of research on educational outcomes for the newest technologies as used by completely computer-literate post-secondary students.

From Katy Campbell, "The promise of computer-based learning: designing for inclusivity." *IEEE Technology and Society Magazine* (Winter 1999/2000) pp. 28-34. Reprinted by permission.

Feminist theory about technology argues that the rational, objectivist design of computing environments reflects their military and masculine origins. From these origins come a reliance on an aggressive technical vocabulary, overuse of abstract problem-solving approaches, industrial and utilitarian design of computers and classrooms, and the action-oriented, competitive and arcade-style of much of the software available in classrooms.

How can women negotiate and transform a world of instructional technology that is, in effect, premised on their absence? Can new learning technologies and new learning designs support new teaching and learning opportunities? I think they can, and in ways that creatively promote inclusivity through representation and design, by:

1) allowing for alternative representations through dynamic processes and the linking of verbal, visual, and aural information to support diverse learning styles, preferences, and experiences;

2) including large databases of resources previously unavailable to learners, inviting the inclusion of experiences of women and other marginalized groups for the first time, and supporting the interrelatedness of perspectives;

3) supporting rational ways of knowing and being in the world, ways that may be preferred by women;

4) inviting the instructional designer to step outside linear, objectivist, traditional models of instruction to create environments reflecting knowledge that is both intuitive and rational.

Learning Styles

The design of learning technologies and environments has reflected a view of cognitive development in which the "received knowing" of the rational Western intellectual endeavor is contrasted with the relational position of "connected knowing" described by Belenky, Clinchy, Goldberger, and Tarule [2]. Until the mid-1990s computer-based learning had to be delivered on stand-alone microcomputers, so learning programs were self-contained in diskettes or interactive formats such as CD-ROMs. Learning designs were limited in two ways. They reinforced gender ideologies n content and images [3], and they were constrained by technological environments that encouraged autonomous learning, since cooperative learning was difficult to implement in fixed computer labs in which data could not easily be shared. When designs use abstract, formal operations they privilege the rational learner and disadvantage those whose cognitive styles tend to be more concrete and associative [4]. The increase in networked learning, which supports more interconnected learning activities, has ironically also perpetuated very flat, text-based designs, as multimedia elements have not been easily delivered via the Internet. Broad-band technology shows great promise in this regard, but it has not been widely available, or evaluated, for instructional purposes.

In the past decade learning theorists have suggested different learning styles that are somewhat gender-related: the *autonomous,* separate, or independent style, which typifies the majority of men (and some women); and the *relational,* connected, or interdependent style, which typifies the majority of women (and some men). Both Magolda [5] and MacKeracher [6] describe learning style preferences on a *continuum* of intellectual development. Their work has important implications for the design of inclusive-learning environments.

Magolda for example, examined 100 college students, trying to identify patterns of knowing and intellectual development over time in a post-secondary context [5]. She started with the premise that students interpret, or make meaning of, their educational experiences as a result of their assumptions about the nature, limits, and certainty of formal knowledge. She then described a developmental scheme in which ways of knowing are evolving, continuous and fluid, context-bound, socially constructed, and gender-related.

From the students' accounts Magolda identified four ways of knowing and intellectual reasoning from absolute knowing ("Truth is absolute") through transitional, independent, and finally contextual knowing ("multiple, valid perspectives exist"). Each category contains two distinct and gender-related patterns. Through the continuum, males tended to prefer challenge and debate, individual activities, and the use of external evidence, while females tended towards interindividual, collaborative activities, and demonstrated interchange and attenuation as discourse styles. Magolda's findings thus suggest that the strategies traditionally reflected in much of the highly structured computer-based designs available are counter-intuitive for women learners [7]. These environments have been based on traditional perspectives on structuring learning; that is, they have been designed to reflect mostly knowledge-based (low-level), criterion-referenced, identifiable outcomes, on which controlled activities are based and assessed. The control of information presentation rests with the computer, rather than the learner, and the instructional strategies tend to be didactic and expository rather than supportive of knowledge construction. While appropriate for some learning tasks, these environments do not encourage the cognitive flexibility described by Spiro *et al.* and Jonassen *et al.,* and reflected in women's connected learning styles [8], [9].

Implicit and Explicit Content

Issues

If *how* one learns—learning style—is influenced by gender, then *what* one learns is equally so. The military language of computing (e.g., killing a job, fatal errors, crashing), as well as programs containing cultural and emotional associations hostile to women, do little to promote an interest in computing among women [10]. Themes, metaphors, and settings from sports, action/adventure, and battle exemplify competition and violence. The assumption that a user interface must be arcade-like to be engaging ignores the fact that such structures and images are familiar and intuitive only to those who have played or have been exposed to video games. Since boys outnumber girls in video arcades and in other informal computing environments, these interfaces are familiar primarily to the boys who come to computing as a recreation [11].

As an example, I received from a major publisher an evaluation copy of a CD-ROM based supplement for a first-year psychology course (*CyberPsych*™). The interface is based on a medieval castle that spins rapidly in the air. In order to open the program one must have some dexterity with a mouse and be able to click on a particular part of the castle while it is spinning. When asked to rationalize the interface, the publisher's representative confessed that the program was designed to resemble *Myst*™, a very popular action/adventure video game, that only 13% of the female student population had ever played![1] Similarly, a Web-course design tool (*WebCT* ™) uses language such as "hold your horses" and images such as a red metal toolbox, from which a hammer partially emerges, to represent a set of learning activities that include annotated notetaking. Because the images evoked by these representations of the activities draw from traditionally male occupations (cowboys and carpenters), they are tacitly gender biased even though they do not contain explicitly negative or stereotypical images of women [12]–[14].

Scientific and mathematical examples also dominate in software; and accompanying simulations tend to be abstract, whereas females prefer real-life contexts with a social focus [2], [15], [16]. In these environments, software design is often text-based, expository, and sequenced, and learning tasks are set up to support individual, procedural problem solving and/or competitive and abstract activities, rather than being cooperative, collaborative, and narrative-based. In Inkpen's study, for example, women/girls preferred to work on tasks creating characters or finishing a story rather than creating new task levels [16].

To the degree that the software draws primarily from traditionally male activities for images and content, then organizes the information in ways consistent with most men's but not most women's learning styles, women confront challenges to using the software successfully that men do not. However the division between women and men in cognitive styles is not a mutually exclusive one. Belenky and her colleagues, for example, point out that the women they interviewed did not reject abstraction as such but did attend to the context of the abstraction. They resisted the learning activity, in the sense that they refused to become engaged, when abstractions preceded authentic experiences or pushed them out entirely [2].

Inclusive Design Solutions

With improved bandwidth over the Internet and multimedia technologies such as streaming audio and video, multiple representations of information are possible. Since not all learners fit neatly into our research categories, multimodal designs that include graphical and dynamic representations (such as motion video, audio, and animation) will support more diverse cognitive and learning styles.[2] We are beginning to see educational Web sites that offer not only information in a diversity of forms, but also represent that content from multiple perspectives. Examples of such hypermedia, problem-based sites, include *The Shell Island Dilemma* (http://www.ncsu.edu/coast/shell/index.html) and *Planet Earth Conflict: Yellowstone Wolf* (http://powayusd.sdcoe.k12.ca.us/mtr/ConflictYellowestoneWolf.ht).

Although hypertext and online social environments may support the connected ways in which many women prefer to learn, some may find these associative environments unfamiliar and difficult to navigate [17]–[19]. These learners tend to feel lost in hypertext/hypermedia designs as they link nodes that lead them to even more choices, especially if their exploration is not evaluated. Some researchers suggest a design and cognitive strategy known "as learner control with advisement" which appears to be a gender-based preference [17], [20].[3]

To summarize, inclusive learning design guidelines include:

- no arcade-style designs, thus no competition, hierarchical information, violence; portray women as problem-solvers rather than victims or prizes;
- stress characterization and relationships;
- avoid competitive and aggressive metaphors from games, sports, adventures, and wars:
- evaluate visual imagery and design for bias;
- emphasize harmony with nature, concern for others; empathy and compassion. Women show a preference for working with scientific concepts with social value, concern with consequences of action on others, and an ethic of care;
- represent objects or issues studied holistically;
- gender-neutral, open-ended creative tasks such as collaborative writing.

Learning Environments

Issues

Even when the learning context and content are theoretically designed for inclusivity, the users do not necessarily come to computing activities untouched by social practices associated with gender. Communications technologies such as computer-mediated conferencing, virtual worlds, and microworlds can challenge ideas about computing as an individual (male) activity and hold promise for redefining computing as an opportunity for learning through interactions that promote inclusivity. In particular, teaching about, and for, social and political activism and agency may be enhanced by online worlds that focus on gender and identity issues. Especially interesting questions about the use of these worlds include those related to how people learn and practice a "disembodied" gender identity online.[4]

It has been assumed that some gender inequalities would be lessened in computer-mediated communications (CMC), since in face-to-face interactions equalities emerge through non-verbal cues. A lack of social cues, plus the advantage of asynchronicity, may make the online conversation more equitable and safer for women. But despite the potential in CMC, there is some evidence that women have been silenced and even pursued and frightened in the online environment, thus transferring physical vulnerability into cyberspace [21].

There is also evidence of gender differences in how people talk, and so online interactions can be shaped by gender-based practices. Deborah Tannen argues that men and women have different speech patterns, men preferring expository "report talk," while women like exploratiory "rapport talk" [22]. Kirkup contends that the style of talk in CMC is very dialogue-oriented, privileging the expository style [23]. This style is observed in males online, whose behavior is consistent with adversarial relationships: put-downs, strong, often contentious assertions, lengthy and/or frequent postings, self-promotion and sarcasm. Females' style of talking, on the other hand, has two co-occurring aspects: supportiveness and attenuation. A report in the *ASEE Prism* cites a number of examples of conflicting and exclusionary discourse styles in engineering classrooms [24]. For example, the "devil's advocate" role is common among men, but is not comfortable for women who would rather cooperate and affirm. In one classroom, several engineering situations involving problem-solving were set up by adversarial-type interactions that involved the defender of an idea and an attacker, but this approach is seldom part of a women's verbal experience. In a later study [45], described in the same report, Hall and Resnick-Sandler claimed that in academic settings women are interrupted more often, that their contributions are mistakenly attributed to others—or to luck—more often than men's, and they receive less attention and encouragement from instructors. This difference appears to be sustained in the roles people take in online conversations. Women will behave consistently with maintenance of socio-emotional group process roles and men will behave consistently with a task-oriented role [25].

Although many institutions have developed strong policies for pornography and harassment, both continue to be problems. Women must be cautious about publishing any personal information. Men have adopted female pseudonyms in order to belong to restricted conversations and once included then have harassed participants for their views. Some women have also enjoyed more credibility by using male pseudonyms [4].

Herring found that in studies of Internet discussion groups involving both women and men, men contributed more consistently than did women [26]. In fact, if women contributed more than 30% of the conversation, they were perceived to be dominating the conversation, by both men and women. These findings have been supported in more recent studies [27].

Inclusive Design Solutions

In the classroom, many of these problems can be addressed by a discussion of social protocols online, a conversation during which all participants consider the effects of lack of social cues. Issues to be discussed may include identity, language use and tone, acceptable ways to disagree with or challenge the views of others, and length and number of postings. In some cases, the use of pseudonyms is acceptable, although anonymous postings can encourage inappropriate, even abusive behavior. Because one often chooses to use CMC as a way to build learning communities, facilitator modeling and support for diverse views and experiences, expressed in safety, must be explicit. Swift interventions are essential when interactions go awry.

The Internet can bring women together in communities across national and cultural boundaries, can enhance women's creative potential, and can provide an opportunity to extend or re-define one's gender identity. Formerly inaccessible information sources are available to share through online support structures. Hypertext writing and CMC may encourage the building of online, activist communities for social justice. Online environments may be empowering for women if/when they support connected, inter-relational, collaborative, and non-linear learning. Indeed, such innovations promise the most equitable context yet for learning about and through computer technology.

Access

Issues

The issue of access to computers and, by extension, information, is of central concern as numerous studies have shown that computer ownership and computer use is predominantly male, likewise the pattern of online use and access [28]. Unequal access begins in the home and at school, ranging from a 2:1 ratio to a 3:1 ratio in favor of male ownership of computers [29], [30].[5] The ratios increase, too, when the *kind* of computer is considered.[6]

Spenneman speculates that the level of computer ownership and use reflects the socioeconomic differential between men and women in the industrialized world [30].

Gender differences in access to computer technology spill onto a variety of related issues. Males tend to participate in more informal computing experiences than females and feel more comfortable with technology [30]. Access relates directly to experience by influencing attitude and achievement [31]. Unless we address these inequities, women and other marginalized groups are in danger of becoming "the disappeared" in educational, economic, and employment initiatives that rely on computer technologies [32], [3].

For instance, distance education is one area in which access is of paramount concern to educators. As traditional institutions make more flexible options available for off-campus students, equitable access be comes an effective gatekeeper. High percentages of distance, and/or non-traditional learners are women. Funding is cited as a problem for this group by von Prummer, as well as lack of institutional support for the family issues that concern women [33]. Women may have different needs for support than men, but their needs are often dismissed as unaddressible by the institution.

This lack of support translates into inflexible schedules and deadlines for assignments and exams, requirements for technological tools that may be out of their economic reach, designs for the solitary learner that are uncomfortable for women, and learning activities that may require travel, extra fees, and special arrangements, such as videoconferencing.

Their families and other social structures in the community may marginalize women who are otherwise candidates for distance learning [12], [13], [33]. This marginalization is characterized by von Prummer as "sabotage" by family and friends, including the destruction of materials, increased demands for attention and help, "guilt-tripping," and refusing to set aside time or space in the home for study.[7] Ironically, women may place higher demands and standards on themselves to compensate for self-perceived "selfishness" in pursuing their goals and interests.

Inclusive Design Solutions

The issue of access is a widespread and globally political one that resists simplistic formulations and solutions, but we can try to minimize inequitable access among our own students. As post-secondary institutions wrestle with the notion of flexible learning and the "laptop university," a number of creative approaches are possible.

Several institutions have experimented with "rent-to-own" or "work-to-own," leasing, "ever-greening" and interest-free loan programs, among them Wake Forest University. (See http://www.wfu.edu/Computer-information/thinkpad/2000.htm).[8] In Alberta, a consortium of post-secondary institutions formed "Alberta North," to develop and foster community-based learning centers with guaranteed access to standardized learning technologies.

On-campus, too, access for women can be improved through:

- requiring computer literacy classes for all students;
- locating computing facilities in campus areas where women learners and women faculty members are concentrated;
- designating "women-only" lab time, with a less competitive climate and more personal interactions around problem solving and computer anxieties;
- creating same-sex computer classes, as one learning option available to women students who would like it;
- using alternative designs of computer spaces, such as pods of four to encourage cooperative work;
- supervising computing facilities at all times, or especially in the evenings.

New Design Tools and Approaches

In Kirkup and Keller's The Social *Construction of Computers,* Sherry Turkle speaks of technological environments in the 1990s as "a new social construction," in which we are freed from the social conventions of specific cultures, professional or personal roles, and gender [34]. In these environments the cultural context in which knowledge was produced is examined with the questions *whose authority?* and *whose knowledge?* as critical lenses. Learners are encouraged to use their own feelings, intuition and imagination as resources and strengths for learning as they work towards self-empowerment. Designs based on cognitive flexibility [8] encourage learners to "crisscross the landscape" of multiple perspectives and constructions of reality, so that learning based on social interaction helps clarify meanings and achieve consensus [35]. These kinds of relational designs include problem-based and case-based models in which learners work together to gather evidence to support critical solutions. Social discourse is central to this process, and is often supported through asynchronous means such as online conservations or threaded discussions, or synchronous conversations through audio or video conferencing.

At the University of Alberta, we have designed and delivered numerous courses that reflect inclusive design guidelines. For example, "Interpretive Inquiry: Hermaneutic Phenomenology", a graduate nursing course, includes a mix of technologies and activities. We provided participants with a number of issues, or anchors, related to bioethics. The issues were presented through multiple representations: readings, links to medical research sites, a videotape of a simulated genetic counseling session, and a television episode of the series, "Law and Order." The students, who were from Guam, Thailand, Canada, and the United States, reflected on the nature of embodied knowledge (a phenomenological concept) by following a videotaped yoga lesson, and shared stories of health practices. They joined threaded issues-based online discussions, completed a cooperative project, which they negotiated with one another through a synchronous chat room, and participated in three audioconferences. Although several students encountered technical problems, and thus found it difficult to participate consistently, most were actively engaged by the mix of approaches. A community emerged from their experiences and they have continued their network of personal and professional relationships online beyond the classroom.

The University of Alberta project is one attempt to fully utilize the educational potential of computer technologies to create an inclusive environment for learning; but there are too few models available to us to address the persisting gender inequality in technology-based learning experiences. Designs limited by over-reliance on male-centered experiences have constrained the development of innovative approaches to content, design environments, learning strategies, and access considerations. With the advent of networked technologies and new instructional models, women have an improved chance of learning in more interconnected, authentic, and relational ways. Scholarship from women's and gender studies is a valuable and underutilized resource for the development of computer-based learning technologies. If we are aware of exclusionary learning designs and environments, and consciously adopt new teaching strategies and processes to address inequities, then all of us—teachers and students—can make the most of our educational settings and opportunities.

Notes

1. This figure is based on Culley's estimates of an 8:1 ratio of boys to girls regularly involved in video games [11]. This estimate could be somewhat different if adolescent girls in 1999 were surveyed.
2. Schiller has pointed out that North American sites dominate the Internet, so that most information, language, and cultural representations on the Internet should be designed for cultural inclusivity.
3. Advisement typically provides advice like the optimal path through the lesson, the appropriate lesson sequence, or the optimal amount of instruction. Clariana noted that females that received advisement completed more sessions than either the females with no advisement, or the males with or without advisement [20]. In other words, advisement may be more frequently sought and more effectively used by females than by males, since there seems to be a relationship between achievement and motivational effects for women.
4. See, for example, Sherry Turkle's accounts of fluid identities in "the age of simulations" [4].

5. Figures vary wildly in this area and must be evaluated in light of the context in which they are quoted. For example, Sadie Plant, as a notable exception, estimates female Internet usage at 50% of the total users [35].

6. In Spenneman's study, for example, 48.6% of males and only 6.3% of females had World Wide Web (WWW) capable computers [36].

7. I witnessed this phenomenon first-hand as a distance educator working with First Nations communities in northern Manitoba, in 1995. For example, female adult learners would be denied childcare assistance by their families, without which they could not continue studying.

8. This initiative, and others, were described at a panel at The International Conference on Computers in Education, in October 1998, Beijing, China [38].

References

[1] L.R. Shade, "Gender issues in computer networking," presented at Community Networking: Int. Free-Net Conf., Carleton Univ., Ottawa, Ont., June 1993.

[2] M.F. Belenky, B.M. Clinchy, N.R. Goldberger , and J.M. Tarule, *Women's ways of knowing: The development of self, voice, and mind.* Basic, 1986.

[3] C. Winkelman, "Women in the integrated circuit: Morphing the academic/community divide," *Frontiers: J. Women Stud.,* vol. 18, no. 1, pp. 19–42, 1997.

[4] S. Turkle, *Life on the Screen: Identity in the Age of the Internet.* New York, NY: Simon & Schuster, 1995.

[5] M.B.B. Magolda, *Knowledge and Reasoning in College: Gender-Related Patterns in Students' Intellectual Development.* San Francisco, CA: Jossey-Bass, 1992.

[6] D. MacKeracher, *Making Sense of Adult Learning.* Toronto, Ont.: Culture Concepts, 1996.

[7] J.M. Ewing, J.D. Dowling, and N. Coutts, "Learning using the World Wide Web: A collaborative learning event,"*J. Educational Multimedia & Hypermedia,* vol. 8, no. 1, pp. 3–22, 1998.

[8] R.J. Spiro, P.J. Feltovich, M.J. Jacobson, and R.L. Coulson, "Cognitive flexibility, constructivism, and hypertext: Random access instruction for advanced knowledge acquisition in ill-structured domains," *Educational Technol.,* vol. 31, pp. 24–33, 1991.

[9] D, Jonassen et al., "Cognitive flexibility hypertexts on the Web: Engaging learners in making meaning," in *Web-based instruction,* B.H. Khan, Ed. Englewood Cliffs, NJ: Educational Technology Pub., 1997, pp. 119–133.

[10] E.F. Provenzo, *Video Kids: Making Sense of Nintendo.* Cambridge, MA: Harvard Univ. Press, 1992.

[11] L. Culley, "Gender equity and computing in secondary schools: Issues and strategies for teachers," in *Computers into Classrooms: More Questions than Answers.* H. Mackay and J. Beynon, Eds. London, U.K.: Falmer, 1993.

[12] E.J. Burge, Women as learners: Issues for visual and virtual classrooms. *The Canadian Journal for the Study of Adult Education,* vol. 4, no. 2, pp. 1–24, 1990.

[13] E.J. Burge, "Learning in computer conferenced contexts: The learners' perspective." *J. Distance Education,* vol. 9, no. 1, pp. 19–43, 1994.

[14] B. Elkjaer, "Girls and information technology in Denmark: An account of a

socially constructed problem," *Gender & Education,* vol. 4, No. 1/2, pp. 25–40, 1992.

[15] S.K. Damarin, "Rethinking science and mathematics curriculum and instruction: Feminist perspectives in the computer era," *J. Education,* vol. 173, no. 1, pp. 107–123, 1991.

[16] K. Inkpen et al., "We have never-forgetful flowers in our garden': Girls' responses to electronic games," *J. Computers in Mathematics & Science Teaching,* no. 13, vol. 4, pp. 383–403, 1994.

[17] Cognition and Technology Group at Vanderbilt (CTGV), "Designing learning environments that support thinking," in *Designing Environments for Constructive Learning,* T.M. Duffy, J. Lowyck, and D.H. Jonmassen, Eds. Berlin, Germany: Springer-Verlag, 1993.

[18] S.O. Tergan, Misleading theoretical assumptions in hypertext/hypermedia research, *J. Educational Multimedia and Hypermedia,* vol. 6, no. 3/4, pp. 257–283, 1997.

[19] K. Oliver, "Computer-based tools in support of Internet-based problem-solving," presented at *Annual Meet. Assoc. Educational Communication Technology,* Houston, TX, Feb. 1999.

[20] R.B. Clariana, "The motivational effect of advisement on attendance and achievement in computer-based instruction," *J. Computer-Based Instruction,* vol. 20, no. 2, pp. 47–51, 1993.

[21] H. Taylor, C. Kramarae, and M. Ebben, *Women, Information Technology and Scholarship.* Univ. of Illinois Press, 1993.

[22] D. Tannen, *You Just Don't Understand: Women and Men in Conversation.* New York, NY: Ballantine, 1990.

[23] G. Kirkup, "The importance of gender as a category in open and distance learning," presented at Conf. on Putting the Learner First: Learner-Centered Approaches in Open and Distance Learning. Cambridge, U.K., July 1995.

[24] J. Taylor, "Warming a chilly classroom," *ASEE Prism,* Feb. 29–33, 1997.

[25] V. Savicki, M. Kelley, and D. Lingenfelter, "Gender and small task group activity using computer-mediated communication," *Computers in Human Behavior,* vol. 12, pp. 209–224, 1996.

[26] S.C. Herring, "Gender and democracy in computer-mediated communication," in *Computerization and Controversy: Value Conflicts and Social Choices,* 2nd ed., Rob Kling, Ed. San Diego, CA: Academic, 1996, pp. 476–489.

[27] K.D. Blum, "Gender differences in CMC-based distance education," *Feminista,* vol. 2, p. 5, 1998; online at http://www.feminista.com/v2n5/

[28] E. Balka and L. Doucette, "The accessibility of computers to organizations serving in the province of Newfoundland: Preliminary study results," *Arachnet Electronic J. Virtual Culture,* vol. 2, p. 3, 1994.

[29] L. Gilbert and C. Kile, *Surfer Grrrls.* Seattle, WA: Seal, 1996.

[30] D.H.R. Spenneman, "Gender imbalances in computer access among environmental science students," 1996; online at http://www.usq.edu.au/electpub/e-jist/spenne.htm

[31] Yuen-kuang Liao, "Gender differences on attitudes towards computers: A meta-analysis," presented at Ann. Meet. World Conf. Educational Multimedia, Hypermedia, and Telecommunications, Seattle, WA, June 1999.

[32] L.R. Shade, "Preliminary actions towards achieving gender equity," presented at Int. Council of Women, Ottawa, Ont., June 1997.

[33] C. von Prummer, "Women-friendly perspectives in distance education," keynote address presented at Feminist Pedagogy and Women-Friendly Perspectives in Distance Education at the International WIN Working Conference, Umea, Sweden, June, 1993.

[34] S. Turkle, "The social construction of computers: Hammers or harpsichords?," in *Science, Technology, and Gender,* G. Kirkup and L. S. Keller, Eds. Cambridge, MA: Basil Blackwell, 1992.

[35] N.G. Stacey, *CompetencE [sic], without credentials.* Washington, DC : U.S. Dept. of Education, Office of Educational Research and Improvement, 1999.

[36] S. Plant, *Zeros and Ones: Digital Women and the New Technoculture.* New York, NY: Doubleday, 1997.

For Further Reference

[37] C. Beardon and S. Worden, "The virtual curator: Multimedia technologies and the roles of museums," in *Contextual Media: Multimedia and Interpretation,* E. Barrett and M. Redmond. Eds, Cambridge, MA: M.I.T. Press, 1995.

[38] C. Blurton et al., *"Assured access/Mobile computing initiatives on four university campuses,"* presented at Ann. Meet. Int. Conf. Computers in Education, Beijing, China, Oct. 1998.

[39] K. Borland, "That's not what I said": Interpretive conflict in oral narrative research," in *Women's Words: The Feminist Practice of Oral History,* S.B. Gluck and D. Patai, Eds. New York, NY: Routlege, Chapman and Hall, 1991, pp. 63–76.

[40] R. Braidotti, *Cyberfeminism with a difference;* online at http://www.let.ruu.nl/womens_studies/rosi/cyberfem.htm#bcybspace

[41] H.I. Schiller, *Information Inequality: The Deepening Social Crisis in America.* New York: NY: Routledge, 1996.

[42] D. Spender, *Nattering on the Net: Women, Power, and Cyberspace.* Australia: Spinifex, 1995.

[43] D. Tannen, *"Gender gap in cyberspace,"* Newsweek, vol. 54, May 16, 1994.

[44] K.L. Gustafson and R.M. Branch, *Survey of Instructional Development Models,* 3rd ed. Syracuse, NY: ERIC Clearinghouse on Information and Technology, 1997.

[45] Hall and Resnick-Sandler, "The chilly classroom climate: A guide to improving the education of women," *ASEE Prism,* Feb. 29–33, 1997.

Computers and the Work Experience

Anthony Townsend examines how new information technologies are changing the nature of work. In particular,
he looks at how these technologies affect the way workers view the world and the way work is organized and
unionized.

Anthony M. Townsend

I. Introduction

Information and communications technologies have evolved to where a significant portion of our lives is increasingly shaped less by physical
reality and more by the reality of the media with which we interact (Poster,
1990, 1996). Where once a fairly local community informed our ideas about
ourselves, our social status, and our relations with others, as citizens of the
electronic village we are far less confined by the ideas in our local community. With Internet access, we have the widest diversity of information ever
available. And unlike every preceding media, the Internet is absolutely egalitarian in that anyone can publish and be read by the entire electronic community. With access to this breadth of information, individuals can go far beyond the historically monolithic information sources (newspapers,
television, radio, etc.) and discover both raw information as well as a
tremendous diversity of interpretation of the meaning of events and ideas.

The Internet allows something else to happen too; unlike traditional
media, which send their messages in one direction, an individual on the Internet can communicate back to the electronic community. In doing so, individuals can redefine themselves in a much greater context than ever before, as they interactively determine their positions in this diverse universe.
Since individuals are no longer bounded by the physical and cultural realities of their neighborhoods, they may well abandon their old self-defini-
tions, philosophical conventions, and class loyalties.

In addition to changes in the forces that influence an individual's social
perspective, radical changes n the nature of work itself have changed the
bases on which individuals assess their relations with others. The information revolution takes place during a radical transformation of the work-

From Anthony M. Townsend, "Solidarity.com? Class and collective action in the electronic
village." *Journal of Labor Research* (Summer 2000) 21. Reprinted by permission.

place; the post-industrial landscape offers few smokestack factories staffed by legions of union workers. Instead, contemporary workers are much more likely to work with their heads than their hands and are paid for performance more than by job category and seniority. Accordingly, union membership has declined precipitously as these structural changes have eliminated many of the traditional bulwarks of union strength.

In this study, I examine how changes in the community of work and moving out of the "neighborhood" changes individuals' fundamental assumptions about themselves and their social position, specifically in relation to their motivations for collective action. I argue that in a post-industrial economy and an information-rich context, class identification (and union support) becomes a phenomenon created more by the individual and less by economic and political structures. I then offer a theoretical framework to analyze this evolving phenomenon and examine the ramifications of this transformation on union relevance.

II. The Changing Community of Work

The Factory Town

In 1950, U.S. Steel operated factories employing thousands of men, all earning their wages in hard, backbreaking work. These men came to work together, lived in the factory town, and drank at the same bars. They knew each other, maybe not personally, but as members of the same community and as members of the same class. They knew too that there was a difference between themselves and "management." They could see management, in suits and starched white shirts, working with paper instead of with steel; they believed at a visceral level in a wide gulf between workers and managers. Union membership was a natural extension of this sociology, as these men clearly believed that their only means to higher wages and better working conditions was through collective action.

In the ecology of the factory town, union information was disseminated through hand billing, picketing, and mass meetings, and information was controlled because there were few, if any, independent sources of information available to workers. In the factory town, labor was also a restricted commodity, for the cost of bringing in workers from any distance added value to local labor. The final great union advantage in the factory-town union was its ability to enforce conformity to the collective will, either through social pressure or violence. In the factory town, a union was almost inevitable.

However, as factory towns declined in the 1960s and 1970s, unions were marginalized by a social ecology in which they were ill equipped to compete. The change from production to service industries, the economic transformation of the South, suburbanization, and the change in workers' roles within the organization, all represented radical departures from the historical environment of collective action. With the decline of the factory town, the clear sense of class that once spanned generations of workers declined as well.

The Post-Industrial Landscape

With the factory town becoming extinct, new forms of work emerged that are predicated on a fundamentally different economic ecology: radically different organizational structures and worker capabilities are valued in comparison with those in the past. Based largely on information services, this new economy emphasizes individual productivity rather than collective productivity. Information services do not have an assembly line, a shop floor, or large congregations of workers, lunch bucket in hand, passing their counterparts during shift changes. Information services usually have the clean feel of an office for even the most menial jobs. In this context, the classic distinction between blue-collar and white-collar blurred into a continuum of ascending levels of managerial power.

The Rise of the e-Corporation

With the transition to a post-industrial economy well underway, a number of technological and economic factors converged in the mid-1980s to create even greater economic opportunity and a further imperative for change in how people work. Faster computers, new telecommunications technologies, and new information infrastructures created a revolution in the informational and communication resources in industrialized nations. Simplified information retrieval systems and affordable access to the Internet attracted a new breed of information consumer, while at the same time informationally empowering a new class of people.

Additionally, the globalization of trade forced businesses to rethink their operating strategies and to restructure to effectively compete with offshore competitors. Where large and monopolistic organizations had once dominated the economic landscape, smaller and nimbler organizations began to establish themselves as the preeminent organizational form. Gradually, even the most successful of the giant firms began to disassemble into smaller and more adaptive operating units, reducing layers of administrative control and moving decision-making authority into lower levels of the remaining hierarchy. Even low-level jobs began to require decision making, as line workers were taught to manage quality control; the traditional assembly line effectively became a thing of the past.

III. The Electronic Village

Beginning with radio and motion pictures, and then television, American politics, culture, and social mores have been shaped by broadcast[1] media.

These media were expensive to operate, and in the case of radio and television, access was limited by government regulation. While it is beyond the scope of this paper to discuss the ideological bent of these media, I can reasonably assert that the narrow control of these media clearly restricted the range of views presented. Thus, the average person's ideas about class, politics, and even self-identity were largely informed by media information and local custom.

The Internet revolution changes the historical role of mass media with two radical new factors: (1) Mass access, in the sense that anyone (or any institution) that publishes on the web is equally accessible to any web user; and (2) Robust interactivity, in that people can communicate with each other in a variety of different ways and discuss, debate, and critique the ideas of others in an almost unrestricted forum.

Where traditional media were controlled only by relatively powerful institutions (both private and public), the Internet is accessible to virtually anyone; the cost of putting a message in the public domain (at the time of this writing) is only about $20.00 per month.[2] While there is no guarantee that people will actually access a given Internet site, the potential exists. Consider this analogy: In traditional media forms, publishing a book or a newspaper was expensive, and even if you paid to create one that reflected your views, there was little chance that bookstores and newsstands would stock your publication. On the Internet, your publication is "stocked" in every bookstore and newsstand in the world; whether individuals read it is up to their discretion.

Aside from merely providing access to publications, the Internet has another characteristic that increases the likelihood that potentially interested parties will find your web site; the "search engines" (e.g., Altavista, Yahoo, Excite) that locate web resources are absolutely egalitarian. These search engines catalogue the text of virtually every site on the web at any moment and allow the user to find Internet sites that appear to relate to topics of interest; a search for sites related to labor is just as likely to turn up National Right to Work as it is the AFL-CIO. They will also turn up hundreds other sites, both institutional and individual, that have some discussion of "labor." In other words, virtually every web site is subject indexed with equal standing on the Internet.

The Internet's interactivity is important, because it allows users to participate in the broad community of ideas represented on the Internet. Whether it is one-on-one correspondence and a web-site author or participation in a chat room or user group, the ability to go beyond unilateral publication of one's ideas on a web site and to interactively participate in a community of ideas allows the development of a social relationship among members of the electronic community. While not all Internet users participate interactively, seeing the interaction of others is much akin to attending a meeting but not speaking oneself, the participant experiences the discussion and passively participates just as saliently as if the meeting were held at the union hall.

Taken together, this access and interactivity create a potentially powerful social community for the Internet user, what becomes vexing sociologically is that each individual creates his own sociology from a limitless menu of options. Because users determine what ideas they address and how they interpret these ideas, it becomes very difficult to assert what factors in the political and economic environment meaningfully shape any given participant's ideas and self-identity. Thus, the predictable forces that shaped peoples' ideas about themselves and their place in the order of things have become unpredictable; we cannot know what any individual has now been exposed to, nor what has affected his thinking. As the community of ideas has become unbounded, so too has the community of reference; in such a broad community, once simple distinctions—such as class—become enormously complex.

IV. Class in the Electronic Village

Among traditional theorists, socioeconomic class is viewed deterministically (Sowell, 1985); if one works non-managerially, then by definition one is a member of the working class (Lukacs, 1986; Marx and Engels, 1969). In this traditional view, it is less up to individuals to interpret their class membership than it is to discover the membership they already have. Taken in the context of the historical factory town, where a common factory job could span generations and where social and economic institutions were fairly common to all, this deterministic view makes sense. In essence, what traditional class theorists argue (albeit unintentionally) is common to a number of us, we constitute a class. Thus, in the micro environment of the factory town, a dialectic class structure of workers and managers makes sense; if individuals are indeed the product of their environment, and their environment is bounded by the limits of the factory town, then class membership is almost inevitable.

Accepting this view that class is a function of environment, it is clear that as environments change, so too does class affiliation. As workers moved from the factory town to suburbs and as the economy transitioned away from manufacturing, it follows that the historical class affiliations that encouraged union membership and collective action have changed as well. Although there is some resistance to this logical extension of traditional theory,[3] I am assuming for the present discussion that an individual's relevant environment informs a considerable portion of his class affiliation. Thus, as the lines between manager and worker have blurred, the clear dialectic that set them in unionized opposition to each other has lost salience as well.

Although the traditional view of environmentally determined class provides the bases for an evolving delineation of class boundaries, it lacks the necessary analytic to effectively determine actionable class in the individually-constructed community of the electronic village. Because the Internet provides so many options of involvement and sources of information, information relevant to the formation of an individual's self-perception will vary from person to person. Sowell (1985) argues that externally identified class membership is unable to bring the individual to action; rather, it is the individual's perception of his or her environment and its meaning that creates a sense of belonging and a willingness to act in consort with others of a similar disposition.

One final point about class in the electronic village is that I believe that classes will become much smaller, more particularly defined, and much more numerous. Class has always constituted a level of aggregation that is negated by experience; although a "working class" should by definition include all those who labor for wages, distinctions on the basis of race, gender, and relative income have long been the basis of exclusion. My operational definition of class in the electronic village is that it is a group with common economic and social interests large enough to exert pressure for social and economic change. While this definition is far from perfect, it should provide a point of departure for further discussion on the constitution of class in the electronic village. . . .

V. Conclusion

In detailing the evolution of the economic landscape from factory town to electronic village and in discussing how class and collective action may be analyzed in the context of the electronic village, my goal has been to provide a framework that researchers can use to develop meaningful studies of class and collective action in the electronic village. . . .

I believe that our evolution toward an ever-richer information context will forever change the way that we define ourselves, our class, and our view of others. I also believe that this information richness will create greater precision in class definition and will obviate the cumbersome affiliations based on race, gender, or national identity. I fervently hope that the greater availability of information will end coalitions formed on the basis of demagoguery; although the demagogue has equal access to the Internet, I expect that the pervasive availability of diverse ideas and interpretations will allow people to form better affiliative choices.

Notes

1. [I] use the term "broadcast" inclusively here, referring to any media form that presents a fixed message to the receiver.
2. This represents the current monthly cost of an Internet Service Provider, which usually provides its clients with an Internet address (URL) and an e-mail ad-

dress. For a slightly higher cost, an individual can register a unique address and domain name, which further encourages contact with one's publication. The annual cost of this higher-level type of Internet presence is less than $500.00 per year.

3. Critical theorists (Adorno, 1995; Horkheimer, 1995) argue that there is still a class dialectic between the power elite and the powerless. However, their analysis is confounded by differing definitions of who constitutes the power elite and the powerless.

References

Adorno, Theodor W. *Negative Dialectics.* New York: Continuum, 1995.

Horkheimer, Max. *Critical Theory: Selected Essays.* New York: Continuum, 1995.

Lukacs, Georg. *History and Class Consciousness: Studies in Marxist Dialectics.* Boston: MIT Press, 1986.

Marx, Karl and Friedrich Engels. *The Communist Manifesto.* New York: Washington Square Press, 1969.

Poster, Mark. *The Mode of Information: Poststructuralism and Social Context.* Chicago: University of Chicago Press, 1990.

———. *The Second Media Age.* Cambridge: Blackwell, 1996.

Sowell, Thomas. *Marxism: Philosophy and Economics.* New York: Quill/William Morrow, 1985.

—— 21 ——

Information Technology and Our Changing Economy

Martin Carnoy focuses on growth in information technology and the resulting globalization of production and explores how this growth affects people's work, families, communities, and societies. He argues that changes in work (e.g., grueling hours, intense competition, unavoidable job changes) generate substantial social costs (e.g., social isolation, personal and familial stress). He also considers policy options for responding to these problems.

Martin Carnoy

From Martin Conroy, *Sustaining the New Economy: Work, Family, and Community in the Information Age.* New York, Russell Sage Foundation, and Cambridge, MA, Harvard University Press, 2000, pp. 1–13. Reprinted by permission of Harvard University Press.

Alan Burke works for a small company in North Carolina's booming Research Triangle. His firm processes discount coupons, bills the product manufacturers for the discounts, and refunds the money to the supermarkets that collected them. This is the third job—all in the Research Triangle—Alan has had in the last eight years. The last two were in software sales, but Alan had jumped at this opportunity because he had been a Latin American studies major in college. Alan's company ships the coupons to Mexico, where their codes are keypunched, and the files are then electronically transferred back to North Carolina. He monitors the Mexico operations and is exploring ways to speed up the process. The faster the coupons can be turned around in Mexico, the more business his company can do. Between trips south of the border and the twelve-hour days at the office, Alan does not get to spend much time with his wife, Helen, who also works, and his five-year-old son, Darrin. Alan also worries whether this job will last; but he likes its intensity, and he sees the time he gives up at home as an investment in his future, hoping the sacrifice will lead to more challenging jobs in the future.

The new economy that gets Alan to work so hard and rewards him so well is more than the burgeoning internet, dot-com companies, and interfirm networking. It is a way of work and a way of life. Its core values are flexibility, innovation, and risk. As the new economy becomes the main source of wealth creation worldwide, it infuses old industrial cultures with these values. It requires a workforce that is not only well educated, but also ready to change jobs quickly and to take the risks associated with rapid change.

Alan Burke is just a short step away from social isolation. He has friends at work, but when he changes his job, chances are his friends will change as well. His urban-suburban-sprawl neighbors are, like him, totally engrossed in their work lives, so he knows them only to say hello. His parents are in Minnesota, his only sibling in Arizona. Should he lose his job before securing another one to replace it, there is really no one to count on locally except his wife, and the loss of his job could knock that already stressed relationship over the edge.

The institutions that tie Alan and other workers to one another—jobs, family, community—do not work the way they used to. Because of globalization and changes in technology, firms today need to be flexible in how they structure jobs and employment. This means that workers cannot count on working for the same firm, or even doing the same kind of work, for very long. Workers like Alan and those he employs need to network in the job market to hedge against job loss and to move ahead. They also need the quality education that enables them to perform many different types of tasks related to their career, to adjust to constant change, and to get and use the information required to make complex decisions affecting their economic and social lives. However, the two-adult, one-breadwinner family structure that was instrumental to the education of earlier generations has changed. Now, many households are headed by a single adult, and if there are two adults in the family, they are both likely to work, and there is little time to invest in their children. There is a real question of how well today's children will be prepared to cope with tomorrow's flexible work environment. Communities that integrate adults and children in neighborhood support organizations are also a thing of the past. The time needed for community involvement is dispersed in long commutes, transporting children to and from school, and networking and studying for that next job. With less stable and less supportive communities, adults are forced to rely on their own resources when adversity strikes. When those resources exist, all is well and good; when they do not, it can be all the more difficult to climb back.

If new institutions do not emerge to compensate for these fundamental transformations, the flexible production essential to high productivity in the global new economy will be that much less efficient, with disastrous effects all around. Men's and women's work is being transformed by globalization, new information technologies, and women's fight for equality, but the social institutions needed to support this change lag far behind.

The Individualization of Work and the Erosion of Social Institutions

Alan Burke's work, social relations, and self-definition are the product of historical changes that are transforming our everyday lives. Our national economies and even our national cultures are globalizing. Globalization means more competition, and not just with other companies in the same town or the same state: even flower growers in California have to vie with Costa Rican and Chilean imports, flown up the same day from thousands of miles away. Globalization also means that a nation's investment, production, and innovation are not limited by national borders. Everything, including the way we relate to our family and friends, is rapidly becoming organized around a much more compressed view of space and time. Companies in Europe, the United States, and Japan can produce microchips in Singapore, keypunch data in India, outsource clerical work to Ireland, and sell worldwide, barely concerned about the long distances or the variety of cultures involved. Even children in school or watching television are reconceptualizing their world in terms of the meanings they attach to music, the environment, sports, and race or ethnicity.

People's work has shifted from the production of agricultural and manufactured goods to the production of services and to increasingly sophisticated services at that. The main ingredient in these new services is knowledge—knowledge that increases productivity, provides a closer fit between a client's specific needs and the services delivered, and creates possibilities for the development of new products and new services. With more competition, knowledge also becomes increasingly important in manufacturing and agriculture. Quality of production, design, efficient organization, new products, customized production, and just-in-time delivery are the knowledge-intensive aspects dominating today's manufacturing and agricultural activities in both developed countries and the export sectors of developing countries.

Our lives are being transformed by a massive diffusion of new information and communication technologies. Thanks to computers and internet communication, large firms can restructure around different product lines, and even small firms can now go international and customize production for a vast variety of clients. Each one of us can correspond with people around the world instantaneously on the World Wide Web. We can get the daily news, search encyclopedias, make travel arrangements, do our banking, and buy merchandise directly from our homes. To those who know how to use it, telecomputing gives access to huge amounts of information.

The Changing Workplace

The transformation of work has been misinterpreted and mystified by writers who claim that new information technology means a massive and growing shortage of jobs, particularly good, high-skill jobs. Their claim that the new technology restricts the number of jobs, though seductive, is not supported by facts. New technology displaces workers; but it simultaneously creates new jobs by raising productivity in existing work and making possible completely new products and processes. As postindustrial economies and governments adjust to new realities, employment growth, not displacement, dominates. There will be plenty of jobs in the future, and most of them will be high-paying jobs.

Technology-caused job shortage may be a false alarm, but profound changes are occurring in the workplace. In the future, a job may not mean the same think it does today. More intense competition on a worldwide scale makes firms acutely aware of costs and productivity. The solution arrived at by employers has been to reorganize work around decentralized management, work differentiation, and customized products, thereby individualizing work tasks and differentiating individual workers in relation to their supervisors and employers. This has made subcontracting, part-time employment, and the hiring of temporary labor much easier, because a lot of work can be narrowed down to specific tasks, even as other "core" work is conducted by teams and is organized around multitasking. Socially, workers are gradually being defined less by the particular long-term job they hold than by the knowledge they have acquired by studying and working. This knowledge portfolio allows them to move across firms and even across types of work as jobs get redefined.

The effect of individualization and differentiation is to separate more and more workers from the "permanent" full-time jobs in stable businesses that characterized post-World War II development in Europe, Japan, the United States, and other industrialized countries. Just as an earlier factory revolution drove a wedge between workers and the produce they made, the new transformation is dissolving the identity that workers developed with industrial organizations such as the corporation and the trade union. Workers are being individualized, separated from their traditional identities, which were built over more than a century, and from the social networks that enabled them to find economic security. The job and everything organized around the job—the group of friends in the company, the after-work hangouts, the trade union, even the car pool—lose their social function. They are as "permanently temporary" as the work itself.

Some, mainly highly educated professional and technical workers such as Alan Burke, are building new networks. Instead of just talking to colleagues within the companies they work for, they develop electronic mail and informal information relations across companies. Network technology such as the internet helps; the exchange of information among professionals from a broad range of firms in upscale after-work hangouts serves the same purpose. The main question is what happens to the vast majority of workers who do not have easy access to information about other companies or to workers in other firms, or those highly skilled workers who have fallen out of the communications loop. They tend to be left in an individualized limbo, "disaggregated" from traditional networks but not "integrated" into new ones. New, private networks, such as temp agencies, are emerging to fill this void. With a few striking exceptions, however, such as construction unions that traditionally allocate temp jobs among their members, these networks are not organized for or by workers. They fail to satisfy the need for social integration served by stable jobs, unions, and professional associations.

Changing Families and Communities

Besides workplaces and job-centered social networks, families and communities are the traditional social integrators. In times of transition, whether it be from an agricultural society to an industrial one, industrial to postindustrial, or now local or national to global, families and communities are called upon to bear most of the responsibility in preserving social cohesion. Families also transmit much of the skill and knowledge needed by children to make their way in the adult work world. Thus, it is not surprising that whenever these workplace transitions occur, families and the communities that form around new work organizations are put under a lot of stress. The "industrial family" that emerged in the shift from agriculture to factory work beginning two hundred years ago often worked together in the factory, as if they were still on the farm. That system gradually broke down, however, and women were put in the unenviable position of feeding, caring for, and educating their children on wages controlled by their husbands. Neither did women have much control over the number of children they bore. Mothers were often too old to work for themselves by the time their last child reached working age. Working-class family life in nineteenth-century factory towns was therefore hardly idyllic, and women in these highly stressed families were called on to play a key role in maintaining moral and social cohesion. Middle-class women were better off financially, but if Jane Austen's characterization of nineteenth-century life is accurate, they too were bound tightly by strict, male-ordered conventions.

Families have changed profoundly in the past hundred years. Women have gradually rejected the burden of single-handedly maintaining social cohesion and educating the next generation. They began in the late nineteenth century by reducing family size through sexual abstinence. Middle-class women worked out their menstrual cycles and made themselves unavailable to their husbands during periods of fertility. This practice eventually spread to working-class women. The invention of the condom also helped. Smaller families made social cohesion easier, gave more time for community building, and allowed women to create a social life for themselves outside the family—even, increasingly, in the workplace. However, the latest round of women's revolt, starting in the late 1960s, struck at the underlying gender relations in family and work. Women rejected the identity of "homemaker" that was assigned them by industrial society. Masses of married women entered the workplace, part time at first and then full time. Many women ended up going it alone, heading families without men. All this happened before and independently of globalization and new information technology.

Yet when workplace restructuring did come along a short decade later, employers could not help but be influenced by women's new willingness to work and hired them in great numbers as a new source of relatively highly educated labor. However, the nuclear family with a full-time mother doing the home work—the family that had sustained and nurtured the Industrial Revolution—had been transformed. Moreover, the new organization of work that was successfully responding to the competitive pressures of a globalized economy had come to depend on the relatively cheap, highly productive, and highly flexible labor supplied increasingly by these wives and mothers. This constellation has occurred just when a strong, cohesive family with time and energy to invest in the education and well-being of both adults and children is most needed during the difficult transition period towards new forms of work and personal life.

In addition to the meaning and structure of the family having changed, the communities that had emerged from the Industrial Revolution, such as the factory towns and industrial cities with their ethnic and other highly organized suburban enclaves, had broken down in the postindustrial flight to the new urban formations François Ascher calls "metapoles" (Ascher 1998). A wave of accelerated territorial urban and suburban sprawl has by and large undermined the material base of neighborhood sociability. Globalization produces less secure and more dispersed work arrangements than earlier organizations of production. Families with two working adults are the norm, and parents and children tend to build networks within the variety of institutions in which they spend their time rather than socializing with neighbors. This makes these already semitransitory communities even less relevant to the integration of the disaggregated workers of the globalized age.

The transformation of work and the family is also dissolving the political relations that developed in the industrialized countries between working people and government through publicly provided social services, such as social security and medical insurance, provided mainly to people with full-time lifetime jobs and through civic and political groups organized around traditional communities and families. Government social transfers emerged from nineteenth- and early-twentieth-century industrial worker movements responding to the new work conditions in factories. Once workers had been pulled from their farmhouses and put into factories (and factory towns), they were able to organize and targeted the workplace as a target for bettering their social conditions. Such organizing spread to broader political organizing based on working-class interests and the fight for workers' benefits.

The very notion of government as linked directly to the needs of people in communities and workplaces also emerged from civic organizations based in local communities. They counted on participation by individuals whose conception of time and space were defined by particular notions of community and family. As those notions change, however, civic life also changes, undermining political and social relations that once integrated individuals into a national state.

The Failure of Current Public Policy Responses

With the current economic transformation—every bit as important as the last one in the nineteenth century—trade unions and governments, accustomed to the last Industrial Revolution, are not responding to the new conditions. Indeed, under pressure from both right and left, government reactions are generally off the mark, reverting to models that no longer function very well. The system of work that underlies the very concept of these social programs has changed. Flexible work and flexible employment have difficulty coexisting with rigid social entitlements. The individualization of work and the shrinkage of the public safety net create additional stress for families and communities as they try to help their members adapt to the new requirements of work life. Certain definitions of the company, the job, the family, and the community were all essential to the form of government social programs that emerged in the twentieth century; but these definitions are going through major change, making these programs much less effective.

Today's free market conservative models do not work either. Ironically, they rely on family and a civic culture that reached its high point in the heyday of the welfare state, when the "little woman" stayed home taking care of the kids while Dad earned a wage that could support the family, and this family "team" was extensively involved in voluntary civic activities. These institutional structures existed in the developed countries largely because of a partnership between government and working individuals in the context of a particular work system. Free market conservatives now want to hark back to that family and the civil society it nurtured, but they do not want the kind of government intervention that made it possible. In any case, the current work system does not warrant that kind of partnership between government and individual. The free market conservatives believe that markets in and of themselves will create a society in which high technology and high productivity flourish. This belief is plainly wrong.

Because neither political model works effectively, families, communities, and public institutions are less and less capable of restoring social equilibrium to lives knocked off balance by the individualization of work and drastically changing gender relations. In and of themselves, work and family changes do not necessarily have negative consequences. The resurgence of the individual, with greater freedom and self-directed initiative, frees people from bureaucracies, from the often excessive constraints of workplace microsocial networks, and from the grossly unequal relations dominating families. Such newfound freedom can only be enjoyed, however, if alternative forms of social organization provide people with a web of relationships that can serve as both psychological support and a basis for interaction. The whole system of relationships among these cornerstones of our societies is at stake.

Not every society faces the same problems in confronting these changes. Like all transitions, this one has caught each society at a particular historical moment in its development. Family relations, relations between labor and employers, the individual's relation to government, and community structures are all the product of this history, and they differ from one society to another. To the degree that globalization, increased competition, the new technologies, and changes in relations between men and women have universal dimensions affecting everyone, every society must react, but each may, and probably should, react differently.

A Global Approach

The remainder of this essay addresses the question of how societies can reorganize themselves to meet the new conditions of "flexible production" required for high productivity in a global economy in the context of societies undergoing massive social change. Piecemeal measures destined to increase the number of jobs or to educate and better train workers are not enough. They do not address the interactions triggered by the processes of change at the root of globalization and the new organization of work. Public policies, business strategies, and community organizing strategies need to be changed, and before this can be done we must first understand the connection between labor markets and the simultaneous (and related) changes taking place in families and communities. Once these changes are understood, policies and practices can move to make societies more socially coherent and economically productive in the new context.

These phenomena can be understood from two different vantage points. The first looks at the institutions—the workplace, the family, and community—in which individuals organize their social relations. These social sites are highly interconnected and change simultaneously. No one site takes the lead in the change process. Workplace transformation is still crucial to the change in people's lives. Economic globalization, with its increased competition, and the new information and communications technology, with its massive impact on space and time and the way people connect with one another, are pervasive influences on social relations. However, other changes originate outside the workplace and are as important for grasping the overall process of change. Women's rejection of their male-assigned identities as primarily wives and mothers profoundly affects our social world. It also interacts with globalization and new technology to transform the workplace and family life. Finally, increased individualization and rising levels of education influence identity and the reformation of community, and these, too, interact with globalization, changes in work, and women's redefinition of family to produce an even more complex set of changes in social relations.

The second view is across societies. contemporary societies are similar in many ways, but they also differ socially, politically, and culturally. Their institutional histories are particular to each. As a result, they react differently to global change across social spaces: workplaces, families, and communities. The "Anglo-Saxon" highly developed countries—Australia, Great Britain, Canada, New Zealand, and the United States—tend to follow more "open," free market economic policies. Their labor markets are most "flexible." Women's movements within these countries have been parallel, and family changes similar. Even in this similarity, however, there is much variance. Canada, so like the United States in many ways, is much more protective of its workers as it engages in the new global economy. Canada provides more public support to families and has much less poverty, but unemployment rates are higher. Great Britain also differs from the United States despite years of neoconservative economic and social policies that paralleled the Reaganomics of the United States in the 1980s.

These differences among the more flexible labor markets are small compared with those between the Anglo-Saxon countries and continental Europe, Scandinavia, and Japan—and there is considerable variance within that second group as well. Women are more likely to divorce, and women with children more likely to work, in Scandinavia than in Italy, Spain, or Japan. Families and labor markets in the latter societies are much more "traditional" than those in the former. Unemployment rates are much higher in Italy and Spain, so young people marry later and have fewer children—so few, in fact, that populations in both countries are in danger of declining. Other societies provide support to families through major government subsidies for child care, as in France and Scandinavia, which seems to have an effect on the number of children couples are willing to have. Although youth unemployment rates are as high in France as in Italy or Spain, women in France have about the same number of children as British women or Anglo women in the United States, where youth unemployment rates are much lower and labor markets more flexible.

These varying institutional histories mean that people in different societies have reached high standards of living by somewhat different routes. Today, all societies face a changing global economic and social environment and changing gender roles. People accustomed to certain lifestyles have to make personal and collective decisions on how to adjust. They do not want to abandon these lifestyles; after all, over the past fifty years, the Western way of life has been associated with vast economic and social improvements. Many Americans cannot understand why the French, Italians, and Germans, facing high unemployment rates, do not deregulate their economies to look like that of the United States, with its massive job creation but stagnant wages and increasing work hours. In turn, Europeans, despite unemployment and other problems, cannot understand how Americans can tolerate such high rates of child poverty and the stresses of constant work with little if any vacation time. The United States is also pressuring an economically troubled Japan to reduce regulation, to jumpstart their economy by freeing up markets. The Japanese used these same regulations, however, to become a global high-tech powerhouse in just two generations, and it did so with low unemployment and poverty, a high degree of job security, and almost no social strife.

Because of these institutional differences, each nation, or group of nations, is likely to choose different ways to adjust to all the same transformative forces. Even with these differences, all nations will have to rely to one degree or another on their public sector or the state to successfully reintegrate individuals socially. To reintegrate individuals as they are buffeted about by the reorganization of work and family, nation-states, regions, and local communities will have to focus on enhancing knowledge, especially for those groups least able to participate effectively in flexible labor markets.

This is not going to be easy. A major shift is occurring in the way people regard the traditional source of leadership on such policies—their national governments—and in the way they participate in politics. This change has occurred because, with globalization, nation-states have become steadily less able to satisfy the varied economic interests of diverse groups living within their boundaries. In 1964, almost 80 percent of Americans agreed with the following statement: "You can trust the government in Washington to do what is right just about always, or most of the time." This proportion declined to about 27 percent by 1980 and, after rising back up to 45 percent in 1984, continued a steady decline to 20 percent in 1994 (Inglehart 1997, figure 10.2). Until the latest recession of the early 1990s, Western Europeans did not show a similar trend in attitude toward their political systems, but the reaction to this recession seems to have been much more negative than in the past (Inglehart 1997, figure 10.5).

Under these conditions, it is no accident that nation-states are looking for low-cost social politics that simultaneously enhance growth and reincorporate "disaggregated" workers. Economists have long argued that a major source of economic growth is a society's investment in learning (Schultz 1961). Whatever its contribution to the creation of wealth in the past, human knowledge is an even more important ingredient in the information economy. A primary characteristic of flexible production in the new global environment is that it is human capital intensive, new knowledge intensive, and networking intensive. Relatively low labor and material costs alone are no longer enough to assure a firm or nation a place at the global table. The importance of knowledge is accentuated as innovation becomes increasingly endogenous to firms and firm networks. The globalization of innovation also means that even at the peripheries of global firms, the production of information technology depends on a knowledge-enhancing environment. Because of this defining feature, the production of information technology and the quality of information itself inherently depend on a society's members' access to knowledge, particularly the kind that help them integrate into the new flexible, global environment.

This fact may seem obvious, but it poses a fundamental problem that is bound to dominate societies for years to come. In the past, even the recent past, much of the knowledge creation required for social integration occurred in workplaces, families, and local communities, and this process needs to continue in the future even more intensively. However, if employers want just-in-time knowledge, if families are leading just-in-time lives, if communities are increasingly disparate and spatially ill defined, how can the creation of knowledge take place? It is not just an issue of providing the same educational and information services now available. A high proportion of children in developed societies are being born into less educated families. In the past, this was not a significant problem because these children could expect to find decent, relatively high-paying jobs in an expanding manufacturing sector. That, however, is no longer the case. The amount and diversity of knowledge demanded in higher-paying jobs are increasing; yet, more important, the knowledge base required just to function effectively in flexible labor markets, no matter what the job, is also becoming more complex.

This means that institutions' abilities to integrate individuals around access to knowledge—institutions ranging from local organizations to nation-states to even supranational organizations—define the boundaries of the new communities. I make the case in chapter 5 that this is already happening in many different forms, and it is not just happening among highly educated, highly networked individuals. In some instances, the most innovative responses to the new flexible economy are coming from the most marginalized sectors of society.

On the other hand, any traditional organization unable to deliver the various kinds of broad-based education needed for individuals to cope successfully in the new global environment—what I call "integrative knowledge"—will become superfluous to individuals' conception of community. The most obvious candidate for such superfluousness is the state, because it is the state, especially the nation-state, that has borne the greatest responsibility for socially integrating workers during the late industrial age. If governments prove unable to organize institutions successfully around integrative knowledge and a "livable" form of economic development, they will cease to be central to citizens' lives. Individuals will seek other institutions and communities that they believe will do a better job in delivering integrative knowledge to them and their children. So the stakes are high: those nations and localities without coherent reintegrative institutions will be marked by gradual social disintegration and social conflict. Not all developed societies will adjust quickly to the change taking place, and some will suffer serious consequences as a result. Yet I am optimistic, and the analysis in this book reflects my optimism. Political leaders who see the handwriting on the wall early will be able to organize delivery of integrative knowledge and livable economic development to create the conditions in which flexibility and economic competitiveness can be sustained. I believe that all the member countries of the Organisation for Economic Co-operation and Development (OECD) have the capacity to sustain flexible production and at the same time be enjoyable places to live. Those nations and localities that pull themselves together politically to do so will thrive in the global economy. Those that do not, however, face a difficult future.

References

Ascher, Francois, *La Republique contre la ville*. (Paris: L'Aube, 1998)

Inglehart, Ronald, *Modernization and Post-Modernization*. (Princeton: Princeton University Press, 1997).

Schultz, Theodore W. "Investment in Man," *American Economic Review* 51 (1) 1961: 1–17.

—— **22** ————————————————————————————

Music: Intellectual Property's Canary in the Digital Coal Mine

The following article explains how and why the Internet has affected the music industry so profoundly. A case study in the copyright implications of information technology, the National Research Council's report suggests that the music industry's experience is an important cautionary tale. As more powerful technologies become available, copyright battles are likely to emerge in other industries.

National Research Council

Of all the content industries affected by the digital environment, the music industry has, for a variety of reasons, been thrown first into the maelstrom. Events have proceeded at the dizzying pace that has been called "Internet time," with technical, legal, social, and industrial developments occurring in rapid-fire succession. Yet the problems facing the music industry will likely soon be found on the doorstep of other content industries. . . . The music industry offers an intriguing case study illustrating the problems, op-

NOTE: Underground coal deposits are invariably accompanied by methane gas, which is highly explosive, but colorless, odorless, and tasteless. Before more advanced detectors became available, miners would take canaries into the mines with them because the birds were far more susceptible to methane and thus offered advance warning. The concept has since become a metaphor for anything that serves in that role.

portunities, possible solutions, and cast of characters involved in dealing with digital intellectual property (IP). The focus is not on the day-to-day specifics, as these sometimes change more rapidly than daily newspapers can track. Instead, the perspective is on the underlying phenomena, as a way of understanding the issues more generally. Not all these issues will play out identically in different industries, of course. But some of the problems will be widespread, because they are intrinsic to digital information, no matter what content it carries. The problems include distributing digital information without losing control of it, struggles over standards and formats, and evolving the shape of industries as the new technology changes the previous balance of power.

Why Music?

The problem, or opportunity, has hit music first for a variety of reasons. First, files containing high-fidelity music can be made small enough that both storage and downloading are reasonable tasks. Digitized music on a standard CD requires about 10 megabytes per minute of music; with a format called MP3, that same information can be compressed so that it occupies about one-tenth as much space. As a result, music files currently require about 1 megabyte for each minute of music (or about 45 megabytes for a typical album) yet offer generally acceptable (though not quite CD quality) sound. With multigigabyte disk drives common, dozens of albums are easily stored directly on a hard drive or inexpensively written to writable CDs. Video, by contrast, contains a great deal more information: A digitized 2-hour movie (e.g., on a DVD) contains about 5 gigabytes of information.

Second, access to digitized music is abundant, and demand for its is growing rapidly. Numerous MP3 sites offer free MP3 playback software, songs, and albums. With a 56K modem (which provides a sustained transfer rate of about 5K bytes/second), a 5-minute song takes about 17 minutes to download, an album about 3 hours. With access to high-speed network connections growing more commonplace (e.g., at work and on campuses), sustained download speeds of 50K bytes/second and higher are widely available, making possible the transfer of a song in under 2 minutes and of an entire album in about 18 minutes.

But you need not go to the Web to find digitized music. A very large percentage of the music industry's current content is already available in an unprotected digital form: CDs. Widely available software programs know as "rippers" (or "digital audio extractors," in more polite circles) can read the digital data from CD tracks and rewrite it in a variety of formats, notably as MP3 files. These files are easily shared among friends or posted around the Web.

The third reason that the problem has surfaced first in the music world is that music is popular with a demographic group (students in particular, young people generally), many of whom have easy access to the required technology, the sophistication to use it, and an apparently less than rigorous respect for the protections of copyright laws. Students also constitute a well-defined and geographically proximate community, which facilitates the sharing of digital music files.

Fourth, music can be enjoyed with the existing technology: Good speakers are easily attached to a computer, producing near-CD quality sound, and a variety of portable players (e.g., the Rio from Diamond Multimedia) are available that hold 30 minutes to an hour of music. By contrast, even if it were available on the Web, downloading a best-selling novel is not enough; it would still have to be printed before you could enjoy the work.

W(h)ither The Market?

What are the consequences for the recording industry? It is facing an age-old question that lurks in the background of most innovations that affect intellectual property: Something is about to happen, but will it be a disaster or an opportunity? New technology and new business models for delivering content are almost always greeted with the belief that they will destroy the existing market. In 17th century England, the emergence of lending libraries was seen as the death knell of book stores; in the 20th century, photocopying was seen as the end of the publishing business, and videotape the end of the movie business. . . . Yet in each case, the new development produced a new market for larger than the impact it had on the existing market. Lending libraries gave inexpensive access to books that were too expensive to purchase, thereby helping to make literacy widespread and vastly increasing the sale of books. Similarly, the ability to photocopy makes the printed material in a library more valuable to consumers, while videotapes have significantly increased viewing of movies. . . . But the original market in each case was also transformed, in some cases bringing a new cast of players and a new power structure.

Will digital information do the same for music? Some suggest that the ability to download music will increase sales by providing easy purchase and delivery 24 hours a day, opening up new marketing opportunities and new niches. For example, the low overhead of electronic distribution may allow artists themselves to distribute free promotional recordings of individual live performances, while record companies continue to focus on more polished works for mass release. Digital information may also help create a new form of product, as consumers' music collections become enormously more personalizable (e.g., the ability to create personalized albums that combine individual tracks from multiple performers). Others see a radical reduction in aggregate royalties and, eventually, in new production, as pirated music files become widely distributed and music purchases plummet.

The outcome for digital music is still uncertain; there is of course no guarantee that the digital music story will play out in the same way as it has in these other industries. But past experience is worth considering, reminding us as it does that at times innovation has contributed to a resurgence in the market rather than a reduction.

What Can Be Done?

There are two major lines of response to the challenges outlined above: find an appropriate business model, and develop and deploy technical protection mechanisms. Each is considered below.

The Business Model Response

"The first line of defense against pirates is a sensible business model that combines pricing, ease of use, and legal prohibition in a way that minimizes the incentives for consumers to deal with pirates." [Lacy, J., J. Snyder, and D. Maher. 1997. "Music on the Internet and the Intellectual Property Protection Problem," pp. SS77–SS83 in *Proceedings of the International Symposium on Industrial Electronics*. New York: IEEE Computer Society Press]. This view nicely characterizes the business model response, suggesting that one way to cope with piracy is to provide a more attractive product and service. The difficult part of this approach is that it may require rethinking the existing business model, industry structure, and more.

Make the Content Easier and Cheaper to Buy Than to Steal   One example of that rethinking is the suggestion by Gene Hoffman, CEO of EMusic, Inc. (formerly GoodNoise, a digital music provider): "We think the best way to stop piracy is to make music so cheap it isn't worth copying." EMusic sells singles in digital form for 99 cents.

But if those singles are in the form of MP3 files, they are unprotected—nothing prevents the purchaser from passing a file on to others or posting it on a Web site (illegal though these actions may be). So how could there be a market in such things, when it appears that all the value in the item could be extinguished by the very first sale?

One answer becomes evident to anyone who has actually tried to download MP3 music from any noncommercial site: The service is terrible and the experience can be extraordinarily frustrating. Search engines can assist in finding songs by title, performer, and so on, but you have to know how to look: Can't find what you're looking for when you type in "Neil Young"? Try "Niel Young." In any collection, quality control is a problem; when the data are entered by thousands of individual amateurs, the problem is worse.

When the links are found, the next question is, How long are you willing to keep trying, when receiving responses such as "Host not responding," "Could not login to FTP server; too many users—please try again later," and "Unable to find the directory or file; check the name and try again"? The computers containing the files are often personal machines that are both unreliable and overloaded.

Even once connected, the speedy download times cited earlier are ideals that assume that both the computer on the other end and its connection to the Internet are up to the task. The real-world experience is often not so good: Creating a Web site with a few music files is easy; providing good service on a site with hundreds or thousands of songs is not: The hardware and software requirements are considerably more complex.

Where is the business then, if files are unprotected by technical mechanisms (even if legally still protected)? It may be in the service, as much as the content. Why experience 30 minutes or an hour of frustration, if for a dollar or so you can have what you want easily, reliably, and quickly? This is one example of how, in the digital age, content industries may mutate, at least in part, into service companies. The key product is not only the song; it is also the speed, reliability, and convenience of access to it.

There is also a more general point here about the relative power of law and business models. Although legal prohibitions against copying are useful against large-scale pirates (e.g., those who would post MP3 files for sale and hence have to be visible enough to advertise), they are unlikely to be either effective or necessary against individual infringers, where detection and enforcement are problematic. Where such private behavior is concerned, business models may offer a far more effective means of dealing with IP issues.

Use Digital Content to Promote the Traditional Product   Another business model approach sees free online distribution of music as a way to build the market for the traditional product. In March 1999 Tom Petty put a song from his new album online; it was downloaded more than 150,000 times in 2 days. Other groups have made similar efforts, releasing digital versions before the albums were available in stores . . . , all in the belief that distribution of a sample track will increase sales of the traditional product.

In October 1999 the rock group Creed made the most popular song from their CD release "Human Clay" available for free download at more than 100 sites. The Creed CD jumped to the number one spot on the Billboard top album sales when it debuted, notwithstanding the free give-away of what was believed to be its first hit. This phenomenon calls into question the conventional wisdom that, although one may choose to give away free songs as a promotional tool, to give away the most popular song will eliminate some motivation to buy the entire album. The utilization of the digital download of free songs in their entirety in order to drive sales of traditional "packaged goods," in the form of CDs and audio cassettes, is perhaps yet another example of the so-called "clicks and mortar" business strategy, under which the Internet does not replace brick and mortar sales, but can be used as an adjunct to traditional brick and mortar retailing methodologies.

Give Away (Some) Digital Content and Focus on Auxiliary Markets   A more unconventional approach takes the position that most digital content is so difficult to protect that a more sensible business model would treat it as if it were free. . . .

The value instead is in the auxiliary markets. The classic example is the Grateful Dead, who have long permitted taping of their live shows (and have taken the additional step of permitting fans to trade digitized versions of those recordings on the Web. . . . They gave away their live performances (which were generally not released as records) and profited from the increased draw at concerts, and the income from related merchandise and traditionally produced studio recordings.

The breadth of applicability of this model is of course not immediately clear. The model may be idiosyncratic to a particular band, audience, and tradition. But the thought is at least worth entertaining that the model might be used in other musical genres and perhaps in other publishing businesses, as well.

This variety of approaches illustrates the challenge and the opportunity of finding an appropriate business model in the world of digital IP. One challenge is in determining whether the existing models and existing industry structure can be made to work in the face of the new technology. In some cases it can; for example, movie theaters remain viable in the presence of VCRs and rental tapes. But in other cases the existing business model and industry structure cannot be maintained, no matter how vigorous the legal or technical efforts. In such cases some form of adaptation and creative rethinking can be particularly effective; the business model responses noted above offer a few examples of that type of thinking.

The Technical Protection Response

Many technical protection mechanisms are motivated by the key issue noted earlier, lying at the heart of the difficulties with digital IP: the liberation of content from medium. When content is bound to some physical object, the difficulty of duplicating the physical object provides an impediment to reproduction. However, when digitally encoded, text need no longer be carried by a physical book, paintings by a canvas, or music by a record or CD, so reproduction becomes easier. What options does technology offer for controlling reproduction?

Mark the Bits   One response is to "mark" the bits, that is, add to the content the digital equivalent of a watermark that identifies the rights holder. While it does not prevent the content from being copied and redistributed, this technique can at least make evident who owns the material and possibly aid in tracking the source of the redistribution.

Music can be watermarked by very small changes to some of the digital samples. . . . Music is typically digitized by measuring the sound intensity 44,100 times a second, using a 16-bit number (0 to 65,535) to indicate intensity level. If the intensity of a sample is actually 34,459, it can be changed slightly and the human ear will never hear the difference. This permits encoding information in the music, by deciding, say, that the last two bits in every 150th sample will not encode the music, but will instead encode information about the music (e.g., the identity of the rights holder). This change to the music will be imperceptible to a person but will be easily read by a computer program.

A variety of such watermarking techniques is commercially available, including those that are "robust" (i.e., difficult to remove without affecting the music) and those that are "fragile" (i.e., distorted by most modifications to a file, as for example compression using MP3). One proposed plan is to embed both a robust and a fragile watermark in newly released CDs and then require that licensed portable players refuse to play digital music that has a robust watermark but lacks the fragile watermark. The presence of the robust watermark indicates that the music file is no longer in its original form (and hence may have been copied).

Reattach the Bits   A second, more ambitious approach is to find a way to "reattach" the bits to something physical that is not easily duplicated. A number of technical protection mechanisms are motivated by this basic observation, the description that follows draws on features of several of them as a way of characterizing this overall approach.

One relatively straightforward technique for reattaching the bits is to employ special hardware that enforces copy protection. Digital audio tape players, for example, have a serial copy management system (SCMS) in which the hardware itself enforces the prohibition against making digital copies of copies. The first-generation copy contains an indication that it is a copy rather than the original, and any SCMS-compliant device will not copy this copy.

This technique works well but is limited to single-purpose devices. It will not work on a general-purpose computer, because the user would be able to gain access to the original information and make copies by means other than the SCMS. As a result, the challenge of reattaching the bits becomes more difficult for a general-purpose computer. A succession of increasingly more sophisticated and complex mechanisms can be used to approach this goal:

• *Encrypt the content.* This mechanism provides, at a minimum, that the consumer will have to pay to get a decryption key; without it, a copy of the encrypted content is useless. Buy a song, and you get both an encrypted file and a password for decrypting (and playing) the song.

• *Anchor the content to a single machine or user.* Simply encrypting the content is not enough, as the purchaser can pass along (or sell) both the encrypted content and the key, or simply decrypt the content, save it, and pass that along. There are a variety of ways to anchor the content; one conceptually simple technique encodes in the decryption key (or the song file) information about the computer receiving the encrypted file, such as the serial number of its primary disk. The decryption/playback software then checks for these attributes before it will decrypt or play the song.

• *Implement persistent encryption.* The scheme above is still not sufficient, because a consumer might legally purchase content and legally decrypt it, then pass that on (or sell it) to others who can modify the decrypted file to play on their machine. Some technical protection mechanisms attempt to provide additional security by narrowing as much as possible the window of opportunity during which the decrypted information is available. To do this the information must be decrypted just in time (i.e., just before it is used), no temporary copies are ever stored, and the information is decrypted as physically close as possible to the site where it will be used. Just-in-time decryption means that decrypted information is available as briefly as possible and then perhaps only in very small chunks at a time. Decrypting close to the usage site reduces the number of places inside (or outside) the machine at which the decrypted information might be "siphoned off." Persistent encryption is complex to implement in its most ambitious and effective form, because it requires the IP protection software to take control of some of the routine input and output capabilities of the computer. If this is not done, there are a large number of places (e.g., in the operating system) from which decrypted information might be obtained. . . .

Another element of technology provides a useful additional capability. Differences among consumers make it useful to offer content on a variety of different terms. For music, for example, one might want to sell the right to a time-limited use, a finite number of uses, or an unlimited time and usage count. A variety of systems have been developed to provide an easy way to specify a wide variety of such conditions. When a music file is downloaded, then, in addition to the music it will contain information indicating the license conditions under which the music may be used. The playback software checks these conditions and enforces them ppropriately.

Note that the technology picture outlined here is optimistic. . . . Note, too, that as with any security mechanisms, the key question in the real world is not the purely technical issue of whether it can be defeated. All mechanisms can be, eventually. Instead the key questions go back to the three fundamental factors: technology, business models, and the law. The legal system sets the basic rules on what may be controlled; technology and business models then work in tandem: Is the technology strong enough to provide a meaningful disincentive for theft, yet not so expensive (for either the distributor or the consumer) that the added costs drastically curtail demand? At this point in the development of digital content delivery mechanisms, companies have relatively little real-world experience on which to make such judgments.

A Scenario

A system using some of the technology described above is easy to imagine; the details used here are intended to convey the general idea rather than describe any particular system. The user downloads and installs software that provides for music playback and assists with online purchasing. He or she then connects to a Web site offering music in that form, selects a song or album, and provides a credit card number to pay for it. As part of the transaction, the vending site is provided with information specific to the computer requesting the file (e.g., the serial number of its disk); this information is embedded in the decryption key supplied with the file. The vending site may, in addition, mark the music file with a unique ID that enables linking back to this transaction, in the event that the decrypted audio file is later found to have been distributed.

The customer now has the song, the vendor has the money, and the consumer can use the song according to the terms of use that are embedded in the file. Redistribution of the file is pointless, as the song won't play on another computer. Yet all the other advantages of digital audio are maintained: The user can store large amounts of music compactly, have random access to any track on any album, and create personalized albums containing selected tracks from selected albums in a particular order.

The same basic model applies to portable players: . . . To anchor the bits (i.e., make them playable on only one portable player), a hardware identifier may be built into the file, such as the serial number of the player. Just as on the PC, the player's software can check for this information and refuse to play the song unless the identifier in the file matches the device.

Constraints on Technological Solutions

The scenario above sounds simple, but there are inherent difficulties. First, no protection scheme lasts forever. Any time content is valuable, some people will be motivated to find ways to break the protection mechanism, and some of them will be more than willing to share their techniques. . . .

One plausible countermeasure is to design protection to be renewable (i.e., easily changed so that the new protection scheme can quickly replace the old). This solution protects content from that point forward, limits the profits from piracy, and keeps the protection a moving target for those trying to break it.

A second difficulty in developing technical protection solutions is that consumer devices must be easy to use. Cumbersome content protection schemes may discourage use, particularly as consumers are likely to be impatient with mechanisms that they perceive are intended to protect someone else's interests. This requirement puts stringent performance demands on a system (e.g., decryption must be fast enough to become imperceptible) and requires careful design, to ensure that the system is conceptually simple.

A third difficulty arises with any system that "anchors" content to a specific device: the potential loss of all of that content if the device in question fails or is replaced. Does the consumer have to repurchase every piece of music that he or she owns if the portable player fails, is lost, or is replaced?

A fourth difficulty is the diversity of interests at work here, including the computer owner (i.e., music consumer), computer manufacturers (of both hardware and software), music publishers, and performers. Consumers have expectations about the ability to share and the ongoing use of content, publishers are concerned about the overall market, and performers are concerned about their audience and royalties. Getting significant content protection machinery in place and widely distributed would require a concerted and coordinated effort, yet each of the players has its own goals and aims that may not necessarily align. . . .

A fifth difficulty is the inherent complexity of providing end-to-end protection within a general-purpose computer. PCs have been successful to a significant degree because they have open architectures; that is, components of the machine can be replaced by the user (e.g., replacing a hard drive with a larger one or buying a new sound card). As long as the machine is designed this way—to be accessible to users—decrypted information can be captured in numerous ways as it passes from one place to another inside the machine. One could modify the software used by the sound card, for example, so that it not only generates the signal for the speakers but also stores away the decrypted music samples. Clearly, hardware and software designers could make such steps progressively more difficult, but the effort they must expend and the consequential costs would be substantial.

A sixth difficulty arises from the installed base of PCs. With more than 100 million computers in use, any scheme that requires new hardware faces a significant barrier to acceptance. Clearly the benefits have to outweigh the cost and inconvenience of changing machines. One benefit that may encourage the adoption of new hardware is the interest in electronic commerce. Efforts have been mounted to create new hardware and software with security built in at all levels. If this succeeds, PCs may routinely come with technology that makes possible secure electronic commerce, and that may also be usable for enforcing intellectual property rights.

A second mitigating factor here is the relatively short lifetime of computers, at least in the corporate environment, where 3 years is a common figure for turnover. A related opportunity arises with new technology: With portable players, a relatively recent development, there is not a major installed base requiring compatibility, offering the chance to set security measures in place near the outset of the new technology. . . . The installed base problem here is more likely to arise from the need to be compatible with the existing MP3 format, widely and legally used by consumers to make personal copies of CDs they own and who are likely to want players capable of playing those files.

There is also a traditional chicken and egg problem involving technology development and content owners. Investing in new content delivery technology is risky without content to deliver, yet content owners are reluctant to release their content for digital distribution until they feel the delivery system has been tested in real use, is secure, and will be accepted by consumers. . . .

Finally, there is the problem of the digital infrastructure, one element of which is transaction support: Buying content online requires systems for secure transactions, in high volume, possibly involving rather small amounts of money (e.g., $1 for a song). A second element of infrastructure, public-key cryptography, is effective at protecting content but requires a substantial infrastructure to make it easy to use on a wide scale. . . . Although some progress has been made on creating the infrastructure to support electronic commerce, these and other elements of this digital infrastructure are not yet in place for routine use and will require both a sizable investment for their creation and a major effort at agreeing on standards.

Industry Consequences of the New Technology

The digitization of music in general and the availability of an easily used format like MP3 in particular have wide-ranging consequences for the industry, consequences that are being played out in a number of struggles.

One consequence is the possibility of a radical shift in power. . . . One of the fundamental changes brought about by the Web is the availability of an inexpensive publishing and distribution medium with worldwide reach. If composers and performers choose to take advantage of that medium, what is to be the role of traditional music publishers and distributors?

This phenomenon has been called disintermediation, referring to the elimination of middlemen in transactions. In the view of some, traditional publishers are becoming unnecessary, because authors, composers, and performers will be able to publish and distribute their product online themselves. Some performers have already done so, though generally offering their products as free samples. A variety of MP3 Web sites have also emerged, modeled on the notion of artists' cooperatives: Composers and performers can post their work and receive royalties, with no effort on their part other than the original posting.

Even as ease of publication may provide alternatives to and hence reduce the demand for one kind of intermediary—traditional publishers and distributors—it may simultaneously increase the demand for another kind. If anyone can be a creator and publisher, content will proliferate, producing a world of information overload. The consumer's problem will not be obtaining content, but rather wading through it all. This difficulty has long been recognized: Nearly 30 years ago Herbert Simon suggested that "a wealth of information creates a poverty of attention." . . . In the content-rich world, then, information intermediaries may become even more important because, although content may proliferate, attention is on an immutable budget.

But these intermediaries would not be publishers in the traditional sense; hence the phenomenon may not be so much disintermediation in general, as the diminishing need for one variety of intermediary and an increasing role for another. The new role of publishers in an information-rich world may require a different kind of company with a different focus. This scenario presents the possibility of a significant shift in the power structure of the music industry and a significant economic impact. Little wonder, then, that battles are emerging over the future character of the industry.

The Broader Lessons

Three general lessons can be learned from the early years of the struggle over digital music. First, what has happened there may happen in other content industries as well, as other products become digitized.

Books and movies have begun to feel the effects. Electronic books are appearing, with several Web sites selling full-length books in digital form, while others offer reloadable book-sized portable display hardware. This development is made possible in part by the creation of more secure forms for the content. . . .

With electronic publishing of books come many of the same issues concerning the role of the publisher. Various sites on the Web offer electronic publication of works, presenting an alternative to traditional publishers, while also promising 40 to 50 percent royalty rates and author retention of copyright, practices far from common in the print publishing business.

Movies in digital form are currently saved from widespread illegal copying because of their large size, but this barrier is likely to be overcome before too long. A number of sites have begun already to sell full-length movies in digital form, but at upwards of 200 megabytes for a (compressed) movie, and 5 megabytes for even a trailer, the space requirements and download times are still quite substantial. Others are exploring the possibility of Internet distribution of movies. Digital movie piracy has also appeared. . . . These copies are relatively low-quality, still sizable to download and store, and not easy to find (they are generally traded in low-profile news groups and chat rooms). But the struggle over digital movies has clearly arrived and will grow worse as storage capacity and transmission speeds increase.

The second lesson is that struggles over protecting intellectual property take many forms and reach into a variety of areas, including battles over technology, standards, industry structure, and business models. Keeping this in mind often makes it easier to decode the disparate agendas and strategies of the many players engaged in the struggle.

The third lesson is that among the various battles, the struggle over standards is often the most intense as it typically has the most far-reaching effects, with consequences for authors, publishers, and consumers alike, as well as the shape and character of the industry.

—— 23 ——————————————

The Case of Collective Violence

The authors use the term "collective violence" to denote war, genocide, environmental destruction, systematic violations of human rights, and other large-scale harmful actions. Because computers are useful in all large-scale projects, computer professionals make crucial contributions to most cases of collective violence. This reading discusses the psychosocial mechanisms that allow decent individuals to participate, as part of a group, in such actions.

Craig Summers and Eric Markusen

This article extends the emerging debate and discussion over ethical dimensions of computer science from issues such as software piracy, viruses,

Reprinted by permission of the publisher from "Computers, Ethics, and Collective Violence," Craig Summers and Eric Markusen, *Journal of Systems Software*, pp. 91–103. Copyright 1992 by Elsevier Science Inc.

and unauthorized systems entry to the realm of collective violence. We view collective violence as actions by large numbers of people that contributes to large-scale destruction. Several ways in which computer professionals may contribute to actual or potential violence are briefly discussed. Then, to understand how well-meaning computer professionals can do work of the highest technical quality, but which is routinized and isolated from its social effects, we discuss three types of psychosocial mechanisms: (1) psychological-level aspects of one's own role; (2) bureaucratic factors routinizing individual involvement, and (3) specific factors in scientific and technological work affecting perceived responsibility. To understand why these mechanisms occur, the importance of perceived short-term economic needs for day-to-day living are considered against values and ethics. A predictive model of temporal and social "traps" is outlined that explains when individuals may contribute to harmful projects regardless of social values and human welfare. . . .

Introduction

Professions in contemporary society can be characterized by four defining features: they possess specialized knowledge; they are important to society; they enjoy a high degree of autonomy and self-regulation; and they are guided by an ideology of public service [1]. The latter two features involve ethics, defined here as moral guidelines for behavior. Thus, most professions have codes of ethics to which all members in good standing are expected to adhere.

However, simply having codes of ethics does not guarantee ethical behavior. As society and technology change, new situations emerge which create new ethical dilemmas. Also, is students and practitioners of a profession are not carefully instructed about ethical issues and concerns relevant to their profession, it is unlikely that they will guided by them.

Ethics are every bit as relevant to the profession of computer science as they are to other contemporary professions. There has been widespread and influential dissemination of computer technology in recent years, although this profession is still relatively young. . . . Examination of ethical issues that relate to computer professionals[1]—as embodied in this special issue of *The Journal of Systems and Software*—is therefore both welcome and necessary. Practices such as illegal duplication of software, insertion of harmful viruses, and unauthorized entry and retrieval of private files all need careful exposure and analysis in terms of ethical principles.

This article, however, examines a rather different ethical dimension that is nonetheless relevant to computer scientists. Rather than focus on ethical issues such as viruses, abuse of passwords, privacy, and copyrights, we are concerned with the possibility that computer professionals may lend their expertise to activities and projects that involve harm to other human beings on a large scale. We are, in short, concerned with the relations among computers, ethics, and collective violence. By "collective violence" we mean large-scale destruction to which many people have contributed.

This article has [four] primary objectives, which are examined in the sections that follow. First, we will briefly address the problem of collective violence. Second, we hope to persuade readers that they should be concerned with the problem of collective violence. Third and fourth, we will summarize relevant literature from psychology and sociology to explain how and why normal individuals—including professionals—contribute to collective violence. . . .

Collective Violence during the Twentieth Century

Anyone who reads the newspaper or watches the news on television is painfully aware of the prevalence of collective violence throughout the world. In this section, we discuss a number of relationships between professionals and collective violence.

First, collective violence can occur in a wide variety of forms. Warfare, which can take place between nations or groups of nations (international war) as well as between groups within a nation (civil war), is perhaps the most widely recognized and thoroughly studied form of collective violence. Genocide, a term invented only in 1944, refers to the deliberate destruction of groups of human beings because of their racial, ethnic, religious, or political identity. When governments permit and enforce official discrimination and violation of human rights—for example, apartheid in South Africa and torture and "disappearances" in Argentina—large numbers of people suffer and some lose their lives. Likewise, certain corporate practices, such as exploitation of the environment or tolerance of dangerous workplace conditions, can hurt many people. Finally, the nuclear arms race, even though it has been justified as a deterrent, poses the ever-present threat of collective violence on an unimaginable scale.

Second, some scholars have argued that the scale of collective violence was greater in the twentieth century than at any other period in history [2]. One analyst of genocidal violence estimates that more than 100,000,000 people were killed by governments during the twentieth century [3]. Another scholar counted 22 wars underway in 1987—more than in any other single year in human history [4]. Military historians and weapons experts argue that the intensity and lethality of war in the twentieth century exceeds anything in history [5, 6]. Projections of the possible results of a nuclear war have estimated that more than one billion people could be killed [7] and the planetary ecosystem catastrophically damaged [8]. The unprecedented levels of collective violence probably do not reflect any increase in aggressiveness or brutality among human beings, but rather their possession of more effective technologies for killing [9].

A third aspect of professionals and collective violence is that most of the individuals who contribute to collective violence are psychologically normal and motivated by idealistic concerns. Studies of the Holocaust, for example, have found that the vast majority of Nazi perpetrators were ". . . normal people according to currently accepted definitions by the mental health profession" [10, p. 148]. This finding has been corroborated by numerous other scholars [1].

Finally, professions and professionals make crucial contributions to most forms of collective violence. Again using the Holocaust as an illustration, there is strong consensus among scholars that educated professionals played indispensable roles in rationalizing and implementing the extermination of the Jews [11]. In his study of German doctors in the Holocaust, Robert Lifton [12] found that these health care professionals made crucial contributions to the killing process, even peering through peepholes in the gas chamber doors to determine when the victims were dead.

Why Computer Professionals Should Be Concerned about Collective Violence

If psychologically normal professionals could be implicated in violence as repugnant and brutal as the Holocaust, it is also conceivable that other professionals could make equally destructive contributions now, particularly if the effects are less apparent. Therefore, the primary reason that computer professionals should be concerned about collective violence is as potential contributors. . . .

Computer technology may adversely affect human warfare through military weapons use. One of the first computer professionals to recognize this was Norbert Wiener, the developer of cybernetics [18–20]. A substantial portion of government research (in North America as least) is through military agencies [4, 21, 22]. This involves a broad cross-section of scientists and researchers who have little or no control over how their published work is subsequently developed or used.

The greatest threat of computers in the military is in nuclear weapons systems. A war fought with nuclear weapons would constitute a human and environmental disaster. Such a war would not be possible without computers and computer professionals. Computer professionals contribute to preparations for nuclear war in at least four ways: 1) computers and the professionals who operate them are essential components of the early warning and command and control systems for nuclear weapons. Malfunctions in these systems may be catastrophic [23, 24], yet in an 18-month period in 1979–1980 alone, the U.S. Senate Armed Services Committee reported 151 "serious" false alarms, and 3,703 others [25]; 2) computer professionals help devise and use computer simulations of nuclear war—so-called "war games" [26]. While computer game simulations are designed to alert officials to the uncertainties and complexities involved in the actual use of nuclear weapons, some analysts have expressed concern that this makes preparations for nuclear war routine [26]; 3) computer professionals may obtain scientific results with eventual applications to nuclear weapons. Scientists conduct basic research without knowing how it will be used; and 4) the most direct way in which computer scientists "up the stakes" for global destruction is in the actual design and development of nuclear weapons and missile guidance systems.

Therefore, computer professionals can do work of the highest technical quality, yet be isolated from the potential human costs. Even those computer professionals who have no direct involvement with these or other forms of collective violence should nevertheless be concerned about the problem, since they and their families are potential victims.

How Destructive Professional Work Is Justified

It is disturbing and regrettable to have to consider violent images and atrocities in relation to our everyday, comfortable lives. But perhaps recognizing the problems, and that the corporations and government agencies we work for have vested interests independent of human needs, is the first step in differentiating economic practicalities from values and human welfare.

In the preceding section, we showed how apparently legitimate work routines can threaten human welfare in the most inhumane ways. Therefore, it is logical to ask how well-meaning individuals perceive their role in the profession. Psychological and social mechanisms related to this are listed in Table 23.1. This is not necessarily intended to be the definitive taxonomy or to cover every possible example, but it should provide a useful summary of processes that may be new to the computer professional. These have been defined from the few existing case studies [27–29], autobiographies [30], ethnographies [31] and related theoretical works [32–35].

We have attempted to list mechanisms which are applicable in many different situations. These have been classified as 1) general psychological processes, 2) processes specific to work in large bureaucracies and organizations, and 3) mechanisms that allow scientific and technological work independent of social values.

Psychological Mechanisms

The mind is capable of playing subtle tricks on us. We do not always take the most rational alternative, or pay equal attention to equally important information. Therefore, we are susceptible to the following psychological mechanisms in many different types of dilemmas.

Dissociation.   This involves a separation of different parts of conscious knowledge. The effect is to continue thinking and cognitive functioning by isolating incapacitating feelings and emotional responses [29]. It prevents full awareness of disquieting or unsettling information. Lifton and Markusen [29] state that this may ultimately involve "doubling" of one's personality, as if separate roles or personalities develop for more and less humane behavior. It may be invoked when a role at work begins to contradict one's personal role [36].[2] As an illustration, Del Tredici [37] recorded the following dialogue with the spouse of a nuclear plant worker:

> "He was just real happy about being hired at Rocky Flats. We were a young couple, expecting a family, and the benefits were very good. The pay was great—you get what they call `hot pay' for working with radiation, so that's why he wanted the process operator's job. . . "
> Did Don ever talk to you about the fact that he was making bombs?
> "He never did go into that." [37], pp. 173–174).

Several other authors have also described dissociation [1, 31, 38]. A similar procedure is often used in everyday life, e.g., when conscious attention is not used in an activity such as driving, changing gears, or locking a door. We can then devote complete attention to something else, such as an ongoing conversation (although we may later find ourselves wondering whether we actually locked that door).

"Psychic numbing" is a type of dissociation. Lifton [39] documented this in nuclear survivors in Hiroshima. He argues that in the nuclear age, it functions to mask the threat of instant extinction in our daily lives. Ironically, it operates in perpetrators as well as victims, and may allow either one to shut out recognition of brutality.

Table 23.1   Mechanisms That Could Maintain Conflict Between Job Actions and Personal and Social Values in Work with Computer Technology

Psychological mechanisms	Dissociation
	Rationalization
Organizational factors	Compartmentalization
	Hierarchical authority structure
	Amoral rationality
Facilitating factors in science and technology	Technological curiosity
	Distancing effects

Rationalization.   This involves after-the-fact explanations of actions. Festinger developed a theory explaining how a post hoc shift in attitudes results from "cognitive dissonance" [40]. When we become aware that our actions contradict our values, we may rearrange our values after the fact to reduce inconsistency. When we are drawn into taking risks, we may adjust our beliefs out the likelihood of negative outcomes. This style of justification for one's actions is typified by commonly-heard explanations for why a particular project was accepted: "Better I do this than someone else"; "If I don't do this, someone else will."

Bureaucratic Factors

Most computer scientists work within bureaucracies, often as specialists on sections of large projects. People who work in large organizations are susceptible to the following ways of separating work and values.

Compartmentalization.   A diffusion of responsibility tends to occur naturally with complex technology, since technological work relies on numerous different specialists [35]. Therefore, most individuals have only small parts in the ultimate product, for which they do not feel responsible. (There are also situations in which a compartmentalized product is benign, but could be developed in future for either beneficial or harmful applications.) Lempert [27] reports interviews with four engineering students with summer jobs at Lawrence Livermore (nuclear weapons) Labs: "All four seemed to agree that in only a few months one could not possibly make a large enough contribution to feel one had personally helped to develop a new nuclear arms" ([27], p. 63). This type of perception then leads to logic of the following sort: "I only——, I don't actually use them." One may fill in the blank with any application: "*write* viruses," "*assemble* the weapons," etc.

Although the division of labor in a large project may contribute to knowledge compartmentalization, it may also be the case that the "big picture" is purposely withheld. Diffusion of responsibility is explicit in cases of military compartmentalization for security reasons [30]. This was true of the thousands of people who moved to the Hanford nuclear reservation for a "top secret" project in the 1940s [31]. Soviet scientist and dissident Andrei Sakharov also noted this in the case of Soviet military research: "I was thankful that I was not told everything, despite my high-level security clearance" ([41], p. 268). However, in military or civilian work, compartmentalization and diffusion of responsibility lead to situations in which no one seems to actually have responsibility, as illustrated by three examples of work that is heavily reliant on computer technology:

> It's not like I'm designing the weapons. The guys who design them are in physics. *An engineer at Lawrence Livermore (nuclear weapons) Labs* ([27], p. 63).
>
> Savannah River is the only facility that is producing weapons-grade plutonium to the defense programs. It is also the sole source of tritium. But we don't have anything to do here with the actual fabrication of weapons. *James Gaver, Public Relations Officer for the U.S. Department of Energy, Savannah River Plant, North Carolina* ([37], p. 141).
>
> Sandia's role in the U.S. nuclear weapons program extends from applied research through development of new weapons and evaluation of their reliability

throughout their stockpile lifetimes. We do not manufacture or assemble weapons components. . . . Sandia does not produce weapons and components. *Sandia National (nuclear weapons) Labs* ([42], p. 5).

A hierarchical authority structure.   In a classic study of obedience, Milgram [32] told individuals in an experiment to administer electric shocks to people making mistakes on a learning test. He found that individuals would follow orders from a stranger to what they thought were life-threatening extents (see update and social applications in Kelman and Hamilton [33]). Although computer professionals in most contemporary jobs do not receive explicit orders (except in the military), there can still be penalties for not following procedures and instructions from superiors: these include implicit sanctions such as loss of status, or the possibility of being passed over for promotion [30]. The hierarchical authority structure is usually quite clear in most organizations.

It is sometimes argued that technicians and computer professionals should leave decisions about ethics and values to government leaders. Individual employees are not elected, and not authorized to make autonomous decisions affecting policy [43, 44]. However, this does not recognize the expertise of those directly involved in a particular project. This logic leads to what Johnson calls the "guns for hire" doctrine [45],. This view suggests that computer professionals should let society regulate what is acceptable through government representatives. Noting that the government cannot always be trusted to provide objective information, however, Sussman [46] states that our "leaders' deliberate avoidance of true debate, the contempt they show the public during political campaigning, their use of refinement of propaganda techniques, the attentiveness of so many of them to moneyed interests and not to the people generally, are all major causes of resentment and distrust" ([46], p. 49).

Amoral rationality.   This is a preoccupation with procedural and technical aspects of work, while ignoring its moral, human, and social implications. The focus is on how to best do a job, with little attention to broader values and social effects. Responsibility for the work is perceived to be limited to technical aspects. In the Nazi death camps, amoral rationality allowed health professionals to serve as professional killers. Lifton reports that "an S.S. doctor said to me, `Ethics was not a word used in Auschwitz. Doctors and others spoke only about how to do things most efficiently'" [12, p. 294]. Albert Speer, Minister of Armaments and War in the Third Reich and a primary director of slave labor, directly addressed this in a 1944 note to Hitler: "The task that I am to perform is unpolitical. I have felt very good about my work so long as both I and my work were evaluated purely on the basis of my professional performance" ([38], p. 3; [47]). Wooten refers to this as a system of amoral functionalism, "one essentially devoid of morals and ethics in its decision-making process and one concerned only with *how* things get done and not *whether* they should get done" ([48], p. 21; emphasis in original). Computer science can be similarly promoted as highly technical, but independent of value considerations.

Once more fundamental social considerations are recognized, it becomes apparent that these questions must be addressed first. As the inventor of the hydrogen bomb in the Soviet Union, Sakharov notes that

> Our reports, and the conferences where we discussed a strategic thermonuclear strike on a potential enemy, transformed the unthinkable and monstrous into a subject for detailed investigation and calculation. It became a fact of life—still hypothetical, but already seen as something possible. I could not stop thinking about this, and I came to realize that the technical, military, and economic problems are secondary; the fundamental issues are political and ethical" ([41], p. 268).

It will be argued in the final section that this way of thinking is reflected in codes of professional ethics and in educational curricula on science and technology.

Facilitating Factors in Science and Technology

These are processes encountered in professions based on science and technology. Again, they are distorting mechanisms that separate individual judgments from the collective effects of work.

Technological curiosity.   Regardless of the overall consequences, intelligent computer systems can be inherently interesting and can distract the worker from thoughts about the ethical implications of his or her work. Chalk describes a "primitive fascination" [30] with new technology (also see [27]). Since any type of basic research has by its nature no direct application, this must be a primary motivation for work on many scientific projects. Lifton and Markusen [29] discuss this general "passion for problem solving" in the work of nuclear physicists. Hayes [49] argues that work has changed as it has become more technology based; this may be due in part to this curiosity. "What mattered was the product's capacity to provide more interesting work—a capacity that usually dovetailed with the corporate concern for profitability." However, "among computer professionals, work was so self-referential, so thoroughly personalized, that it no longer required a public rationale in order to yield meaning" ([49], p. 32).

Distancing effects of technology.   By operating as an intermediate processor in some situations, computers make eventual effects seen more distant. Just as pilots dropping bombs are removed from the human suffering that results, computers can remove the human initiator even more from personal involvement. This can occur in time, with contributions to a project or product to be implemented at a later date. A situation more unique to the computer industry, though, is where the human operator is present at the same point in time, but simply removed from the decision-making process: a preplanned procedure is carried through with automated control. (Not that bureaucracies also serve to distance policy makers from front-line effects, and front-line workers from responsibility for policies.)

Why Destructive Professional Work Occurs: A Predictive Model

Taken together, these mechanisms can result in a situation where many highly-trained people work on projects that ultimately have very large human costs. Use of mechanisms such as these could be reinforced by socialization and professional training [30]. Recruitment, selection, and promotion may all depend on one's ability to go along with routines unquestioningly. The atmosphere in many settings may not allow open discussion of the effects of a project on society and on human welfare, and may emphasize distinct roles and hierarchies (e.g., with the use of uniforms or titles).

These mechanisms are factors affecting or in response to decisions we make. However, it is not the mechanisms per se that cause contributions to collective violence. For example, although obedience to a higher authority is often cited as a cause of irresponsible individual behavior [32, 33], we make autonomous decisions before following orders. We are not reflexively and automatically obedient to any higher authority (although we may decide that it is in our interest to be obedient). As another example, dissociation can not fundamentally explain behavior in dilemmas at work. We dissociate as a result of an earlier decision or an event. It is not dissociation that causes computer professionals to work on weapons of mass destruction; rather, they may do so because of practical employment needs, but then dissociate knowledge of destructive effects. To better explain these underlying causes, we will now present a predictive model. It explains why we contribute to large-scale risks that are not in our own or society's long-term interests, and therefore why mechanisms such as psychic numbing, rationalization, and obedience are needed.

It seems fundamental to the human condition that although we expose certain values, individual actions ultimately come down to economic practicalities. For example: "Marie is a mother of two living in a small village in Vichy France in 1941 under Nazi control. Everyone is hustling for a position in the new regime, a pass for curfew, a bit of meat; resistance is not an option . . ." [50]. The demands of daily living [51] were a priority for survival, and still figure prominently in many cases. But even when extreme affluence is attained, the focus on self-interest in the short term does not change. We can see the same process in the following biographical note on a defense electronics executive:

RAYTHEON. Thomas L. Phillips, Lexington, Mass. 617-862-6600. SALES: $8.8 bil. PROFITS: $529 mil. Career path—engineering/technical; tenure—42 years, CEO 22 years. Compensation: 1989 salary & bonus, $1,215,000; ownership, 136,000 shares. Not fretting about defense cuts, thanks to his electronics, commercial businesses, now 40% of sales. . . . One soft target: $40 billion Milstar communication satellite—for use after nuclear war. Scheduled to retire at yearend to enjoy New Hampshire lakefront home. [52].

Of course, wealth is not unethical in and of itself. But certainly when profiting from nuclear war, it is reasonable to wonder how justifications, vested interests, and psychological mechanisms are related. Obviously, day-to-day practicalities for this business executive do not mean actual survival, as they did for the oppressed mother in Nazi-occupied France. In both cases, though, there are immediate, tangible incentives for individuals to contribute to a system in which maximizing their own interests adds to the risk of harm for others later on.

The incentives for decisions that we are faced with can be defined in terms of a number of interacting parameters, such as the value of different alternatives, the probability associated with each alternative, and the type of each alternative [53]. In computer work, one might have to decide between

1. developing a profitable computer project with a 10% chance of eventual misuse or failure, or

2. not developing this project, therefore creating no chance of misuse or failure but possibly incurring negative consequences for one's job.

Note that the two alternatives differ in both probability (0% vs. 10%) and value (profit vs. negative consequences). The value can be conceptualized as coming in positive (reinforcing) or negative (punishing) forms. Either type can elicit behavior, although positive incentives are much more desirable. For example, a programmer would obviously rather work for intellectual or monetary rewards, than because he or she was forced to under threat of penalty (e.g., by an oppressive government, or simply because of monetary losses).

Parameters such as the value or magnitude of rewards and punishments tend to be relative, rather than absolute. For example, the difference we perceive between $20 and $30 is likely to be seen as more valuable than the difference between $1,020 and $1,030 (also a difference of $10). The interesting thing for dilemmas faced by computer professionals, though, is not a choice based on the perceived value of a single dimension. In alternatives where two parameters interact, each parameter has to be weighed, and trade-offs evaluated. Therefore, the computer professional may be faced with choosing between a profitable but low-probability project, for example, or one which offers less profit but a better chance of success.

Another important parameter in the subjective value of different alternatives is time delay. A basic principle of learning theory is that as the delay of a reward increases, its value decreases. Just as the subjective value of an additional $10 varies according to whether it is in the context of $20 or $1,020, $10 received now is likely to be seen as preferable to $10 received tomorrow. This in turn has more value than a promise of $10 or more in five weeks. Interestingly, we can obtain the relative importance of magnitude and time delay by asking now much money *would* be equally valuable: "Would you take $12 tomorrow instead of $10 now?" "Would you take $30 in five weeks instead of $10 now?" Regardless of the actual value in dollars, the psychological value is thus a nonlinear function of time ([54]).

Magnitude and time delay trade off in a predictable manner, although some irrational decisions are produced that do not maximize benefits, as will be discussed below. Rachlin notes the disproportional increase in value of some jobs initially because of this: "In the army . . . you get an enlistment (or reenlistment) bonus so that the delay between signing up and your first pay check is very short" ([53], p. 142). Even advertisements for military service stick to payoffs that are both in one's self-interest and immediate: "travel . . . summer employment . . . interesting people . . . earn extra money . . . build on your career . . . part-time adventure" [55]. Recruiting has historically appealed to broad patriotic and nationalist values, but these are apparently not as marketable as early pay checks and the promise of more and earlier money, friends, adventure, and jobs. This situation is not unlike that of many computer professionals, for whom a fundamental motivation for many work decisions is economic: the need for a job that satisfies day-to-day needs [51].

A specific model, based on "social traps" [56, 57] relates incentives for individuals in their jobs to larger collective effects. As is true of all traps, a social trap presents an enticing opportunity, or bait. Like a more tangible trap, a social trap is a situation in which one choice that seems beneficial carries with it other negative consequences. Baron [58] emphasizes that this model is fundamental to dilemmas in many social situations.

> Because so many situations can be analyzed as social dilemmas, much of the philosophy and psychology of morality is contained in this problem. . . . If everybody lies, we will not be able to depend on each other for information, and we will all lose. Likewise . . . cheating on one's taxes (making the government spend more money on enforcement), building up arms stocks in the context of an arms race, accepting bribes, polluting the environment, and having too many children are all examples ([58], pp. 399–400).

Two different types of traps can be defined, both of which are based on conflicting alternatives. Strictly speaking, "social" traps, or social dilemmas, apply only to a choice between self-interest and broader social or

group interests (e.g., [59]). This model has been formally tested in laboratory simulations of conflict and cooperation between individuals and between countries [60]. However, there has been practically no attempt to
collect empirical data or quantitatively model choices between self- and
group interests in real life individual dilemmas, whether political, occupational or ethical.

"Temporal" traps could also be defined, for conflict between an immediate, short-term incentive, and a later one. The significance of these choices
is that one has to wait to obtain the preferable alternative. Experiments with
children on delay of gratification have identified cultural and personality
variables affecting self-control [61], although the process of weighing different alternatives in decisions is more directly relevant in the present context. Quantitative models have been developed in numerous studies on animal learning defining tradeoffs between parameters such as the magnitude
and delay of rewards [62–64]. Nevertheless, until now there have been
very few attempts to apply these to the dilemmas that people face.

. . . . .

For individuals in single-industry towns, the practicality of having to avoid
the consequences of unemployment may be much more salient than the
possibility of producing a weapon that fuels the arms race [65–67]. Moreover, the weightings that we subjectively give to immediate, local needs
over a global consequences at some point in the future can be rationalized
or overlooked with many of the psychological mechanisms discussed earlier. From interviews with computer professionals, physicists, and engineers working on nuclear weapons, Lempert [27] has noted the motivation
that short-term economic needs provides: "in a tight job market, a young
man or woman with a newly-earned degree might abandon a primary academic interest for a tempting salary" ([27], p. 62).

It should be clear that some of our decision preferences may be short
sighted, and lead us into traps in which there are much larger consequences
to suffer. It is also important to emphasize, however, that this model of
social-temporal traps does not specify that individuals always choose the
short term. Rather, decisions involve weighing the parameters of each alternative and evaluating trade-offs. With other things being equal, the
short-term incentive will have greater perceived value.

Looking at decision making in terms of social and temporal traps is useful for explaining work behavior at all levels of organizational hierarchies.
How does the data entry operator perceive and weigh conflicting responsibilities or interests? The model is equally applicable to the executive
policymaker.

Although many of the problems of sustainability that we face at the end
of the 20th century relate to institutions, organizations, industry, and so on,

ultimately these are all made up of individual people. In affirming the importance of individuals and the collective effects of their work, Baron [58] has noted that

> the problems caused by the existence of social dilemmas are among the most important that human beings have to solve. If we could learn ways to cooperate, wars would disappear and prosperity would prevail . . . more cooperation would solve many other human problems, from conflicts among roommates and family members to problems of protecting the world environment" ([58], pp. 403–404).

Practical Applications to Ethical Decision Making

The psychological model and collective effects outlined here suggest that the wheels of the technological machine may be powered more by short-term economic interests and psychological, organizational, and technical mechanisms than by actual scientific or social needs (to say nothing of moral and ethical concerns). This can lead to devastating human costs on a world-wide scale. As Bandura [35] notes,

> Given the many psychological devices for disengagement of moral control, societies cannot rely solely on individuals, however honorable their standards, to provide safeguards against inhumanities. To function humanely, societies must establish effective social safeguards against moral disengagement practices that foster exploitive and destructive conduct ([35], p. 27).

In view of this process, then, what practical alternatives are there to facilitate the choice of the right overall decision, rather than simply the one with immediate rewards?

Summary and Conclusions

Organizations such as governments, companies, and the military involve many professionals, but can have goals independent of human needs. Because of the role computer technology now plays in any large project, computer professionals may face ethical decisions between organizational interests and social values. unfortunately, if there are vested job interests, the reliance on higher authority, regular routines, and technological curiosity may support amoral rationality: do a good job technically, but leave responsibility to the larger organization. Because of this process, professionals have been participants in collective violence.

Social and temporal traps provide a useful framework for evaluating the role of individuals in collective violence. These models look at the value and timing (delay) of the alternatives in a decision. Lawful predictions can then be made for both rational and shortsighted behavior. This approach has the advantage of applying to individuals at all levels of organizational hierarchies, and in many different situations.

Finally, in response to the conflicting interests that may arise for computer professionals, there are several approaches that may help to structure and prioritize the alternatives. Professional codes of ethics, education, and government policies may all facilitate choices that provide benefits individually *and* collectively.

Notes

1. "Professional" is used here in a broad sense, referring to occupations including programmers, systems analysts, engineers, technicians, and computer scientists.
2. It should also be recognized that many individuals would not report any conflict between their personal values and job actions. We are interested in cases, however, where the individual has a vested interest in carrying out organizational goals independent of social values. The psychological mechanisms outlined show how conflict between vested work interests and values can then be obscured.

References

1. E. Markusen, Professions, professionals and genocide, in *Genocide: A Critical Bibliographic Review* (I. W. Charney, ed.), Facts on File Publishing, New York, 1991.
2. P. R. Ehrlich and A. H. Ehrlich, *Extinction: The Causes and Consequences of the Disappearance of Species,* Ballantine Books, New York, 1985.
3. R. Rummel, *Lethal Politics: Soviet Genocide and Mass Murder Since 1917,* Transaction Books, New Brunswick, New Jersey, 1990.
4. R. Sivard, *World Military and Social Expenditures 1987–88,* World Priorities, Leesburg, Virginia, 1988.
5. G. Dyer, *War,* Crown, New York, 1985.
6. R. O'Connell, *Of Arms and Men,* Oxford University Press, New York, 1989.
7. World Health Organization, *Effects of Nuclear War on Health and Health Services,* World Health Organization, Geneva, 1984.
8. C. Sagan and R. Turco, *A Path Where No Man Thought: Nuclear Winter and the End of the Arms Race,* Random House, New York, 1990.
9. E. Markusen, Genocide and total war, in *Genocide and the Modern Age* (I. Wallimann and M. Dobkowski, eds.), Greenwood Press, New York, 1987.
10. I. W. Charny, Genocide and mass destruction: doing harm to others as a missing dimension in psychopathology, *Psychiatry* 49, 144–157 (1986).
11. R. L. Rubenstein and J. Roth, *Approaches in Auschwitz,* John Knox Press, Atlanta, Georgia, 1987.
12. R. J. Lifton, Medical killing in Auschwitz, *Psychiatry* 45, 283–297 (1982).
13. I. Mumford, Memorandum (restricted commercial), *Atomic Energy of Canada Limited,* January 12, 1988.
14. R. Ludlow, N-industry spying, activists allege, *The Vancouver Sun,* Vancouver, British Columbia, Canada, July 19, 1988, p. A7.
15. Office break-ins might be tied to MP's report, *The Ottawa Citizen,* Ottawa, Ontario, Canada, March 15, 1989, p. A4.
16. P. O'Neil, Fulton's fears break-ins linked called paranoia, *The Vancouver Sun,*

Vancouver, British Columbia, Canada, March 15, 1989, p. C8.

17. R. Cleroux, Burglars seek records, not cash from MP, environmental groups, *The Globe & Mail,* March 17, 1989, p. A11.

18. N. Wiener, A scientist rebels, *The Atlantic* 179, 46 (January 1947).

19. T. Winograd, CPSR president Winograd presents Norbert Wiener award to Parnas, *Computer Progessionals for Social Responsibility Newsletter* 6, 10–12 (1988).

20. R. Chalk, Drawing the line, an examination of conscientious objection in science, in *Ethical Issues Associated with Scientific and Technological Research for the Military* (C. Mitcham and P. Siekeitz, eds.), *Ann. NY Acad. Sci.* 577, 61–74 (1989).

21. American Psychological Society, The importance of the citizen scientist in national science policy, *APS Observer,* 4, 10–23 (July 1991).

22. D. D. Noble, Mental material: the militarization of learning and intelligence in U.S. education, in *Cyborg Worlds: The Military Information Society* (L. Levidow and K. Robins, eds.), Free Association Books, London, 1989.

23. D. Ford, *The Button: The Pentagon's Strategic Command and Control System,* Simon & Schuster, New York, 1985.

24. S. Gregory, Command and Control, in *The Greenpeace Book of the Nuclear Age: The Hidden History, The Human Cost* (J. May, ed.), McClelland and Stewart, Toronto, 1989.

25. D. P. Barash, *Introduction to Peace Studies,* Wadsworth, Belmont, California, 1991.

26. T. B. Allen, *War Games,* McGraw-Hill, New York, 1987.

27. R. Lempert, Will young scientists build bombs? *Bull. Atomic Sci.* 37, 61–64 (1981).

28. S. Kull, *Minds at War: Nuclear Reality and the Inner Conflicts of Defense Policymakers,* Basic Books, New York, 1988.

29. R. J. Lifton and E. Markusen, *The Genocidal Mentality: Nazi Holocaust and Nuclear Threat,* Basic Books, New York, 1990.

30. H. T. Nash, The bureaucratization of homocide, in *Protest and Survive* (E. P. Thompson and D. Smith, eds.), Monthly Review Press, New York, 1981.

31. P. Loeb, *Nuclear Culture: Living and Working in the World's Largest Atomic Complex,* New Society Publishers, Philadelphia, Pennsylvania, 1986.

32. S. Milgram, Some conditions of obedience and disobedience, *Hum. Relat.* 18, 57–76 (1965).

33. H. C. Kelman, and V. L. Hamilton, *Crimes of Obedience: Toward a Social Psychology of Authority and Responsibility,* Yale University Press, New Haven, Connecticut, 1989.

34. E. Staub, *The Roots of Evil: The Origins of Genocide and Other Group Violence,* Cambridge University Press, New York, 1989.

35. A. Bandura, Selective activation and disengagement of moral control, *J. Social Issues* 46, 27–46 (1990).

36. J. S. Coleman, *The Asymmetric Society,* Syracuse University Press, Syracuse, New York, 1982.

37. R. Del Tredici, *At Work in the Fields of the Bomb,* Harper & Row, New York, 1987.

38. J. H. Barton, Editorial, *IEEE Potentials* 5, 3 (1986).
39. R. J. Lifton, *Death in Life: Survivors of Hiroshima,* Random House, New York, 1967 (also 1991, University of North Carolina Press).
40. L. Festinger, *A Theory of Cognitive Dissonance,* Stanford University Press, Stanford, California, 1957.
41. A. Sakharov, *Memoirs* (R. Lourie, trans.), Alfred A. Knopf, New York, 1990.
42. *Sandia National Laboratories, A Report for A.T. & T. Shareholders,* A.T. & T., New York, 1990.
43. K. W. Kemp, Conducting scientific research for the military as a civic duty, in *Ethical Issues Associated with Scientific and Technological Research for the Military.* (C Mitcham and P. Siekevitz, eds.), *Ann. NY Acad. Sci.* 577, 115–121 (1989).
44. K. Kipnis, Engineers who kill: professional ethics and the paramountcy of public safety, *Bus. Profess. Ethics J.* 1, 77–91 (1981).
45. D. G. Johnson, The social/professional responsibility of engineers, in *Ethical Issues Associated with Scientific and Technological Research for the Military* (C. Mitcham and P. Siekevitz, eds.), *Ann. NY Acad. Sci.* 577, 106–114 (1989).
46. B. Sussman, *What Americans Really Think, and Why Our Politicians Pay No Attention,* Pantheon Books, New York, 1988.
47. A Speer, *Trial of the Major War Criminals,* International Military Tribunal, Nuremberg, Germany, 1947. (Quoted from [38].) vol. XVI.
48. L. M. Wooten, Albert Speer: how to manage an atrocity, *J. Hum. Psychol.* 21, 21–38 (1981).
49. D. Hayes, *Behind the Silicon Curtain: The Seductions of Work in a Lonely Era,* South End Press, Boston, 1989.
50. *Story of Women* (film, 1989). Advertisement.
51. R. K. Gilbert, The dynamics of inaction: psychological factors inhibiting arms control activism, *Am. Psychol.* 43, 755–764 (1989).
52. The corporate elite: the chief executives of the 1000 most valuable publicly held U.S. companies, *Business Week,* 55–274 (19 October 1990).
53. H. Rachlin, *Judgment, Decision and Choice: A Cognitive/Behavioural Synthesis,* W. H. Freeman and Co., New York, 1989.
54. B. S. Gorman, A. E. Wessman, G. R. Schmeidler, and S. Thayer, Linear representation of temporal location and Stevens' law, *Mem. Cognit.* 1, 169–171 (1973).
55. Canadian Armed Forces, The reserve: part-time adventure (advertisement), *The Tribune-Post,* Sackville, New Brunswick, Canada, Oct. 17, 1990. p. 17.
56. J. Platt, Social traps, *Am. Psychol.* 28, 641–651 (1973).
57. J. G. Cross and M. J. Guyer, *Social Traps,* University of Michigan Press, Ann Arbor, Michigan, 1980.
58. J. Baron, *Thinking and Deciding,* Cambridge University Press, New York, 1988.
59. G. R. Hardin, The tragedy of the commons, *Science* 162, 1243–1248 (1968).
60. A. Rappaport, Experiments with N-person social traps I, *J. Conflict Res.* 32, 457–472 (1989).
61. W. Mischel, Preference for delayed reinforcement: an experimental study of a cultural observation, *J. Abnormal Soc. Psychol.* 56, 57–61 (1958).

62. M. L. Commons, R. J. Herrnstein, and H. Rachlin, eds. *Quantitative Analyses of Behavior, Vol. II: Matching and Maximizing Accounts,* Ballinger Publishing, Cambridge, Massachusetts, 1982.

63. H. Rachlin, R. Battalio, J. Kagel, and L. Green, Maximization theory in behavioral psychology, *Behav. Brain Sci.* 4, 371–417 (1981).

64. R. J. Herrnstein, Rational choice theory: necessary but not sufficient, *Am. Psychol.* 45, 356–367 (1990).

65. P. Sanger, *Blind Faith: The Nuclear Industry in One Small Town,* McGraw-Hill Ryerson Ltd., Toronto, 1981.

66. C. Giangrande, *The Nuclear North: The People, The Regions and The Arms Race,* Anansi, Toronto, 1983.

67. A. G. Mojtabai, *Blessed Assurance: At Home with The Bomb in Amarillo, Texas,* Houghton-Mifflin, Boston, 1986.

24

Activism, Hacktivism, and Cyberterrorism

Dorothy Denning studies how information technology, particularly the Internet, is being used to influence foreign policy. Not only have groups recently employed the Internet for public advocacy, they have also been able to effect activism on a global scale. In this far-reaching article, Denning looks at computer-enabled activism, "hacktivism," and cyberterrorism.

Dorothy E. Denning

The conflict over Kosovo has been characterized as the first war on the Internet. Government and non-government actors alike used the Net to disseminate information, spread propaganda, demonize opponents, and solicit support for their positions. Hackers used it to voice their objections to both Yugoslav and NATO aggression by disrupting service on government com-

From Dorothy Denning, "Activism, Hacktivism, and Cyberterrorism: The Internet as Tool for Influencing Foreign Policy." This paper was sponsored by the Nautilus Institute and presented at The Internet and International Systems: Information Technology and American Foreign Policy Decision Making, The World Affairs Council, San Francisco, December 10, 1999. Full text of the paper can be found at http://www.nautilus.org/info-policy/workshop/papers/denning.html.

puters and taking over their Web sites. Individuals used it to tell their stories of fear and horror inside the conflict zone, while activists exploited it to amplify their voices and reach a wide, international audience. And people everywhere used it to discuss the issues and share text, images, and video clips that were not available through other media. In April, the Los Angeles Times wrote that the Kosovo conflict was "turning cyberspace into an ethereal war zone where the battle for the hearts and minds is being waged through the use of electronic images, online discussion group postings, and hacking attacks."[1] Anthony Pratkanis, professor of psychology at the University of California, Santa Cruz, and author of Age of Propaganda: The Everyday Use and Abuse of Persuasion, observed, "What you're seeing now is just the first round of what will become an important, highly sophisticated tool in the age-old tradition of wartime propaganda. . . . The war strategists should be worried about it, if they aren't yet."

Just how much impact did the Internet have on foreign policy decisions relating the war? It clearly had a part in the political discourse taking place, and it was exploited by activists seeking to alter foreign policy decisions. It also impacted military decisions. While NATO targeted Serb media outlets carrying Milosovic's propaganda, it intentionally did not bomb Internet service providers or shut down the satellite links bringing the Internet to Yugoslavia. Policy instead was to keep the Internet open. James P. Rubin, spokesman for the U.S. State Department, said "Full and open access to the Internet can only help the Serbian people know the ugly truth about the atrocities and crimes against humanity being perpetrated in Kosovo by the Milosevic regime."[2] Indirectly, the Internet may have also affected public support for the war, which in turn might have affected policy decisions made during the course of the conflict.

The purpose of this paper is to explore how the Internet is altering the landscape of political discourse and advocacy, with particular emphasis on how it is used by those wishing to influence foreign policy. Emphasis is on actions taken by nonstate actors, including both individuals and organizations, but state actions are discussed where they reflect foreign policy decisions triggered by the Internet. The primary sources used in the analysis are news reports of incidents and events. These are augmented with interviews and survey data where available. A more scientific study would be useful.

The paper is organized around three broad classes of activity: activism, hacktivism, and cyberterrorism. The first category, activism, refers to normal, non-disruptive use of the Internet in support of an agenda or cause. Operations in this area include browsing the Web for information, constructing Web sites and posting materials on them, transmitting electronic publications and letters through e-mail, and using the Net to discuss issues, form coalitions, and plan and coordinate activities. The second category, hacktivism, refers to the marriage of hacking and activism. It covers operations that use hacking techniques against a target's Internet site with the intent of disrupting normal operations but not causing serious damage. Examples are Web sit-ins and virtual blockades, automated e-mail bombs, Web hacks, computer break-ins, and computer viruses and worms. The final category, cyberterrorism, refers to the convergence of cyberspace and terrorism. It covers politically motivated hacking operations intended to cause grave harm such as loss of life or severe economic damage. An example would be penetrating an air traffic control system and causing two planes to collide. There is a general progression toward greater damage and disruption from the first to the third category, although that does not imply an increase of political effectiveness. An electronic petition with a million signatures may influence policy more than an attack that disrupts emergency 911 services.

Although the three categories of activity are treated separately, the boundaries between them are somewhat fuzzy. For example, an e-mail bomb may be considered hacktivism by some and cyberterrorism by others. Also, any given actor may conduct operations across the spectrum. For example, a terrorist might launch viruses as part of a larger campaign of cyberterrorism, all the while using the Internet to collect information about targets, coordinate action with fellow conspirators, and publish propaganda on Web sites. Thus, while the paper distinguishes activists, hacktivists, and terrorists, an individual can play all three roles. . . .

The main conclusion of the paper is that the Internet can be an effective tool for activism, especially when it is combined with other communication media, including broadcast and print media and face-to-face meetings with policy makers. It can benefit individuals and small groups with few resources as well as organizations and coalitions that are large or well-funded. It facilitates activities such as educating the public and media, raising money, forming coalitions across geographical boundaries, distributing petitions and action alerts, and planning and coordinating events on a regional or international level. It allows activists in politically repressive states to evade government censors and monitors. . . .

Activism

The Internet offers a powerful tool for communicating and coordinating action. It is inexpensive to use and increasingly pervasive, with an estimated 201 million on-line as of September 1999.[3] Groups of any size, from two to millions, can reach each other and use the Net to promote an agenda. Their members and followers can come from any geographical region on the Net, and they can attempt to influence foreign policy anywhere in the world. This section describes five modes of using the Internet: collection, publication, dialogue, coordination of action, and direct lobbying of decision makers. While treated separately, the modes are frequently used together and many of the examples described here illustrate multiple modes.

Collection

One way of viewing the Internet is as a vast digital library. The World Wide Web alone offers about a billion pages of information, and much of the information is free. Activists may be able to locate legislative documents, official policy statements, analyses and discussions about issues, and other items related to their mission. They may be able to find names and contact information for key decision makers inside the government or governments they ultimately hope to influence. They may be able to identify other groups and individuals with similar interests, and gather contact information for potential supporters and collaborators. There are numerous tools that help with collection, including search engines, e-mail distribution lists, and chat and discussion groups. Many Web sites offer their own search tools for extracting information from databases on their sites.

One advantage of the Internet over other media is that it tends to break down barriers erected by government censors. For example, after Jordanian officials removed an article from 40 print copies of the Economist on sale in Jordan, a subscriber found a copy on-line, made photocopies, and faxed it to 1,000 Jordanians. According to Daoud Kuttab, head of the Arabic Media Internal Network (AMIA), the government would have been better off leaving the print version intact. "We found this very exciting," he said. "For the first time the traditional censorship that exists within national borders was bypassed." Kuttab said AMIA opened Jordanian journalists to the non-Arab world and use of the Web as a research tool. "In the Jordanian media, we have been able to detect a much more open outlook to the world as well as to Arab issues," he said.[4]

The Internet itself is not free of government censorship. According to Reporters Sans Frontiers, 45 countries restrict their citizens' access to the Internet, typically by forcing them to subscribe to a state-run Internet service provider, which may filter out objectionable sites.[5] Authoritarian regimes recognize the benefits of the Internet to economic growth, but at the same time feel threatened by the unprecedented degree of freedom of speech. . . .

Publication

The Internet offers several channels whereby advocacy groups and individuals can publish information (and disinformation) to further policy objectives. They can send it through e-mail and post it to newsgroups. They can create their own electronic publications or contribute articles and essays to those of others. They can put up Web pages with documents, images, audio and video clips, and other types of information. The Web sites can serve as a gathering place and source of information for supporters, potential supporters, and onlookers.

One reason the Internet is popular among activists is its cost advantage over traditional mass media. It is easier and cheaper to post a message to a public forum or put up a Web site than it is to operate a radio or television station or print a newspaper. Practically anyone can afford to be a publisher. In addition, the reach of the Internet is global. A message can potentially reach millions of people at no additional cost to the originator. Further, activists can control their presentation to the world. They decide what is said and how. They do not have to rely on the mass media to take notice and tell their story "right."

During the Kosovo conflict, organizations and individuals throughout the world used their Web sites to publish information related to the conflict and, in some cases, to solicit support. Non-government organizations with Kosovo-related Web pages included the press, human rights groups, humanitarian relief organizations, churches, and women's groups.

Government Web sites on Kosovo tended to feature propaganda and materials that supported their official policies. An exception was the U.S. Information Agency Web site, which presented a survey of news stories from around the world, some of which were critical of NATO actions.[6] Jonathan Spalter, USIA Chief Information Officer, commented that "The measure of our success is the extent to which we are perceived not as propaganda but anti-propaganda."[7]

The British government's Foreign Office used their Web site, in part, to counter Serb propaganda. Concerned that the Yugoslav public was getting a highly distorted view of the war, Foreign Secretary Robin Cook posted a message on their Web site intended for the Serbs. The message said that Britain has nothing against the Serbs, but was forced to act by the scale of Yugoslav President Slobodan Milosevic's brutality.[8] British Defense Secretary George Robertson said the Ministry of Defence (MoD) had translated its Web site into Serbian to counter censorship by Belgrade of the news.[9] . . .

Dialogue

The Internet offers several venues for dialogue and debate on policy issues. These include e-mail, newsgroups, Web forums, and chat. Discussions can be confined to closed groups, for example through e-mail, as well as open to the public. Some media sites offer Web surfers the opportunity to comment on the latest stories and current issues and events. Government officials and domain experts may be brought in to serve as catalysts for discussion, debate issues, or answer questions. Discussion can even take place on

Web sites that themselves lack such facilities. Using Gooey software from the Israeli company Hypernix, for example, visitors to a Web site can chat with other Gooey users currently at the site.[10]

Internet discussion forums are frequently used to debate, blast, and maybe even attempt to influence government policies. Encryption policy, for example, is discussed on the e-mail lists "cypherpunks" and "ukcrypto" and on several newsgroups, including alt.privacy and sci.crypt.

The ukcrypto list created was created in early 1996 by two academics, Ross Anderson (Cambridge) and Paul Leyland (Oxford), and one person then in government, Brian Gladman (NATO SHAPE), who was acting outside his official capacity. Motivated by a concern that a lack of public discussion and debate in the United Kingdom on cryptography issues was allowing the government to set policies that they believed were not in the interests of the United Kingdom and its citizens, they formed the list with the objective of impacting cryptography policy. They were concerned both with domestic policy, particularly proposals to restrict the use of cryptography by U.K. citizens, and on foreign policy, particularly export controls. As of May 1999, the list has 300 subscribers, including government officials responsible for U.K. policy and persons in other countries, including the United States. Many of the key contributors held influential positions in other policy making fora. Focus is on U.K. policy issues, but items of international interest are also discussed, including export controls adopted under the Wassenaar Arrangement (31 countries participate); policy changes adopted by France, the United States, and other countries; policy statements from the European Union and other organizations; and some technical issues.[11]

Gladman believes the list has made four contributions: 1) educating many about the policy issues and encouraging journalists and writers to write about them; 2) bringing individual and industry views closer together and allowing U.K. industry to see more clearly that agreeing with their government may not be a good thing if private citizens do not support government policy; 3) encouraging the more progressive voices in government to speak out and argue from within government that their views represent those of the public; and 4) bringing groups together that were previously campaigning separately. "The most significant contribution of ukcrypto is not direct," Gladman said. "It is the contribution that it has made in promoting an educated community of commentators and a forum for the review of what government is doing that is fully open."

On the downside, some postings on ukcyrpto may alienate the very government officials the authors hope to influence. According to Gladman, "discussions n the list can become slinging matches that quickly put those in government on the defensive and hence inclined to discount what is being said. It would be more effective if we had a way of focusing on the issues and not the personalities."[12] But Andrew Brown gave ukcrypto high marks, crediting it with most of the thought and co-ordination behind the successful campaign to keep strong cryptography legal and widely available. "There, for the past two years, the civil servants responsible for policy have actually been available, more or less, to the people who disagree with them," he wrote in *New Statesman*. "They have had to justify their actions, not to the public, but to a small group of geographically dispersed experts. . . . It's a kind of updated version of Lions v Christians."[13]

Nigel Hickson, one of the principal players in the policy debates from the U.K. Department of Trade and Industry, agrees the Internet and ukcrypto in particular have played a role in shaping U.K. cryptography policy.[14] But he was also critical of the list: "Whilst ukcrypto has undoubtedly had an influence on the development of UK encryption policy, it has tended to polarise the debate into extremes. This may be because there tends to be a large silent majority on the list who do not directly contribute because of commercial or policy reasons."[15] Besides participating in ukcrypto, the DTI has published draft consultation documents on the Web for comment. Many of the comments they receive arrive through electronic mail. DTI has also met with industry groups and participated in non-Internet forums such as conferences and seminars. These have also helped shape policy decisions. . . .

Coordination of Action

Advocacy groups can use the Internet to coordinate action among members and with other organizations and individuals. Action plans can be distributed by e-mail or posted on Web sites. Services are cheaper than phone and fax (although these services can also be delivered through the Internet), and faster than physical delivery (assuming Internet services are operating properly, which is not always the case). The Internet lets people all over the world coordinate action without regard to constraints of geography or time. They can form partnerships and coalitions or operate independently.

One Web site was created to help activists worldwide coordinate and locate information about protests and meetings. According to statements on Protest.Net, the Web site serves "to help progressive activists by providing a central place where the times and locations of protests and meetings can be posted." The site's creator said he hoped it would "help resolve logistical problems that activists face in organizing events with limited resources and access to mass media."[16] The site features news as well as action alerts and information about events.

The power of the Internet to mobilize activists is illustrated by the arrest of Kurdish rebel leader Abdullah Ocalan. According to Michael Dartnell, a political science professor at Concordia University, when Turkish forces arrested Ocalan, Kurds around the world responded with demonstrations within a matter of hours. He attributed the swift action in part to the Internet and Web. "They responded more quickly than governments did to his arrest," he said. Dartnell contends the Internet and advanced communication tools were changing the way people around the world play politics. Anti-government groups are establishing alliances and coalitions that might not have existed before the technology was introduced.[17]

The force of the Internet is further illustrated by the day of protest against business that took place on June 18, 1999. The protests, which were set up to coincide with a meeting of the G8 in Cologne, Germany, was co-ordinated by a group called J18 from a Web site inviting people to plan individual actions focusing on disrupting "financial centres, banking districts and multinational corporate power bases." Suggested activity included marches, rallies, and hacking. In London, up to 2,000 anti-capitalists coursed through the city shouting slogans and spray-painting buildings.[18] According to the *Sunday Times,* teams of hackers from Indonesia, Israel, Germany, and Canada attacked the computers of at least 20 companies, including the Stock Exchange and Barclays. More than 10,000 attacks were launched over a 5-hour period.[19] . . .

Lobbying Decision Makers

Whether or not government agencies solicit their input, activists can use the Internet to lobby decision makers. One of the methods suggested by the Kosova Task Force for contacting the White House, for example, was e-mail. Similarly, a Canadian Web site with the headline "Stop the NATO Bombing of Yugoslavia Now!" urged Canadians and others interested in stopping the war to send e-mails and/or faxes to the Canadian Prime Minister, Jean Chretien, and all members of the Canadian Parliament. A sample letter was included. The letter concluded with an appeal to "stop aggression against Yugoslavia and seek a peaceful means to resolve the Kosovo problem."[20]

E-mail has been credited with halting a U.S. banking plan aimed to combat money laundering. Under the "Know Your Customer" policy, banks would have been required to monitor customer's banking patterns and report inconsistencies to federal regulators. Recognizing the value of the Internet to its deliberations, the Federal Deposit Insurance Corporation (FDIC) put up a Web site, published an e-mail address for comments, and printed out and tabulated each message. By the time the proposal was withdrawn, they had received 257,000 comments, 205,000 (80%) of which arrived through e-mail. All but 50 of the letters opposed the plan. FDIC's chair, Donna Tanoue, said it was the huge volume of e-mail that drove the decision to withdraw the proposal. "It was the nature and the volume [of the comments]," she said. "When consumers can get excited about an esoteric bank regulation, we have to pay attention."[21]

Most of the e-mail was driven by an on-line advocacy campaign sponsored by the Libertarian Party. About 171,000 (83%) of the e-mail messages were sent through the party's Web site. The party advertised its advocacy campaign in talk radio interviews and by sending a notice to its e-mail membership list.[22] One could argue that the results were due more to the efforts of a large non-government organization than to a grassroots response from the citizens.

Indeed, many e-mail campaigns have been driven by non-government organizations. The organizations send e-mail alerts on issues to electronic mailing lists, offer sample letters to send to members of Congress and other decision making bodies, and, in some cases, set up e-mailboxes or Web sites to gather signatures for petitions. The petition process can be automated, making it possible to gather huge volumes of signatures across a wide geographic area with little effort and cost. One Web site, e-The People, offers hundreds of petitions to choose from and 170,000 e-mail addresses of government officials.[23]

Computer Professionals for Social Responsibility (CPSR) organized an Internet petition campaign in early 1994 to protest the U.S. government's proposal to adopt the Clipper encryption chip as a standard.[24] The chip offered strong encryption, but would have given law enforcement agencies the capability to decrypt a subject's messages when conducting a court-ordered wiretap against the subject. Despite numerous safeguards to ensure government agencies could not violate the privacy of users of the chip.[25] Clipper was strongly opposed for privacy (and other) reasons, and the general sentiment expressed on Internet newsgroups and e-mail discussion lists was strongly anti-Clipper. CPSR announced their petition through e-mail and set up an e-mail address whereby people could sign on. They collected tens of thousands of signatures, but it is not clear the petition had much impact. The government moved forward with the standard anyway.[26]

Although Clipper was to be a U.S. standard, it was tied in with the government's foreign encryption policy. Because of its back door, it was to be generally exportable, unlike other encryption products with comparable cryptographic strength. Also, the Administration urged other governments to adopt a similar approach. However, after extensive lobbying efforts by industry and civil liberties groups, Clipper met its death. The government moved instead toward a more flexible and liberal approach to encryption export controls. . . .

Hacktivism

Hacktivism is the convergence of hacking with activism, where "hacking" is used here to refer to operations that exploit computers in ways that are unusual and often illegal, typically with the help of special software ("hacking tools"). Hacktivism includes electronic civil disobedience, which brings methods of civil disobedience to cyberspace. This section explores four types of operations: virtual sit-ins and blockades; automated e-mail bombs; Web hacks and computer break-ins; and computer viruses and worms. Because hacking incidents are often reported in the media, operations in this category can generate considerable publicity for both the activists and their causes.

Virtual Sit-Ins and Blockades

A virtual sit-in or blockade is the cyberspace rendition of a physical sit-in or blockade. The goal in both cases is to call attention to the protestors and their cause by disrupting normal operations and blocking access to facilities.

With a sit-in, activists visit a Web site and attempt to generate so much traffic against the site that other users cannot reach it. A group calling itself Strano Network conducted one of the first such demonstrations as a protest against French government policies on nuclear and social issues. On December 21, 1995, they launched a one-hour Net-Strike attack against the Web sites operated by various government agencies. At the appointed hour, participants from all over the world were instructed to point their browsers to the government Web sites. According to reports, at least some of the sites were effectively knocked out for the period.[27]

In 1998, the Electronic Disturbance Theater (EDT) took the concept of electronic civil disobedience a step further. They organized a series of Web sit-ins, first against Mexican President Zedillo's Web site and later against President Clinton's White House Web site, the Pentagon, the School of the Americas, the Frankfurt Stock Exchange, and the Mexican Stock Exchange. The purpose was to demonstrate e solidarity with the Mexican Zapatistas.[28] According to EDT's Brett Stalbaum, the Pentagon was chosen because "we believe that the U.S. military trained the soldiers carrying out the human rights abuses." For a similar reason, the School of the America's was selected.[29] The Frankfurt Stock Exchange was targeted, Stalbaum said, "because it represented capitalism's role in globalization utilizing the techniques of genocide and ethnic cleansing, which is at the root of the Chiapas' problems. The people of Chiapas should play a key role in determining their own fate, instead of having it pushed on them through their forced relocation (at gunpoint), which is currently financed by western capital."[30] . . .

E-Mail Bombs

It is one thing to send one or two messages to government policy makers, even on a daily basis. But it is quite another to bombard them with thousands of messages at once, distributed with the aid of automated tools. The effect can be to completely jam a recipient's incoming e-mail box, making it impossible for legitimate e-mail to get through. Thus an e-mail bomb is also a form of virtual blockade. Although e-mail bombs are often used as a means of revenge or harassment, they have also been used to protest government policies.

In what some U.S. intelligence authorities characterized as the first known attack by terrorists against a country's computer systems, ethic Tamil guerrillas were said to have swamped Sri Lankan embassies with thousands of electronic mail messages. The messages read "We are the Internet Black Tigers and we're doing this to disrupt your communications."[31] An offshoot of the Liberation Tigers of Tamil Eelam, which had been fighting for an independent homeland for minority Tamils, was credited with the 1998 incident.[32]

The e-mail bombing consisted of about 800 e-mails a day for about two weeks. William Church, editor for the Centre for Infrastructural Welfare Studies (CIWARS), observed that "the Liberation Tigers of Tamil are desperate for publicity and they got exactly what they wanted . . . considering the routinely deadly attacks committed by the Tigers, if this type of activity distracts them from bombing and killing then CIWARS would like to encourage them, in the name of peace, to do more of this type of "terrorist activity."[33] The attack, however, was said to have had the desired effect of generating fear in the embassies.

During the Kosovo conflict, protestors on both sides e-mail bombed government sites. According to PA News, NATO spokesman Jamie Shea said their server had been saturated at the end of March by one individual who was sending them 2,000 messages a day.[34] Fox News reported that when California resident Richard Clark heard of attacks against NATO's Web site by Belgrade hackers, he retaliated by sending an e-mail bomb to the Yugoslav government's site. Clark said that a few days and 500,000 e-mails into the siege, the site went down. He did not claim full responsibility, but said he "played a part." That part did not go unrecognized. His Internet service provider, Pacific Bell, cut off his service, saying his actions violated their spamming policy.[35] . . .

Web Hacks and Computer Break-Ins

The media is filled with stories of hackers gaining access to Web sites and replacing some of the content with their own. Frequently, the messages are political, as when a group of Portuguese hackers modified the sites of 40 Indonesian servers in September 1998 to display the slogan "Free East Timor" in large black letters. According to the *New York Times,* the hackers also added links to Web sites describing Indonesian human rights abuses in the former Portuguese Colony.[36] Then in August 1999, Jose Ramos Horta, the Sydney-based Nobel laureate who represents the East Timor independence movement outside Indonesia, warned that a global network of hackers planned to bring Indonesia to a standstill if Jakarta sabotaged the ballot on the future of East Timor. He told the *Sydney Morning Herald* that more than 100 hackers, mostly teenagers in Europe and the United States, had been preparing the plan.[37]

In June 1998, a group of international hackers calling themselves MilwOrm hacked the Web site of India's Bhabha Atomic Research Center (BARC) and put up a spoofed Web page showing a mushroom cloud and the text "if a nuclear war does start, you will be the first to scream. . . ." The hackers were protesting India's recent nuclear weapons tests, although they admitted they did it mostly for thrills. They said that they also downloaded several thousand pages of e-mail and research documents, including messages between India's nuclear scientists and Israeli government officials, and had erased data on two of BARC's servers. The six hackers, whose ages range from 15 to 18, hailed from the United States, England, the Netherlands, and New Zealand.[38]

Another way in which hacktivists alter what viewers see when they go to a Web site is by tampering with the Domain Name Service so that the site's domain name resolves to the IP address of some other site. When users point their browsers to the target site, they are redirected to the alternative site.

In what might have been one of the largest mass home page takeovers, the antinuclear MilwOrm hackers were joined by Ashtray Lumberjacks hackers in an attack that affected more than 300 Web sites in July 1998. According to reports, the hackers broke into the British Internet service provider EasySpace, which hosted the sites. They altered the ISP's database so that users attempting to access the sites were redirected to a MilwOrm site, where they were greeted with a message protesting the nuclear arms race. The message concluded with "use your power to keep the world in a state of PEACE and put a stop to this nuclear bullshit." John Vranesevich, who runs the hacker news site AntiOnline, said, "They're the equivalent to the World Trade Center bombings; [they] want to get their story told and bring attention to themselves."[39] . . .

Computer Viruses and Worms

Hacktivists have used computer viruses and worms to spread protest messages and damage target computer systems. Both are forms of malicious code that infect computers and propagate over computer networks. The difference is that a worm is an autonomous piece of software that spreads on its own, whereas a virus attaches itself to other files and code segments and spreads through those elements, usually in response to actions taken by users (e.g., opening an e-mail attachment). The boundary between viruses and worms, however, is blurry and not important to the discussion here.

The first protest to use a worm occurred about a decade ago, when antinuclear hackers released a worm into the U.S. National Aeronautics and

Space Administration SPAN network. On October 16, 1989, scientists logging into computers at NASA's Goddard Space Flight Center in Greenbelt, Maryland, were greeted with a banner from the WANK worm:

WORMS AGAINST NUCLEAR KILLERS

```
  \ \         / /  / \ \        / \ \        / /    | |  / /
   \ \    /\  / /  / / \ \      / / \ \      / /     | | / /
    \ \ / \ / /  / /——\ \    / /   \ \    / /      | V /
     \ V /\ V /  / /       \ \  / /     \ \ / /      | \ \
      \ V  V /  / /         \ \ / /       \ V /       | | \ \
       \ \ / /  / /          \ \ / /        \ //        | |  \ \
```
Your System Has Been Officially WANKed

You talk of times of peace for all, and then prepare for war.

At the time of the attack, antinuclear protestors were trying to stop the launch of the shuttle that carried the Galileo probe on its initial leg to Jupiter. Galileo's 32,500-pound booster system was fueled with radioactive plutonium. John McMahon, protocol manager with NASA's SPAN office, estimated that the worm cost them up to half a million dollars of wasted time and resources. It did not have its intended effect of stopping the launch. The source of the attack was never identified, but some evidence suggested that it might have come from hackers in Australia.[40]

Computer viruses have been used to propagate political messages and, in some cases, cause serious damage. In February 1999, the *London Sunday Telegraph* reported that an Israeli teen had become a national hero after he claimed to have wiped out an Iraqi government Web site. "It contained lies about the United States, Britain and Israel, and many horrible statements against Jews," 14-year-old Nir Zigdon said.[41] "I figured that if Israel is afraid of assassinating Saddam Hussein, at least I can try to destroy his site. With the help of some special software I tracked down the site's server to one of the Gulf states."[42] The Tel Aviv hacktivist then sent a computer virus in an e-mail attachment to the site. "In the e-mail message, I claimed I was a Palestinian admirer of Saddam who had produced a virus capable of wiping out Israeli websites," Zigdon said. "That persuaded them to open the message and click on the designated file. Within hours the site had been destroyed. Shortly afterwards I received an e-mail from the site manager, Fayiz, that told me to `go to hell.'"[43]

During the Kosovo conflict, businesses, public organizations, and academic institutes received virus-laden e-mails from a range of Eastern European countries, according to mi2g, a London-based Internet software company. "The contents of the messages are normally highly politicised attacks on NATO's unfair aggression and defending Serbian rights using poor English language and propaganda cartoons," the press release said. It went on to say "The damage to the addressee is usually incorporated in several viruses contained within an attachment, which may be plain language or anti-NATO cartoon."[44] In an earlier press release, mi2g warned that "The real threat of cyber warfare from Serbian hackers is to the economic infrastructure of NATO countries and not to their better prepared military command and control network."[45]

It is extremely difficult, perhaps impossible, for an organization to prevent all viruses, as users unwittingly open e-mail attachments with viruses and spread documents with viruses to colleagues. Although anti-viral tools can detect and eradicate viruses, the tools must be kept up-to-date across the enterprise, which may have tens of thousands of machines, and they must be installed and used properly. While viruses bearing political messages may not seem to pose a serious problem, an organization hit by one may have to shut down services in order to eradicate it from its network. . . .

Cyberterrorism

As discussed in the preceding sections, terrorist groups are using the Internet extensively to spread their message and to communicate and coordinate action. However, there have been few if any computer network attacks that meet the criteria for cyberterrorism. The 1998 e-mail bombing by the Internet Black Tigers against the SRI Lanken embassies was perhaps the closest thing to cyberterrorism that has occurred so far, but the damage cause by the flood of e-mail, for example, pales in comparison to the deaths of 240 people from the physical bombings of the U.S. embassies in Nairobi and Dar es Salaam in August of that year.

Is cyberterrorism the way of the future? For a terrorist, it would have some advantages over physical methods. It could be conducted remotely and anonymously, it would be cheap, and it would not require the handling of explosives or a suicide mission. It would likely garner extensive media coverage, as journalists and the public alike are fascinated by practically any kind of computer attack. One highly acclaimed study of the risks of computer systems began with a paragraph that concludes "Tomorrow's terrorist may be able to do more with a keyboard than with a bomb."[46]

In a 1997 paper, Collin describes several possible scenarios. In one, a cyberterrorist hacks into the processing control system of a cereal manufacturer and changes the levels of iron supplement. A nation of children get sick and die. In another, a cyberterroist attacks the next generation of air traffic control systems. Two large civilian aircraft collide. In a third, a cyberterrorist disrupts banks, international financial transactions, and stock exchanges. Economic systems grind to a halt, the public loses confidence, and destabilization is achieved.[47]

Analyzing the plausibility of Collin's hypothetical attacks, Pollitt concludes that there is sufficient human involvement in the control processes used today that cyberterrorism does not—at present—pose a significant risk in the classical sense. In the cereal contamination scenario, for example, he argues that the quantity of iron (or any other nutritious substance) that would be required to become toxic is so large that assembly line workers would notice. They would run out of iron on the assembly line and the product would taste different and not good. In the air traffic control scenario, humans in the loop would notice the problems and take corrective action. Pilots, he says, are trained to be aware of the situation, to catch errors made by air traffic controllers, and to operate in the absence of any air traffic control at all.[48] Pollitt does not imply by his analysis that computers are safe and free from vulnerability. To the contrary, his argument is that despite these vulnerabilities, because humans are in the loop, a cyberattack is unlikely to have such devastating consequences. He concludes that "As we build more and more technology into our civilization, we must ensure that there is sufficient human oversight and intervention to safeguard those whom technology serves."

In a 1997 article titled "How Many Terrorists Fit on a Computer Keyboard?" William Church presents a strong case that the United States does not yet face a compelling threat from terrorists using information warfare techniques to disrupt critical infrastructure. They lack either the motivation, capabilities, or skills to pull of a cyberattack at this time. Church does not rule out a physical attack against the infrastructure, but such a threat is neither new nor matured by U.S. reliance on technology.[49]

There are drawbacks to terrorists using cyber weapons over physical ones. Because systems are complex, it may be harder to control an attack and achieve a desired level of damage. Unless people are injured, there is also less drama and emotional appeal. Further, terrorists may be disinclined to try new methods unless they see their old ones as inadequate.[50]

There is little concrete evidence of terrorists preparing to use the Internet as a venue for inflicting grave harm. However, in February 1998, Clark Staten, executive director of the Emergency Response & Research Institute in Chicago, testified that it was believed that "members of some Islamic extremist organizations have been attempting to develop a hacker network to support their computer activities and even engage in offensive information warfare attacks in the future."[51] And in November, the *Detroit News* reported that Khalid Ibrahim, who claimed to be a member of the militant Indian separatist group Harkat-ul-Ansar, one of the 30 terrorist organizations on the State Department list, declared war on the United States following the August cruise-missile attack on a suspected terrorist training camp in Afghanistan run by Osama bin Laden, which allegedly killed nine of their members. The attempted purchase was discovered when an 18-year-old hacker calling himself Chameleon attempted to cash a $1,000 check from Ibrahim. Chameleon said he did not have the software and did not give it to

Ibrahim, but Ibrahim may have obtained it or other sensitive information from one of the many other hackers he approached.[52]

Given that there are no instances of cyberterrorism, it is not possible to assess the impact of acts that have taken place. It is equally difficult to assess potential impact, in part because it is hard to predict how a major computer network attack, inflicted for the purpose of affecting national or international policy, would unfold. So far, damages from attacks committed for reasons other than terrorism, for example, to seek revenge against a former employer, have generally been confined to immediate targets. No lives have been lost. . . .

Conclusions

The Internet is clearly changing the landscape of political discourse and advocacy. It offers new and inexpensive methods for collecting and publishing information, for communicating and coordinating action on a global scale, and for reaching out to policy makers. It supports both open and private communication. Advocacy groups and individuals worldwide are taking advantage of these features in their attempts to influence foreign policy.

Several case studies show that when the Internet is used in normal, nondisruptive ways, it can be an effective tool for activism, especially when it is combined with other media, including broadcast and print media and face-to-face meetings with policy makers. As a technology for empowerment, the Net benefits individuals and small groups with few resources as well as organizations that are large or well-funded. It facilitates activities such as educating the public and media, raising money, forming coalitions across geographical boundaries, distributing petitions and action alerts, and planning and coordinating events on a regional or international level. It allows activists in politically repressive states to evade government censors and monitors.

In the area of hacktivism, which involves the use of hacking tools and techniques of a disruptive nature, the Internet will serve mainly to draw attention to a cause, as such incidents are regularly reported by news media. Whether that attention has the desired effect of changing policy decisions related to the issue at hand is much less certain. Hacktivists may feel a sense of empowerment, because they can control government computers and get media attention, but that does not mean they will succeed in changing policy. So far, anecdotal evidence suggests that for the majority of cases, they will not.

With regards to cyberterrorism, that is, the use of hacking tools and techniques to inflict grave harm such as loss of life, few conclusions can be drawn about its potential impact on foreign policy, as there have been no reported incidents that meet the criteria. What can be said is that the threat of cyberterrorism, combined with hacking threats in general, is influencing policy decisions related to cyberdefense at both a national and international level. If one looks at terrorism in general for insights into the potential impact of cyberterrorism, one finds that the impact of terrorism on the foreign policy issues at hand is similarly difficult to assess, but here again, the threat of terrorism, particularly chem, bio, and nuclear terrorism, is having a significant impact on national defense policy.

Acknowledgments

I am grateful to Liz Bernstein, Ricardo Dominguez, Ekaterina Drozdova, Peter Ford, Brian Gladman, Sy Goodman, Nigel Hickson, Jason Hunter, Dennis Longley, Diana Owen, David Ronfeldt, Ken Rutherford, Julie Ryan, Brett Stalbaum, and Chuck Weiss for helpful discussions, suggestions, and comments.

Notes

1. Ashley Dunn, "Crisis in Yugoslavia—Battle Spilling Over Onto the Internet," *Los Angeles Times,* April 3, 1999.
2. David Briscoe, "Kosovo-Propaganda War," Associated Press, May 17, 1999.
3. NUA Internet Surveys, www.nua.ie. The site is updated regularly with the latest estimate.
4. Alan Docherty, "Net Journalists Outwit Censors," *Wired News,* March 13, 1999.
5. "The Twenty Enemies of the Internet," Press release, Reporters Sans Frontiers, August 9, 1999.
6. www.usia.gov.
7. David Briscoe, "Kosovo-Propaganda War," Associated Press, May 17, 1999.
8. "Conflict in the Balkans—Cook Enlists Internet to Send Serbs Message," *Daily Telegraph,* London, April 2, 1999, p. 9.
9. Rebecca Allison, "Belgrade Hackers Bombard MoD website in `First-Internet War.'" *PA News,* March 31, 1999.
10. Chris Oaks, "Every Web Site a Chat Room," *Wired News,* June 14, 1999.
11. Personal correspondence with Brian Gladman, May 4, 1999, augmented by my own observations from subscribing to the list since the beginning.
12. Ibid.
13. Andrew Brown, "Editors Wanted," *New Statesman,* April 26, 1999.
14. Private conservation with Nigel Hickson on April 29, 1999.
15. Nigel Hickson, private communication, July 28, 1999.
16. www.protest.net.
17. Martin Stone, "Prof to Build Archive of Insurgency Groups," *Newsbytes,* March 3, 1999.
18. Edward Harris, "Web Becomes a Cybertool for Political Activists," *Wall Street Journal,* August 5, 1999, B11; Barbara Adam, "J18 Hackers Could Target Australian Companies on Friday," Australian Associated Press, June 16, 1999.
19. Jon Ungoed-Thomas and Maeve Sheehan, "Riot Organisers Prepare to Launch Cyber War on City," *Sunday Times,* August 15, 1999.

20. www.aeronautix.com/nato/yugoslavia.html
21. Rebecca Fairley Raney, "Flood of E-Mail Credited with Halting U.S. Bank Plan," *New York Times* (Cybertimes), March 24, 1999.
22. Ibid.
23. Edward Harris, "Web Becomes a Cybertool for Political Activists," *Wall Street Journal*, August 5, 1999, B11. The Web site is at www.e-thepeople.com.
24. The persons organizing the campaign went on to form the Electronic Privacy Information Center (EPIC) shortly thereafter.
25. For example, each chip was uniquely keyed and decryption was not possible without getting the keys to the subject's chip from two separate government agencies.
26. For an interesting discussion of the Internet campaign against Clipper, see Laura J. Gurak, *Persuasion and Privacy in Cyberspace*, Yale University Press, 1997.
27. Information provided to the author from Bruce Sterling; Winn Schwartau, *Information Warfare*, 2nd ed., Thunder's Mouth Press, 1996, p. 407.
28. For an in-depth analysis of the Zapatista's "Anetwar," see David Ronfeldt, John Arquilla, Graham E. Fuller, and Melissa Fuller, *The Zapatista "Social Netwar" in Mexico*, RAND Report MR-994-A, 1998.
29. Niall McKay, "Pentagon Deflects Web Assault," *Wired News*, September 10, 1998.
30. Brett Stalbaum, private correspondence, July 23, 1999.
31. "E-Mail Attack on Sri Lanka Computers," Computer Security Alert, No. 183, Computer Security Institute, June 1998, p. 8.
32. Jim Wolf, "First Terrorist Cyber-Attack Reported by U.S.," Reuters, May 5, 1998.
33. CIWARS Intelligence Report, May 10, 1998.
34. Rebecca Allison, "Belgrade Hackers Bombard MoD Website in First-Internet War," *PA News*, March 31, 1999.
35. Patrick Riley, "E-Strikes and Cyber-Sabotage: Civilian Hackers Go Online to Fight," Fox News, April 15, 1999.
36. Amy Harmon, "Hacktivists of All Persuasions Take Their Struggle to the Web," *New York Times*, October 31, 1999.
37. Lindsay Murdoch, "Computer Chaos Threat to Jakarta," *Sydney Morning Herald*, August 18, 1999, p. 9.
38. James Glave, "Crackers: We Stole Nuke Data," *Wired News*, June 3, 1998; Janelle Carter, "Hackers Hit U.S. Military Computers," Associated Press, Washington, June 6, 1998; "Hackers Now Setting Their Sights on Pakistan," *Newsbytes*, June 5, 1998.
39. Jim Hu, "Political Hackers Hit 300 Sites," CNET, July 6, 1998. The MilwOrm page is shown at http://www.antionline.com
40. Ted Bridis, "Hackers Become An Increasing Threat," Associated Press, July 7, 1999.
41. Tom Gross, "Israeli Claims to Have Hacked Saddam Off the Net," *London Sunday Telegraph*, February 7, 1999.
42. Ibid.
43. Ibid.

44. mi2g Cyber Warfare Advisory Number 2, April 17, 1999, M2 Communications, April 19, 1999.
45. M2 Communications, April 8, 1999.
46. National Research Council Staff *Computers at Risk,* National Academy Press, 1991.
47. Barry Colin, "The Future of Cyberterrorism," *Crime and Justice International,* March 1997, pp. 15–18.
48. Mark M. Pollitt, "Cyberterrorism: Fact or Fancy?" Proceedings of the 20th National Information Systems Security Conference, October 1997, pp. 285–289.
49. William Church, "Information Warfare Threat Analysis for the United States of America, Part Two: How Many Terrorists Fit on a Computer Keyboard?" *Journal of Infrastructural Warfare,* Summer 1997.
50. Kevin Soo Hoo, Seymour Goodman, and Lawrence Greenberg, "Information Technology and the Terrorist Threat," *Survival,* Vol 39, No. 3, Autumn 1997, pp. 135–155.
51. Clark L. Staten, testimony before the Subcommittee on Technology, Terrorism and Government Information, U.S. Senate Judiciary Committee, February 24, 1998.
52. "Dangerous Militant Stalks Internet" Detroit News, November 9, 1998.